TIME STOP HERO

3

STORY & ART BY
YASUNORI MITSUNAGA

CONTENTS

▶START
PAUSE

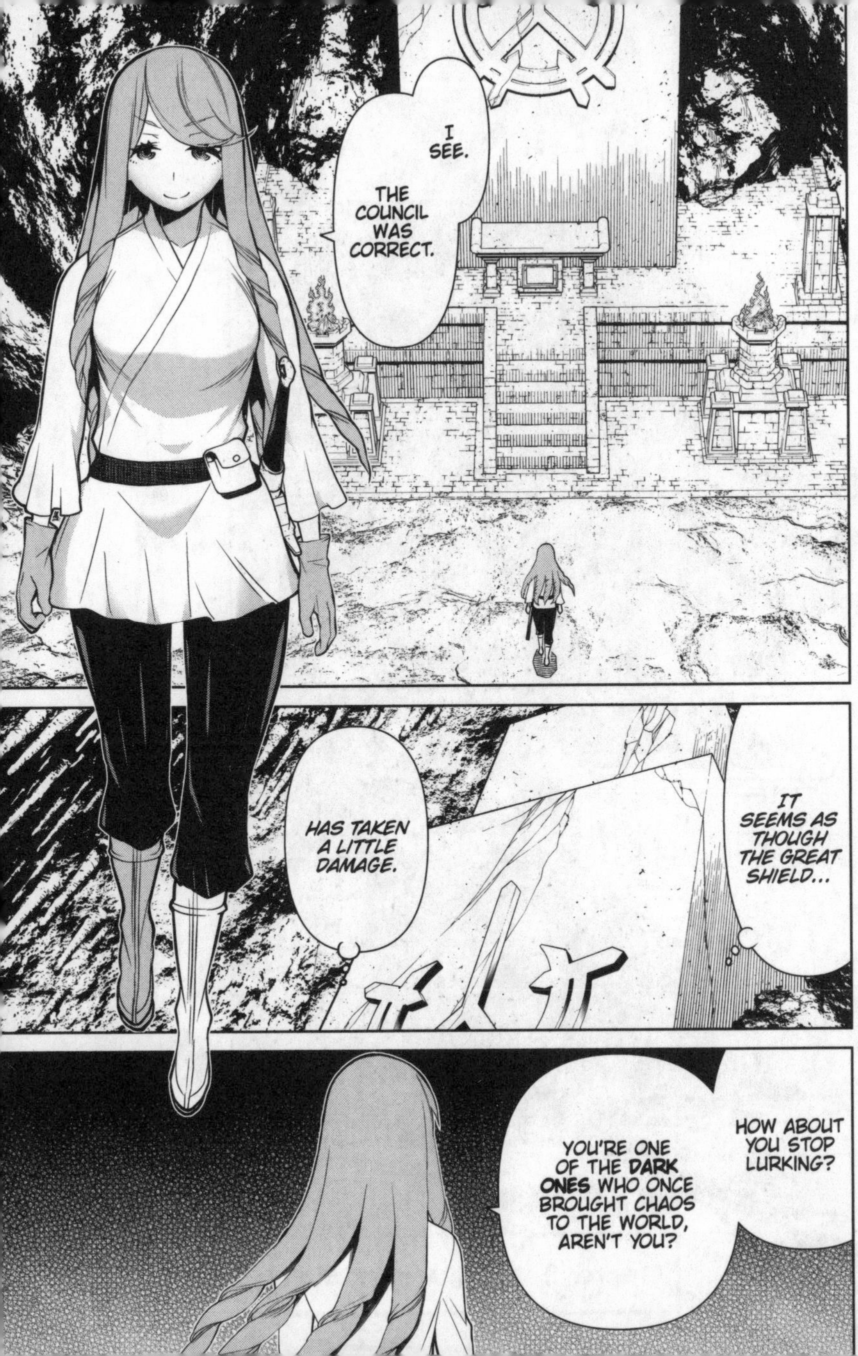
I SEE.
THE COUNCIL WAS CORRECT.
IT SEEMS AS THOUGH THE GREAT SHIELD...
HAS TAKEN A LITTLE DAMAGE.
HOW ABOUT YOU STOP LURKING?
YOU'RE ONE OF THE DARK ONES WHO ONCE BROUGHT CHAOS TO THE WORLD, AREN'T YOU?

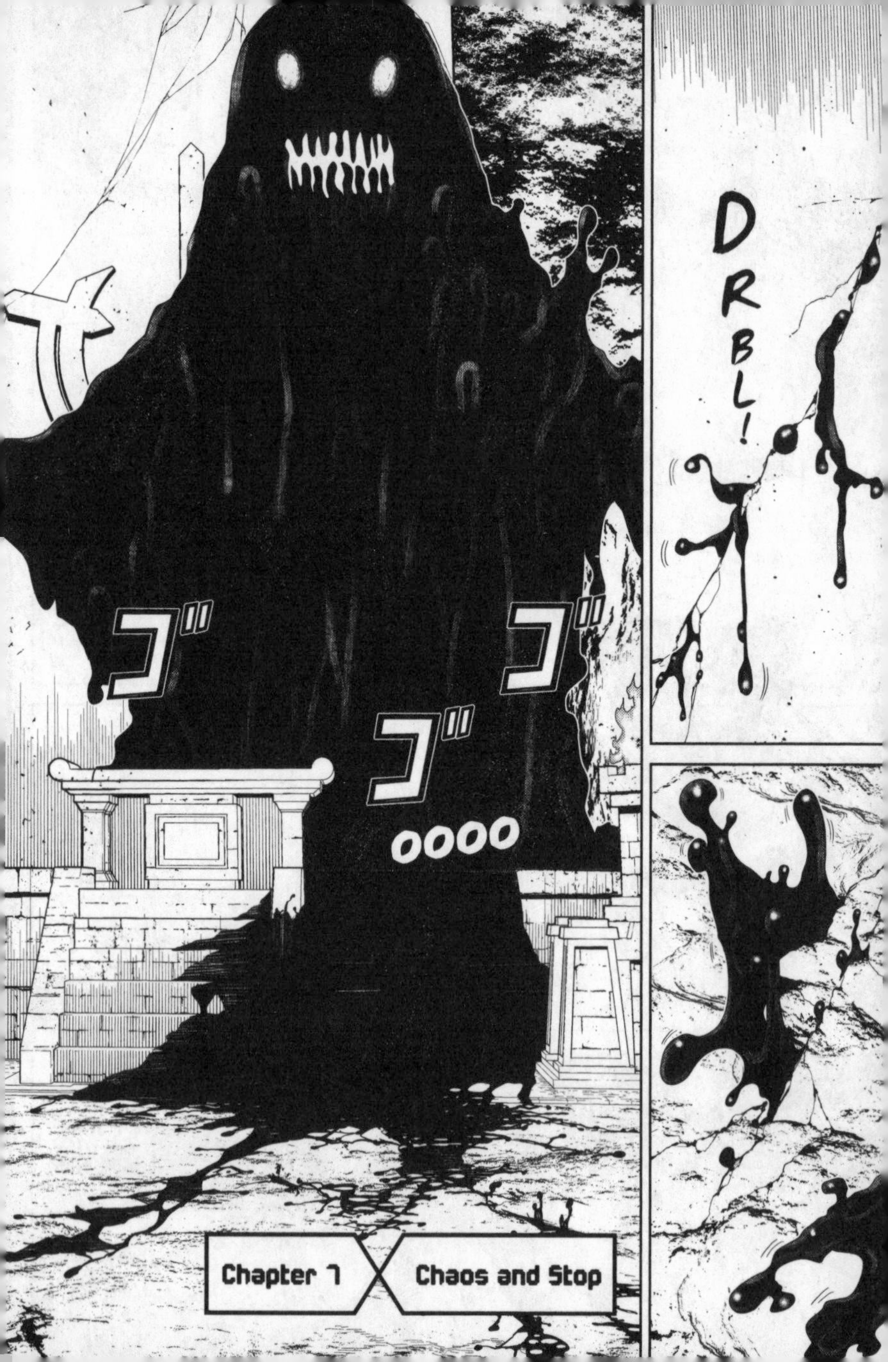
DRBL!
ゴ
ゴ
ゴ
OOOO
Chapter 7
Chaos and Stop

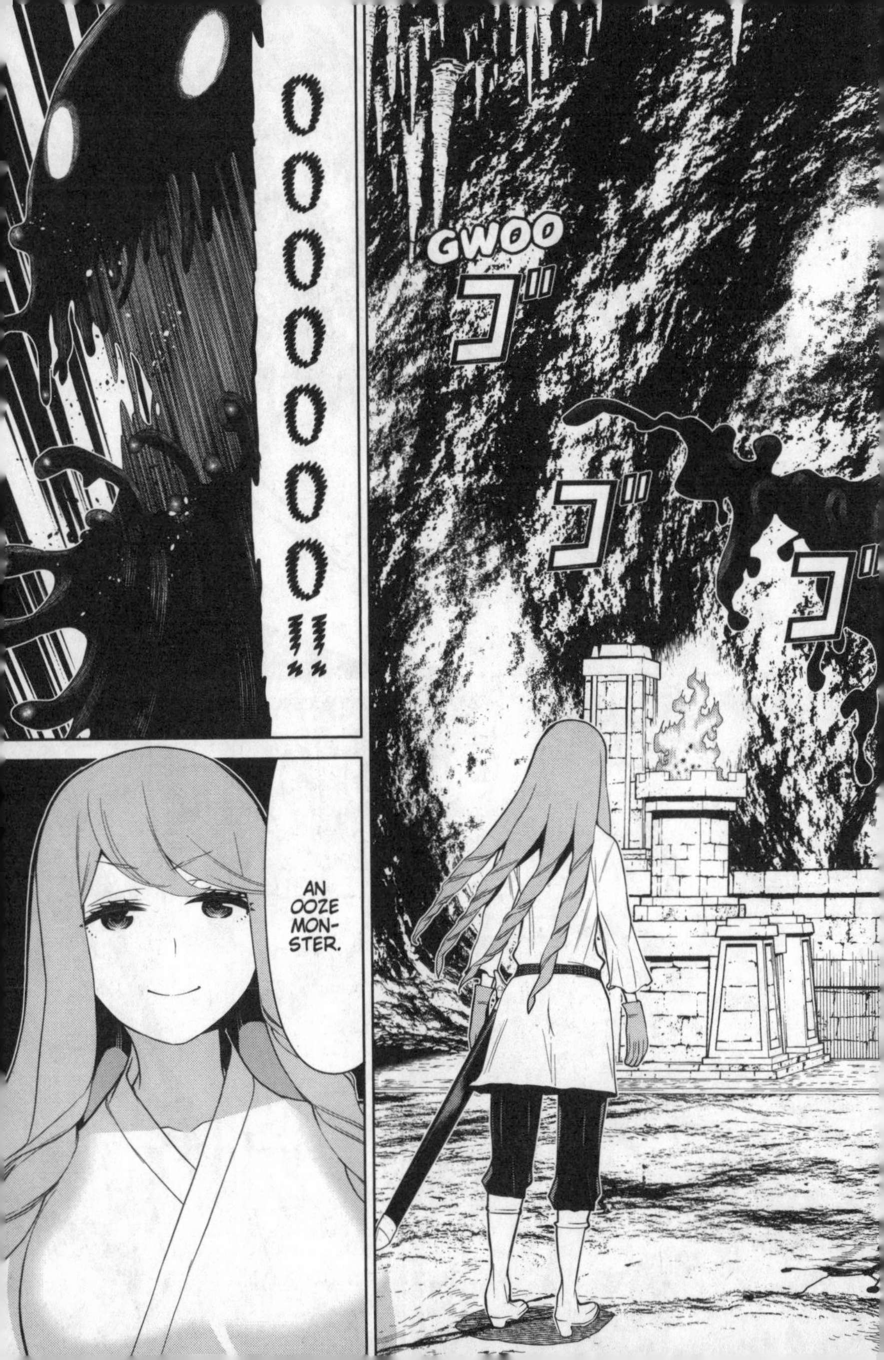
GWOO
ゴ
ゴ
ゴ
OOOOOOOO!!
AN OOZE MON-STER.

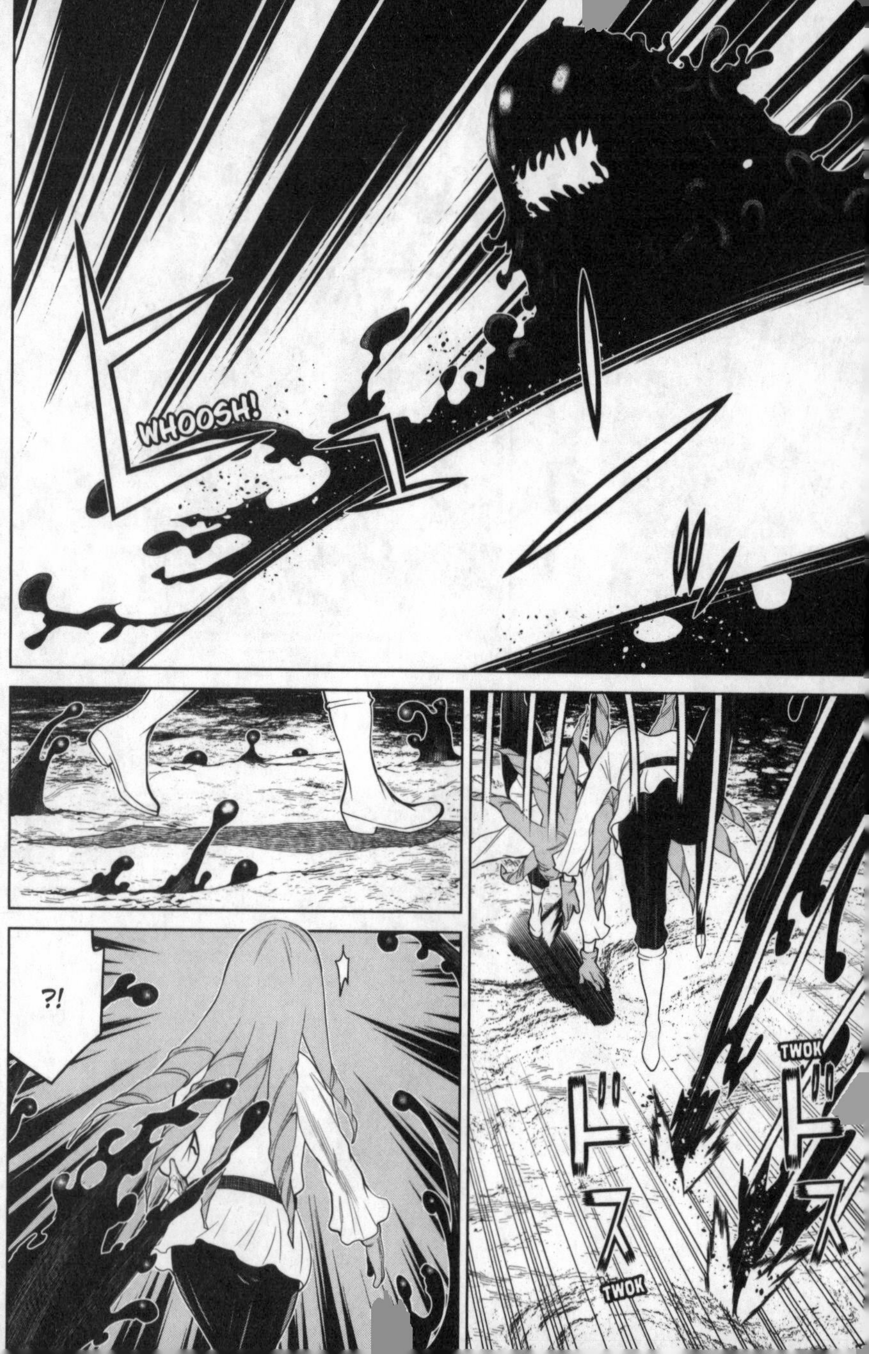

WHOOSH!
TWOK
ドス
ドス
TWOK
?!

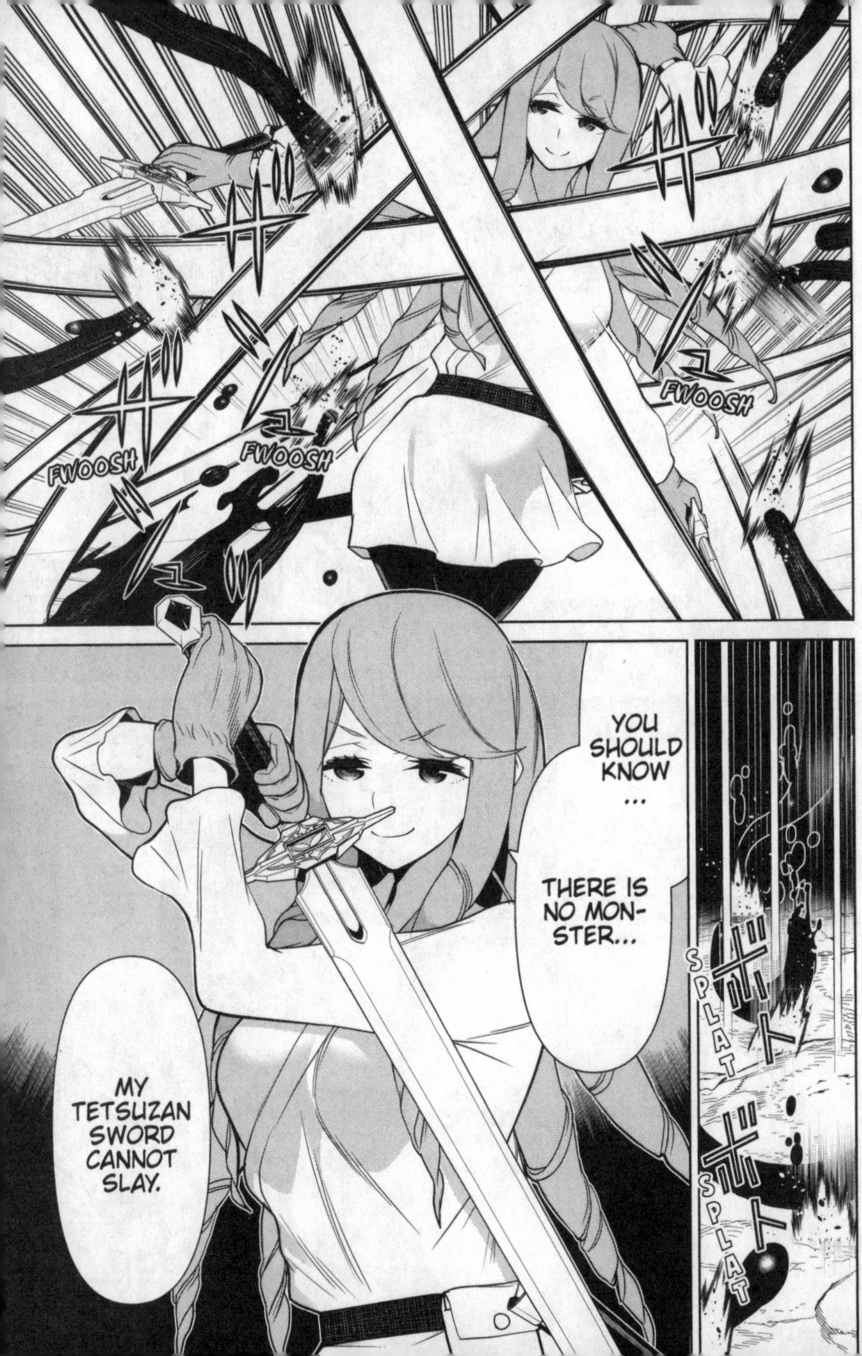
FWOOSH
FWOOSH
FWOOSH
SPLAT
SPLAT
YOU SHOULD KNOW...
THERE IS NO MONSTER...
MY TETSUZAN SWORD CANNOT SLAY.

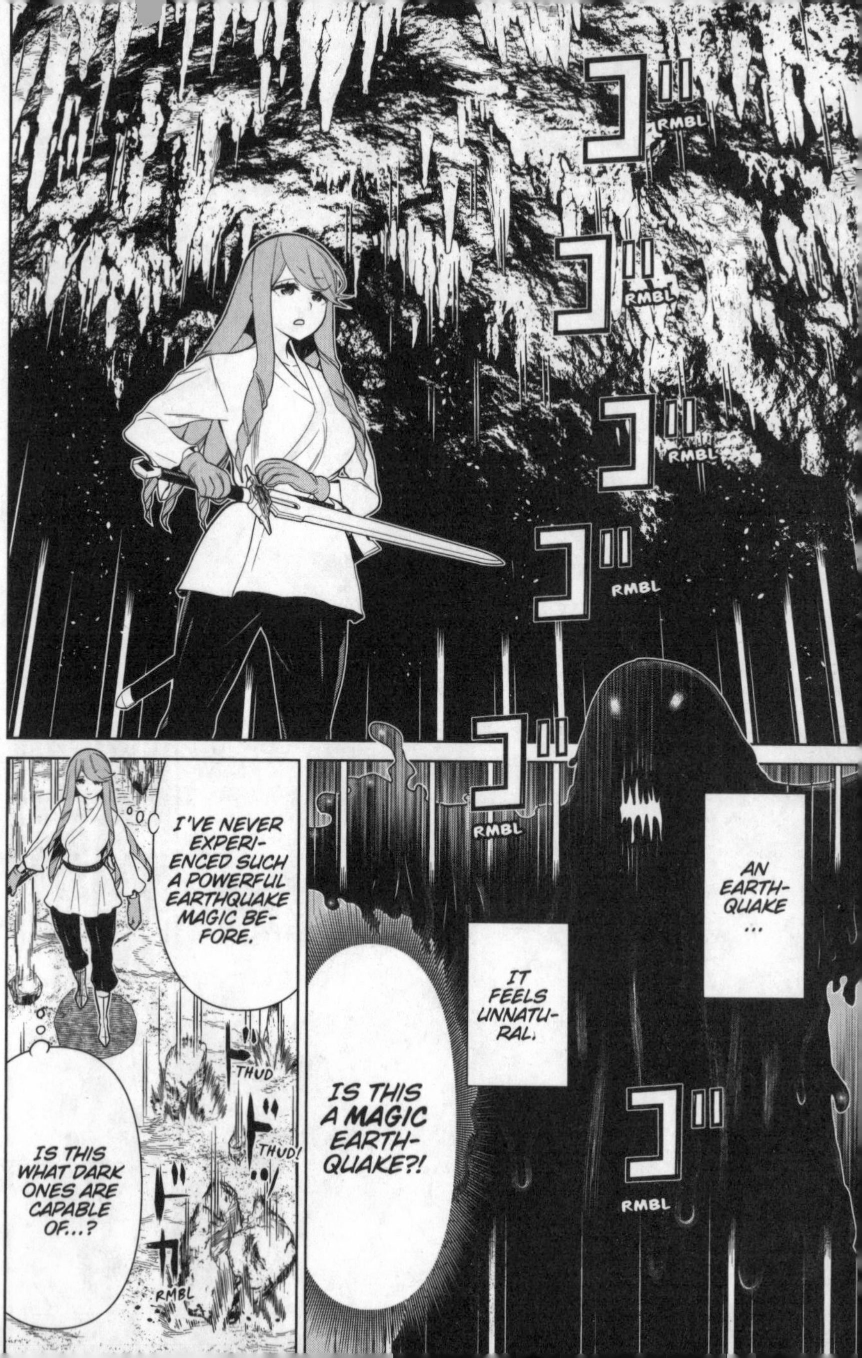
ゴ RMBL
ゴ RMBL
ゴ RMBL
ゴ RMBL
ゴ RMBL
AN EARTH-QUAKE ...
IT FEELS UNNATU-RAL.
IS THIS A MAGIC EARTH-QUAKE?!
ゴ RMBL
I'VE NEVER EXPERI-ENCED SUCH A POWERFUL EARTHQUAKE MAGIC BE-FORE.
IS THIS WHAT DARK ONES ARE CAPABLE OF...?
ド THUD
ド THUD!
RMBL

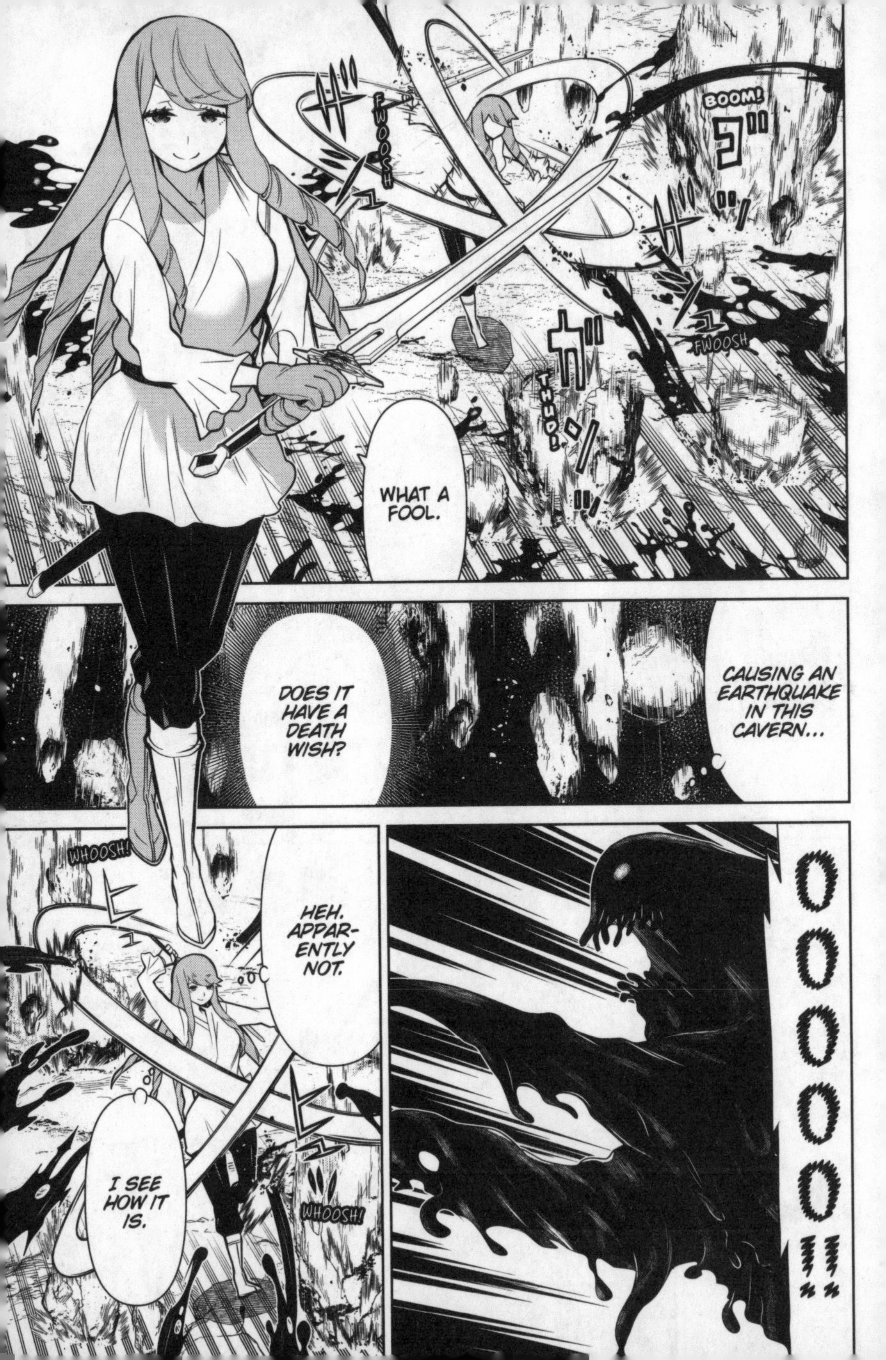
BOOM!
FWOOSH
THUD!
FWOOSH
WHAT A FOOL.
CAUSING AN EARTHQUAKE IN THIS CAVERN...
DOES IT HAVE A DEATH WISH?
WHOOSH!
HEH. APPAR-ENTLY NOT.
WHOOSH!
I SEE HOW IT IS.

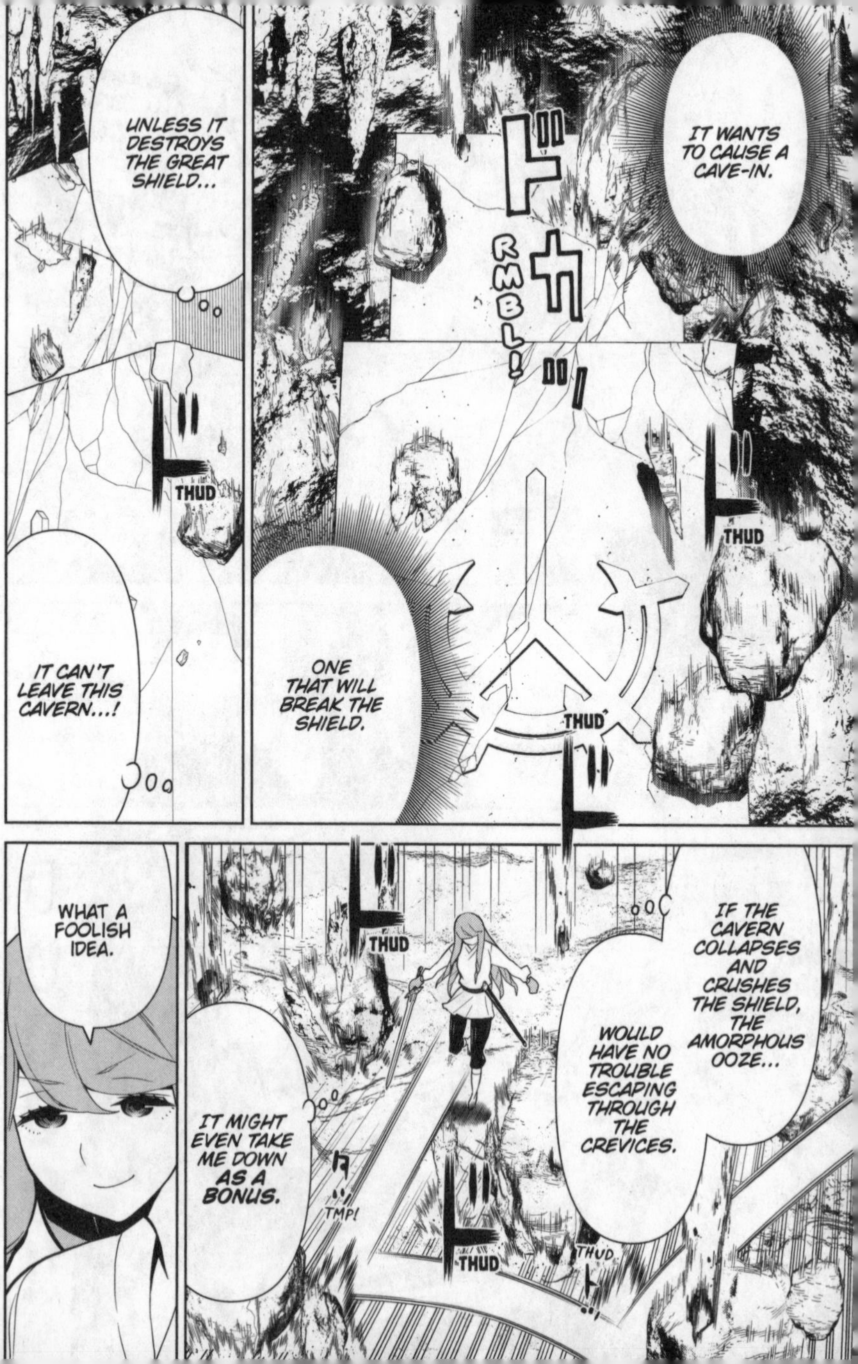
IT WANTS TO CAUSE A CAVE-IN.
RMBL!
THUD
ONE THAT WILL BREAK THE SHIELD.
THUD
UNLESS IT DESTROYS THE GREAT SHIELD...
THUD
IT CAN'T LEAVE THIS CAVERN...!
IF THE CAVERN COLLAPSES AND CRUSHES THE SHIELD, THE AMORPHOUS OOZE...
WOULD HAVE NO TROUBLE ESCAPING THROUGH THE CREVICES.
THUD
THUD
THUD
TMP!
IT MIGHT EVEN TAKE ME DOWN AS A BONUS.
WHAT A FOOLISH IDEA.

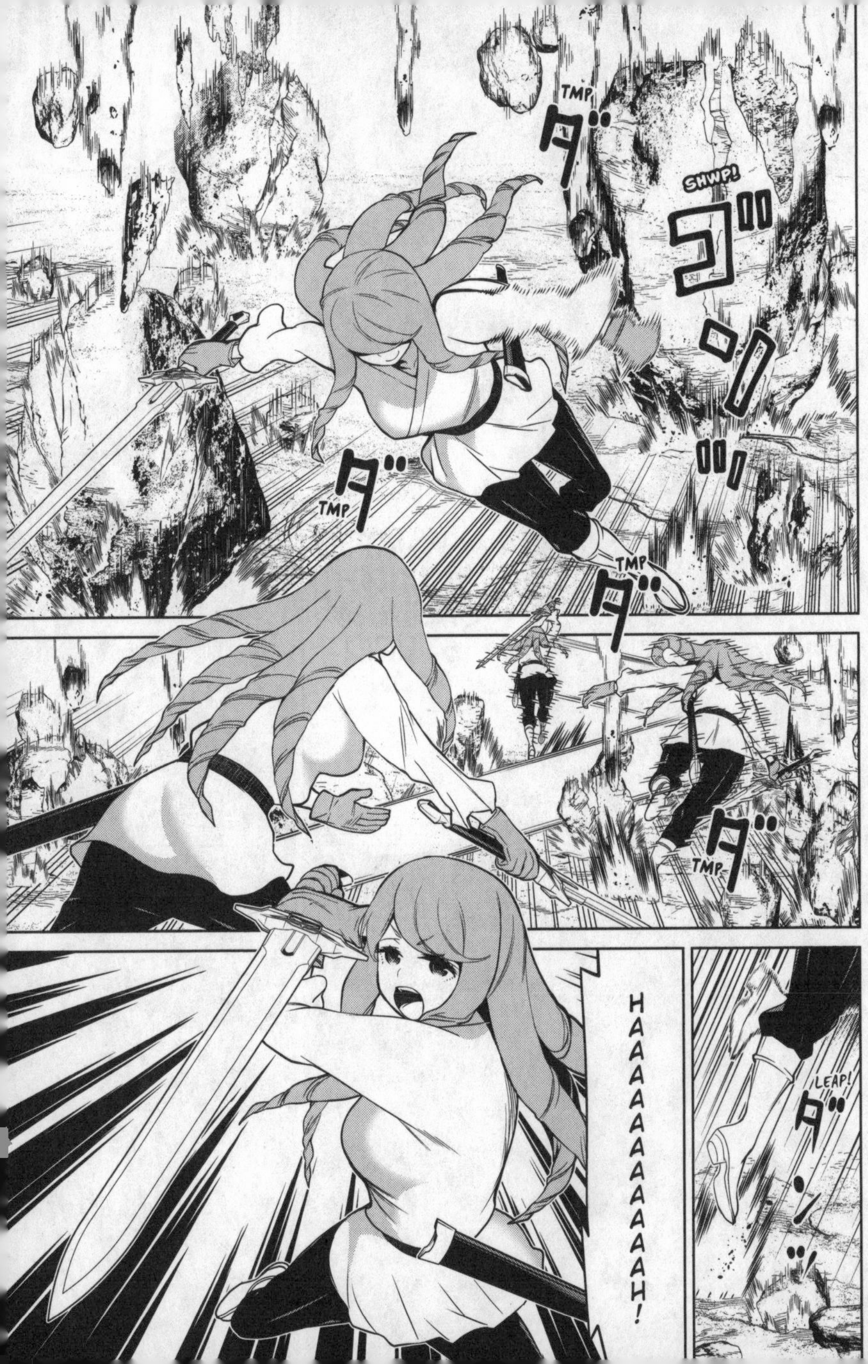
SHWP!
TMP
ダ
TMP
ダ
TMP
ダ
TMP
ダ
LEAP!
ダッ
HAAAAAAAAAAAAH!

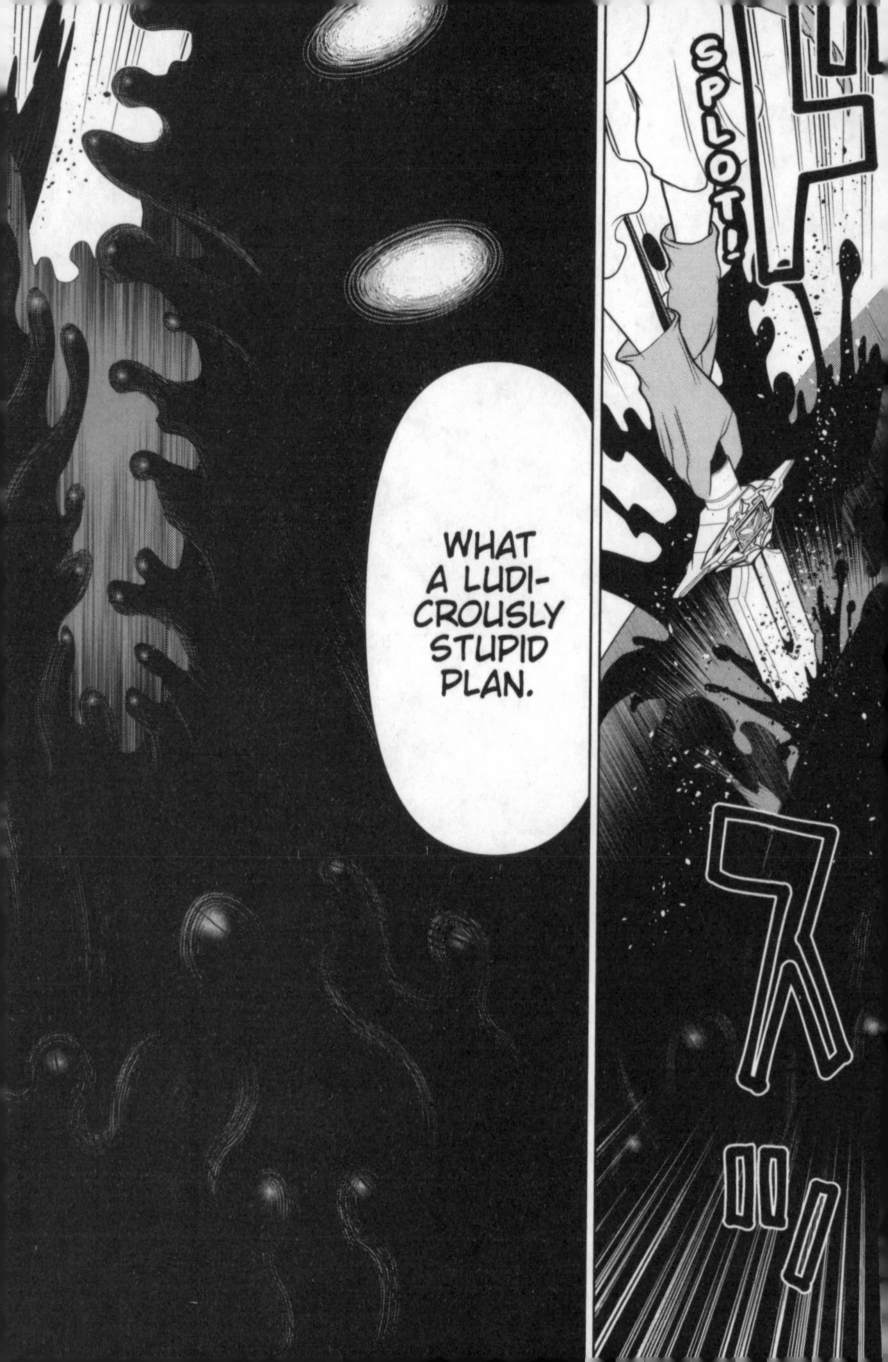
SPLOT!
WHAT A LUDI-CROUSLY STUPID PLAN.

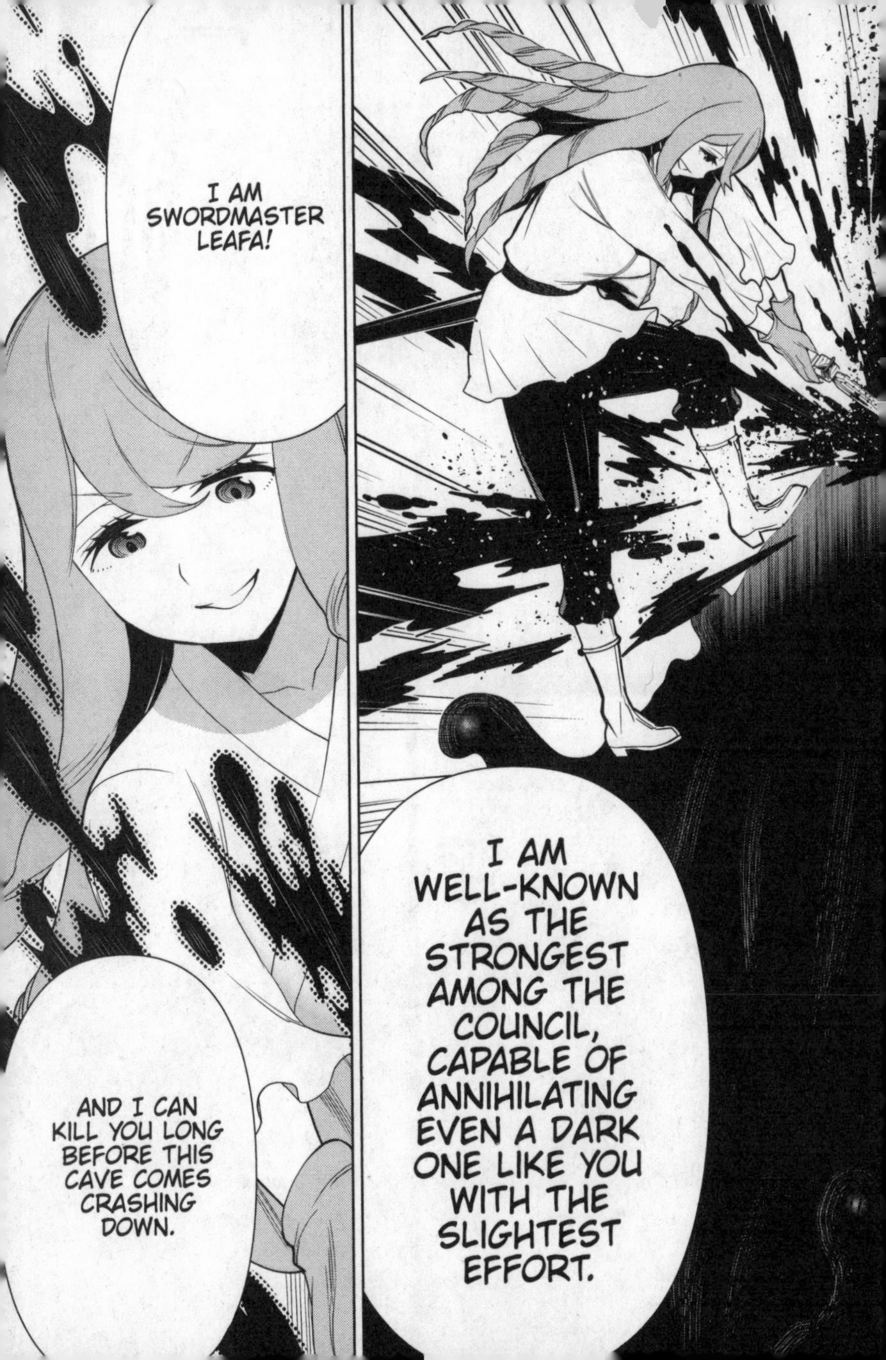
I AM WELL-KNOWN AS THE STRONGEST AMONG THE COUNCIL, CAPABLE OF ANNIHILATING EVEN A DARK ONE LIKE YOU WITH THE SLIGHTEST EFFORT.
I AM SWORDMASTER LEAFA!
AND I CAN KILL YOU LONG BEFORE THIS CAVE COMES CRASHING DOWN.

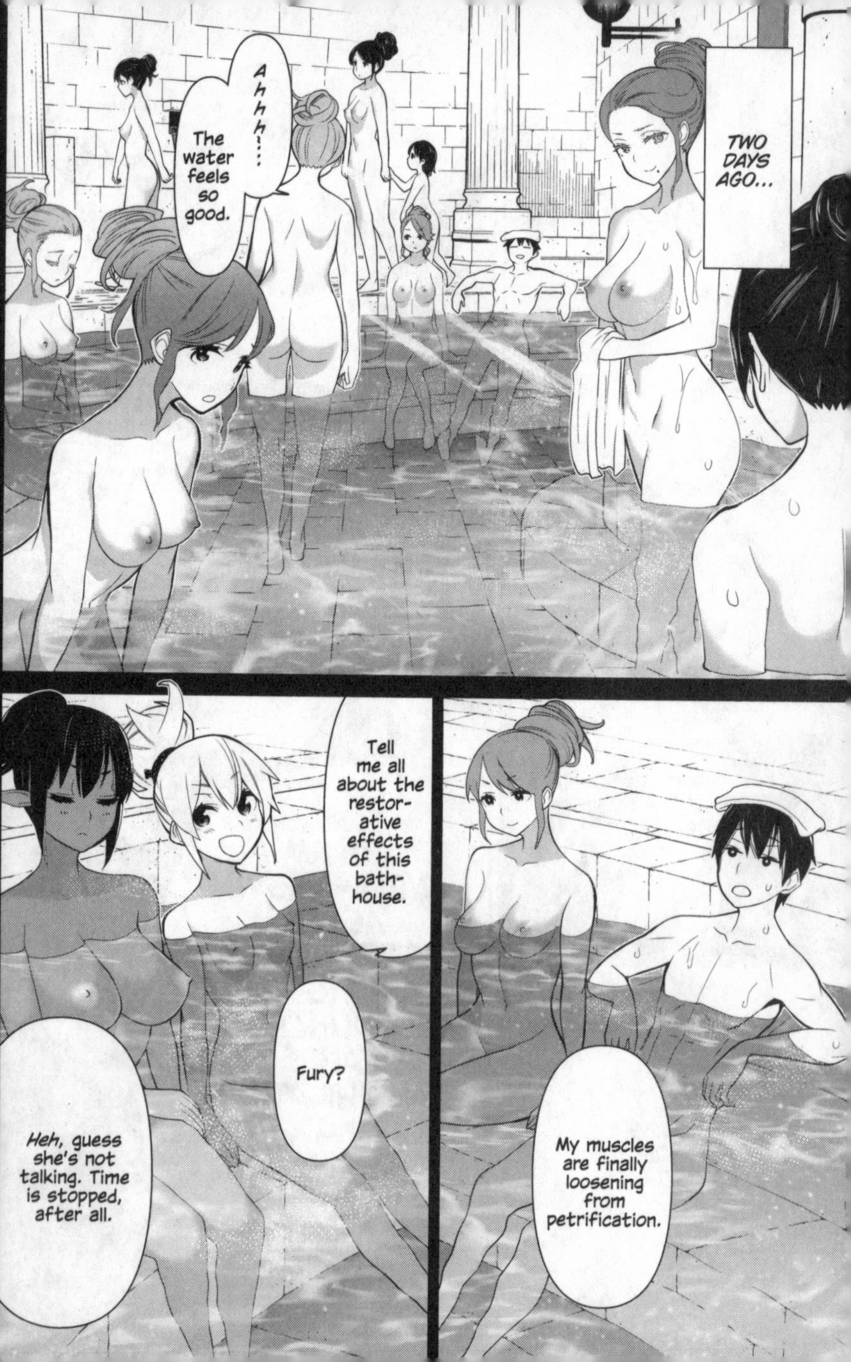
TWO DAYS AGO...
Ahhh... The water feels so good.
My muscles are finally loosening from petrification.
Tell me all about the restor-ative effects of this bath-house.
Fury?
Heh, guess she's not talking. Time is stopped, after all.

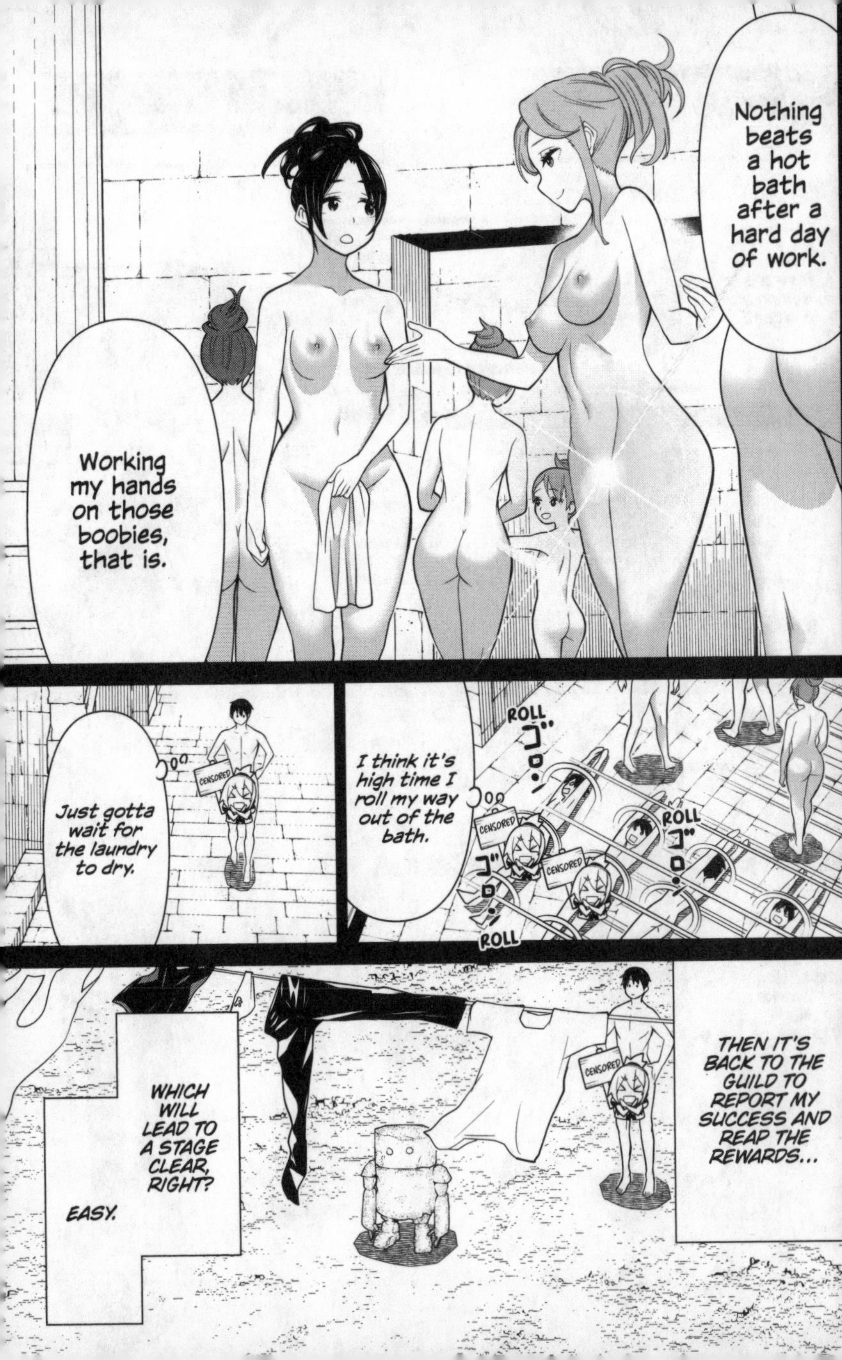
Nothing beats a hot bath after a hard day of work.
Working my hands on those boobies, that is.
ROLL
ゴロ・・
ROLL
ゴロ・・
ゴロ・・
ROLL
CENSORED
CENSORED
I think it's high time I roll my way out of the bath.
CENSORED
Just gotta wait for the laundry to dry.
CENSORED
THEN IT'S BACK TO THE GUILD TO REPORT MY SUCCESS AND REAP THE REWARDS...
WHICH WILL LEAD TO A STAGE CLEAR, RIGHT?
EASY.

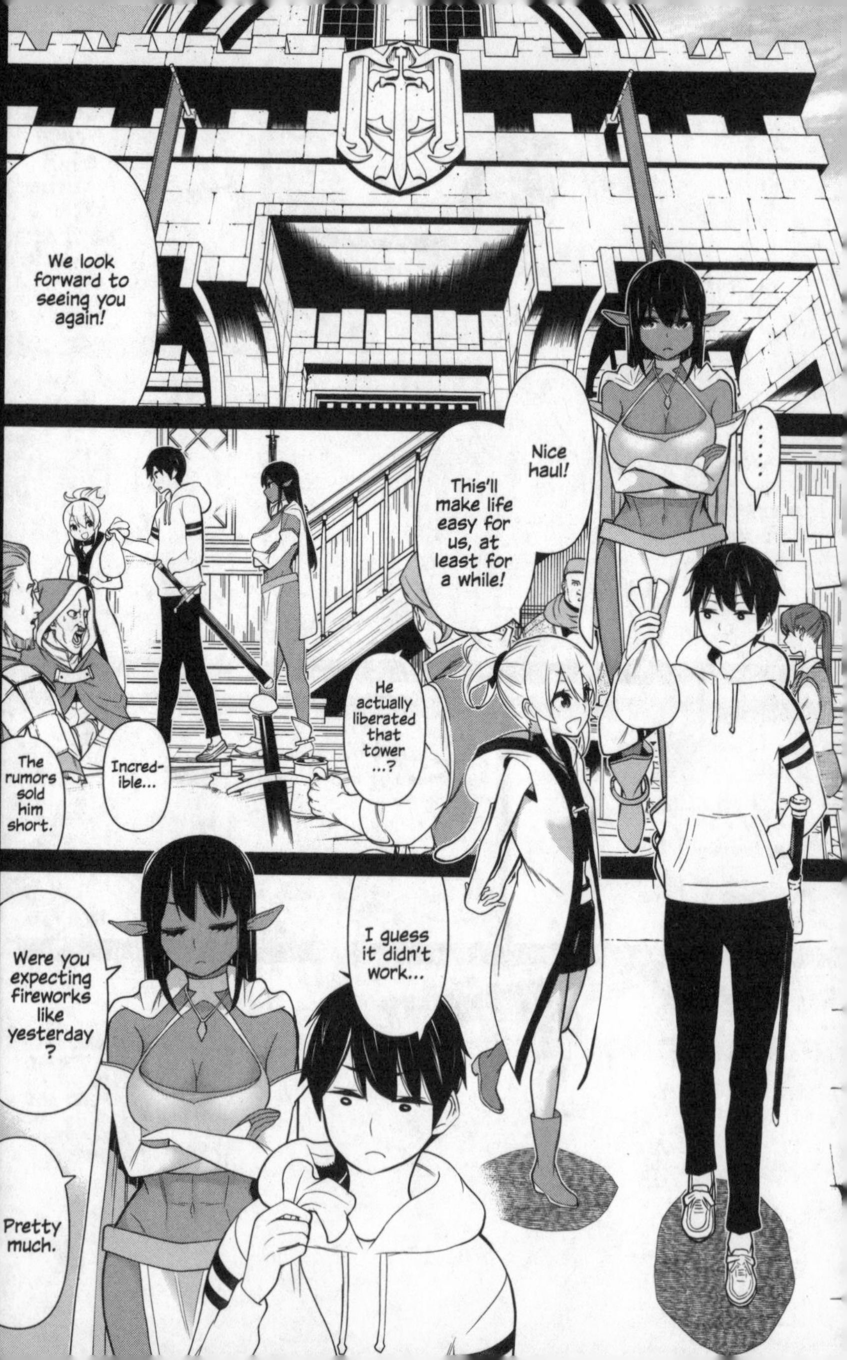

We look forward to seeing you again!
......
Nice haul!
This'll make life easy for us, at least for a while!
He actually liberated that tower ...?
Incred-ible...
The rumors sold him short.
I guess it didn't work...
Were you expecting fireworks like yesterday ?
Pretty much.

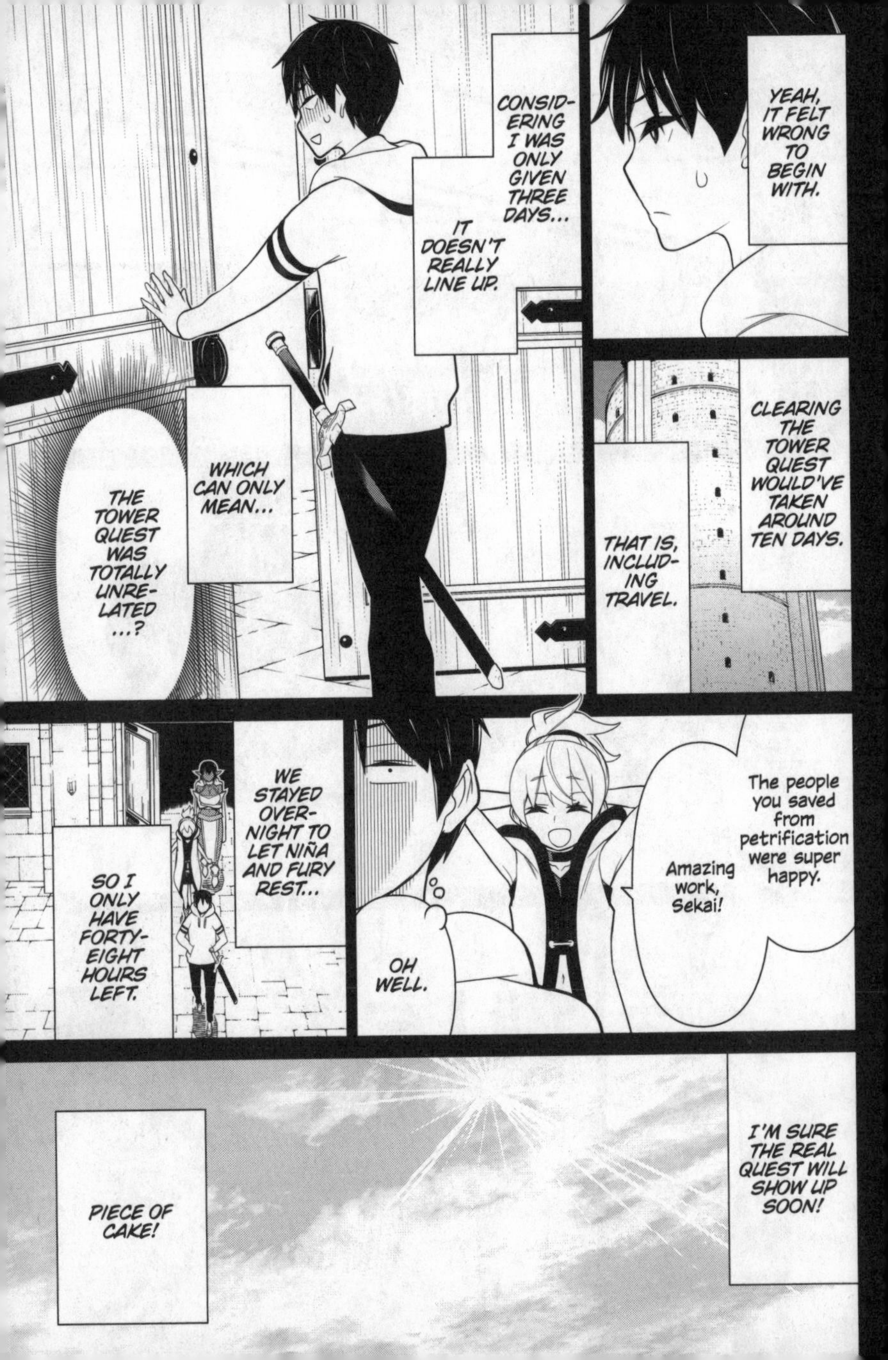
YEAH, IT FELT WRONG TO BEGIN WITH.
CLEARING THE TOWER QUEST WOULD'VE TAKEN AROUND TEN DAYS.
THAT IS, INCLUDING TRAVEL.
CONSIDERING I WAS ONLY GIVEN THREE DAYS...
IT DOESN'T REALLY LINE UP.
WHICH CAN ONLY MEAN...
THE TOWER QUEST WAS TOTALLY UNRELATED...?
The people you saved from petrification were super happy.
Amazing work, Sekai!
OH WELL.
WE STAYED OVERNIGHT TO LET NIÑA AND FURY REST...
SO I ONLY HAVE FORTY-EIGHT HOURS LEFT.
I'M SURE THE REAL QUEST WILL SHOW UP SOON!
PIECE OF CAKE!

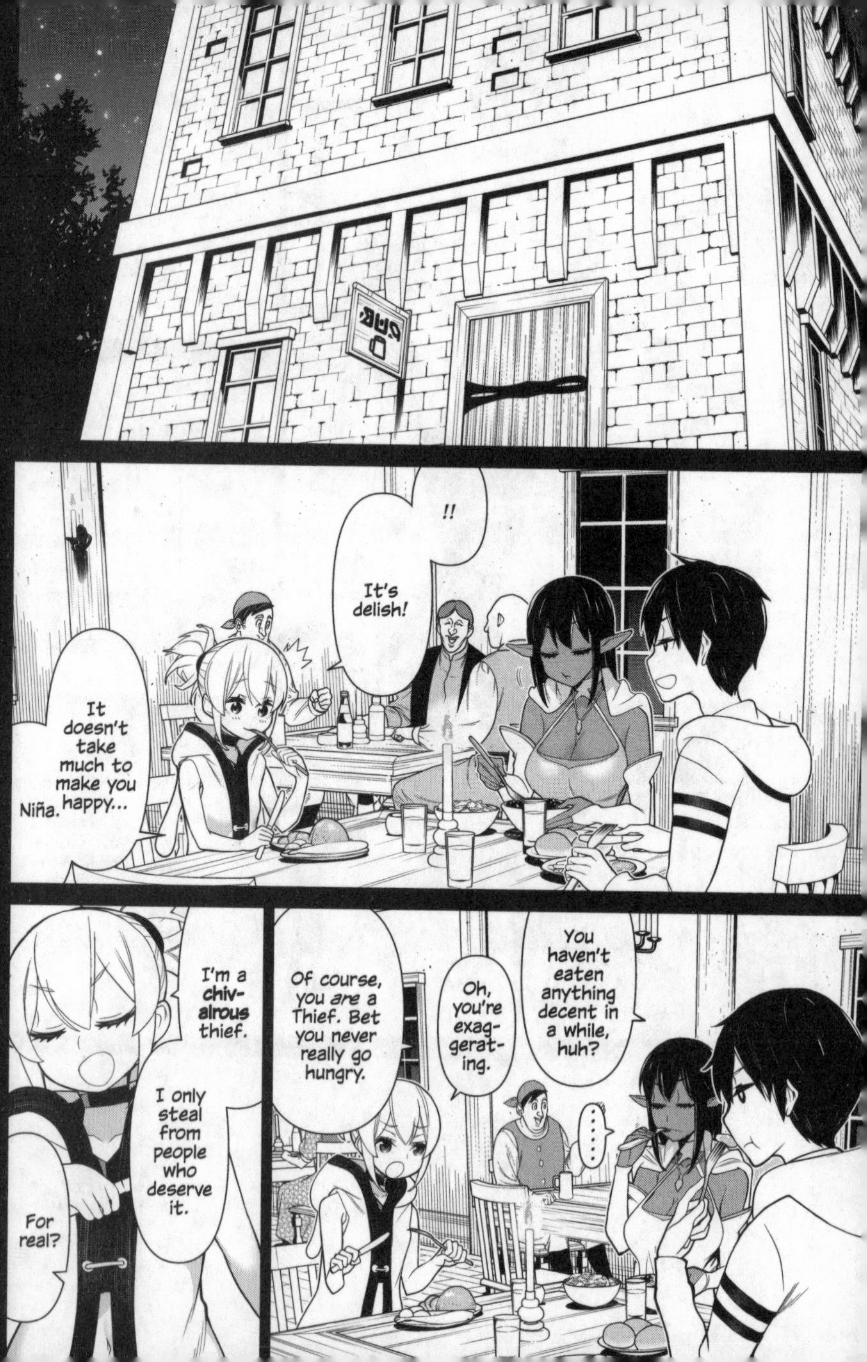
!!
It's delish!
It doesn't take much to make you happy... Niña.
You haven't eaten anything decent in a while, huh?
Oh, you're exaggerating.
Of course, you *are* a Thief. Bet you never really go hungry.
......
I'm a **chivalrous** thief.
I only steal from people who deserve it.
For real?

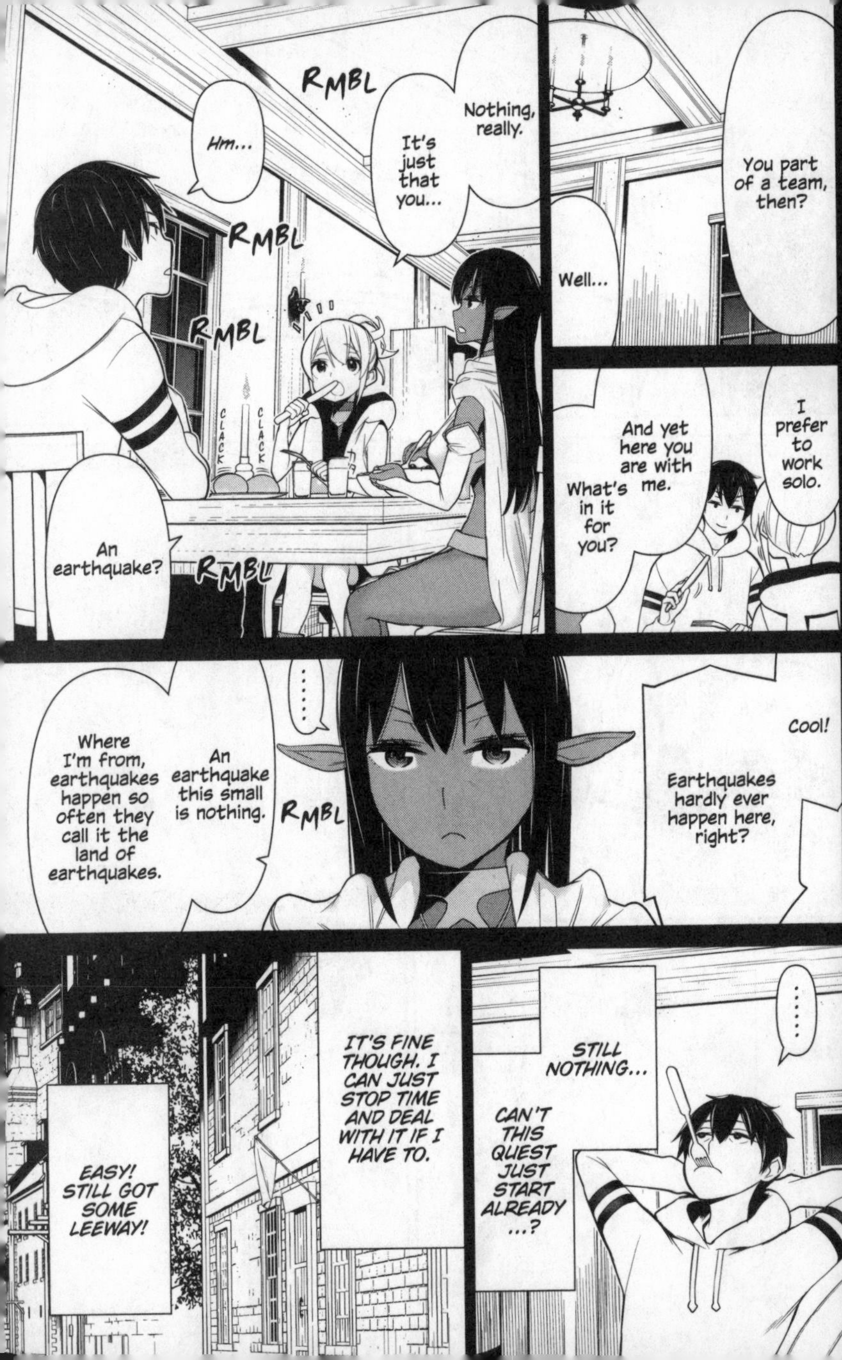
You part of a team, then?
Well...
I prefer to work solo.
And yet here you are with me.
What's in it for you?
RMBL
Nothing, really.
It's just that you...
Hm...
RMBL
RMBL
CLACK
CLACK
An earthquake?
RMBL
Cool!
Earthquakes hardly ever happen here, right?
......
RMBL
An earthquake this small is nothing.
Where I'm from, earthquakes happen so often they call it the land of earthquakes.
......
STILL NOTHING...
CAN'T THIS QUEST JUST START ALREADY ...?
IT'S FINE THOUGH. I CAN JUST STOP TIME AND DEAL WITH IT IF I HAVE TO.
EASY! STILL GOT SOME LEEWAY!

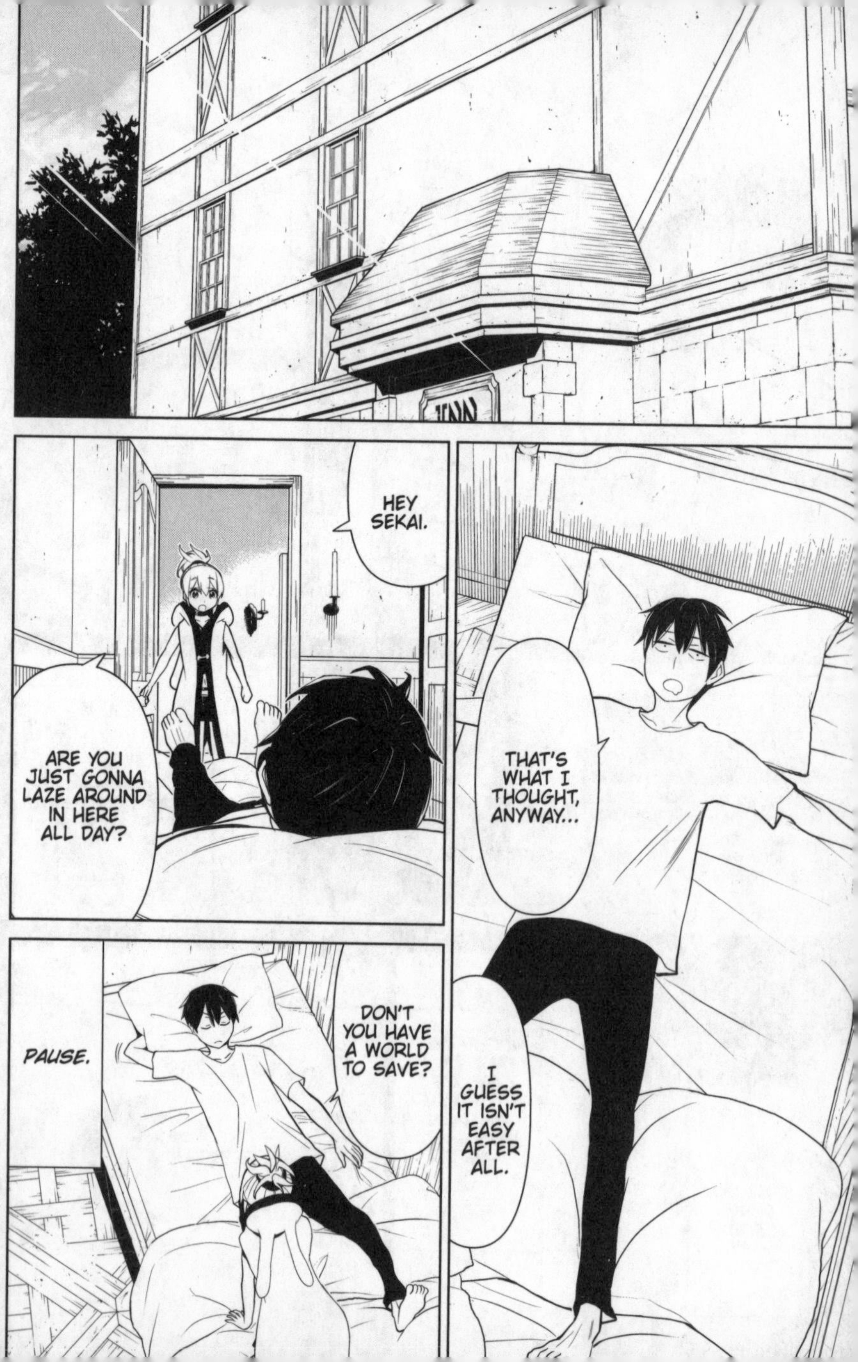
THAT'S WHAT I THOUGHT, ANYWAY...
I GUESS IT ISN'T EASY AFTER ALL.
HEY SEKAI.
ARE YOU JUST GONNA LAZE AROUND IN HERE ALL DAY?
DON'T YOU HAVE A WORLD TO SAVE?
PAUSE.

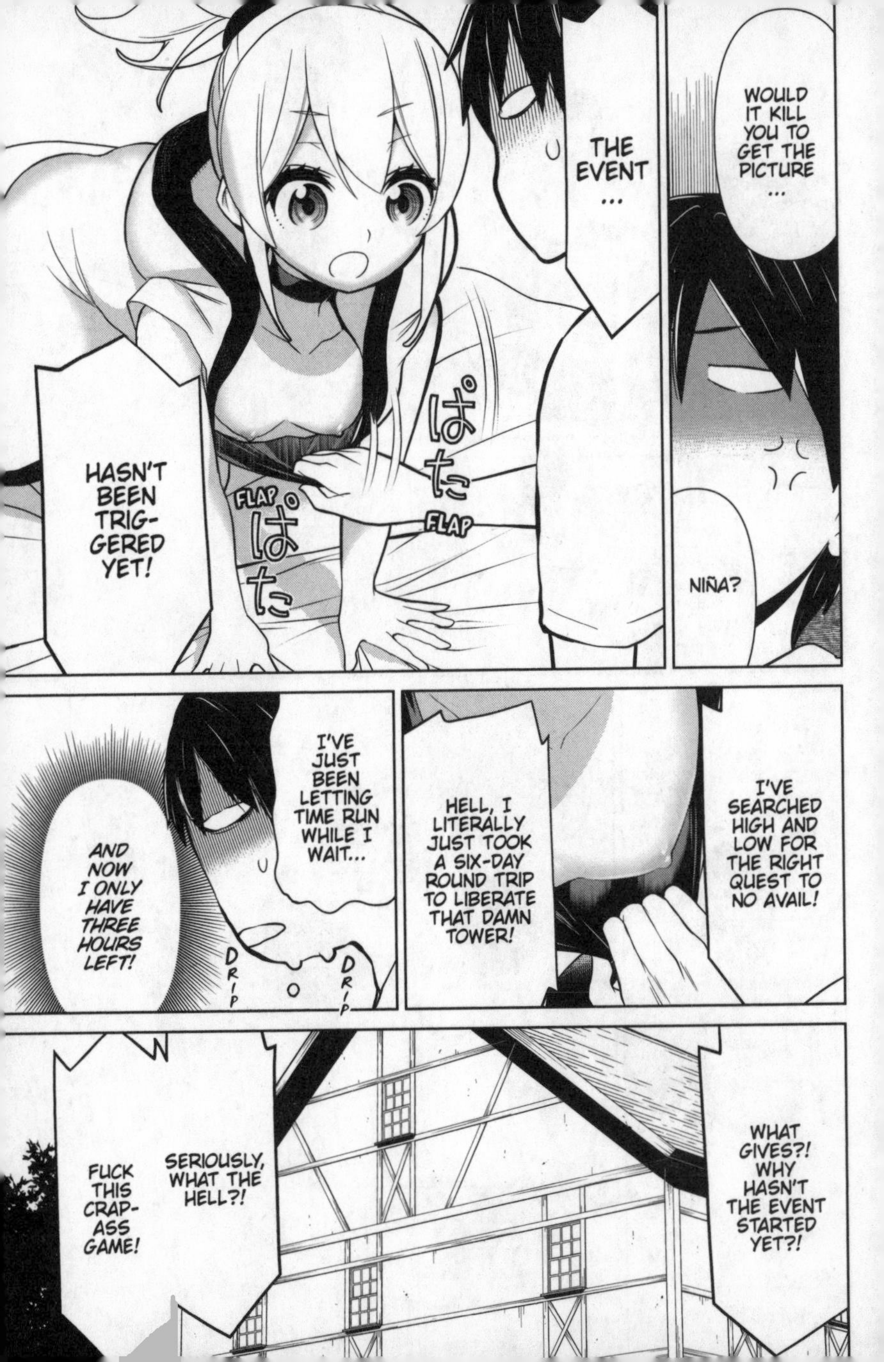
WOULD IT KILL YOU TO GET THE PICTURE ...
NIÑA?
THE EVENT ...
ぱた FLAP
ぱた FLAP
HASN'T BEEN TRIG-GERED YET!
I'VE SEARCHED HIGH AND LOW FOR THE RIGHT QUEST TO NO AVAIL!
HELL, I LITERALLY JUST TOOK A SIX-DAY ROUND TRIP TO LIBERATE THAT DAMN TOWER!
I'VE JUST BEEN LETTING TIME RUN WHILE I WAIT...
AND NOW I ONLY HAVE THREE HOURS LEFT!
DRIP
DRIP
WHAT GIVES?! WHY HASN'T THE EVENT STARTED YET?!
SERIOUSLY, WHAT THE HELL?!
FUCK THIS CRAP-ASS GAME!

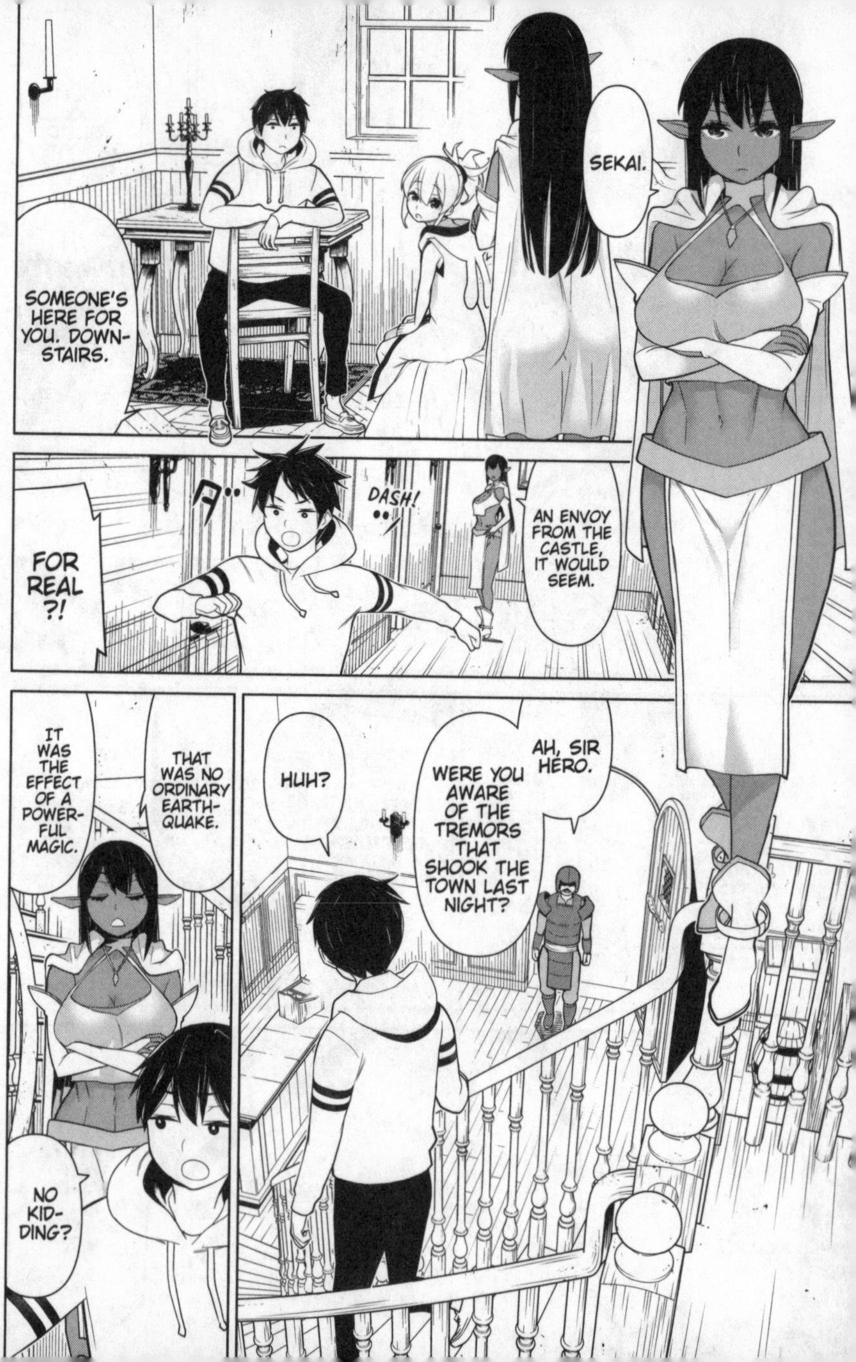
SEKAI.
SOMEONE'S HERE FOR YOU. DOWN-STAIRS.
AN ENVOY FROM THE CASTLE, IT WOULD SEEM.
DASH!
ダッ
FOR REAL?!
AH, SIR HERO.
WERE YOU AWARE OF THE TREMORS THAT SHOOK THE TOWN LAST NIGHT?
HUH?
THAT WAS NO ORDINARY EARTH-QUAKE.
IT WAS THE EFFECT OF A POWER-FUL MAGIC.
NO KID-DING?

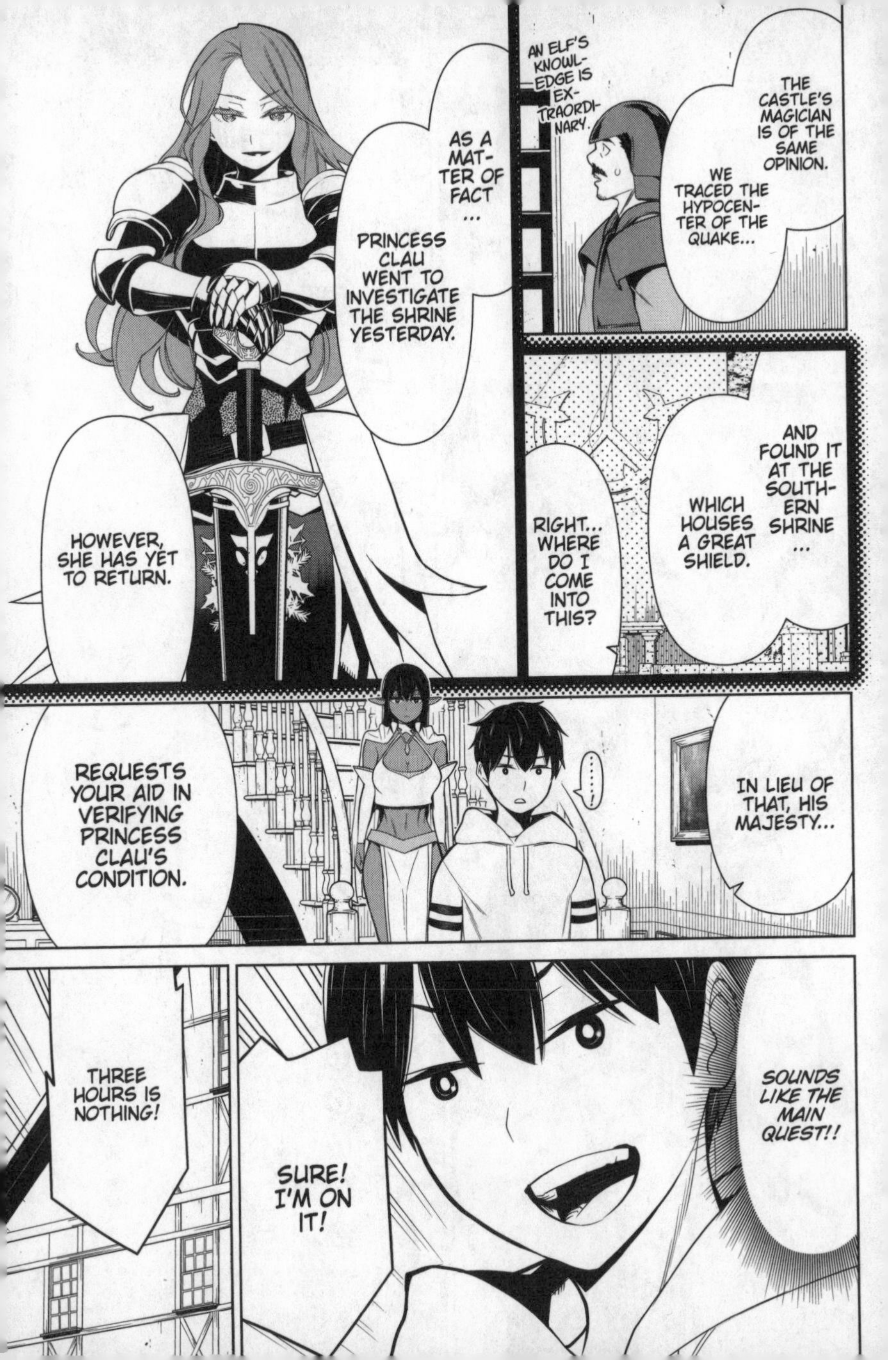
THE CASTLE'S MAGICIAN IS OF THE SAME OPINION.
WE TRACED THE HYPOCENTER OF THE QUAKE...
AN ELF'S KNOWLEDGE IS EXTRAORDINARY.
AND FOUND IT AT THE SOUTHERN SHRINE...
WHICH HOUSES A GREAT SHIELD.
RIGHT... WHERE DO I COME INTO THIS?
AS A MATTER OF FACT...
PRINCESS CLAU WENT TO INVESTIGATE THE SHRINE YESTERDAY.
HOWEVER, SHE HAS YET TO RETURN.
IN LIEU OF THAT, HIS MAJESTY...
...!
REQUESTS YOUR AID IN VERIFYING PRINCESS CLAU'S CONDITION.
SOUNDS LIKE THE MAIN QUEST!!
SURE! I'M ON IT!
THREE HOURS IS NOTHING!

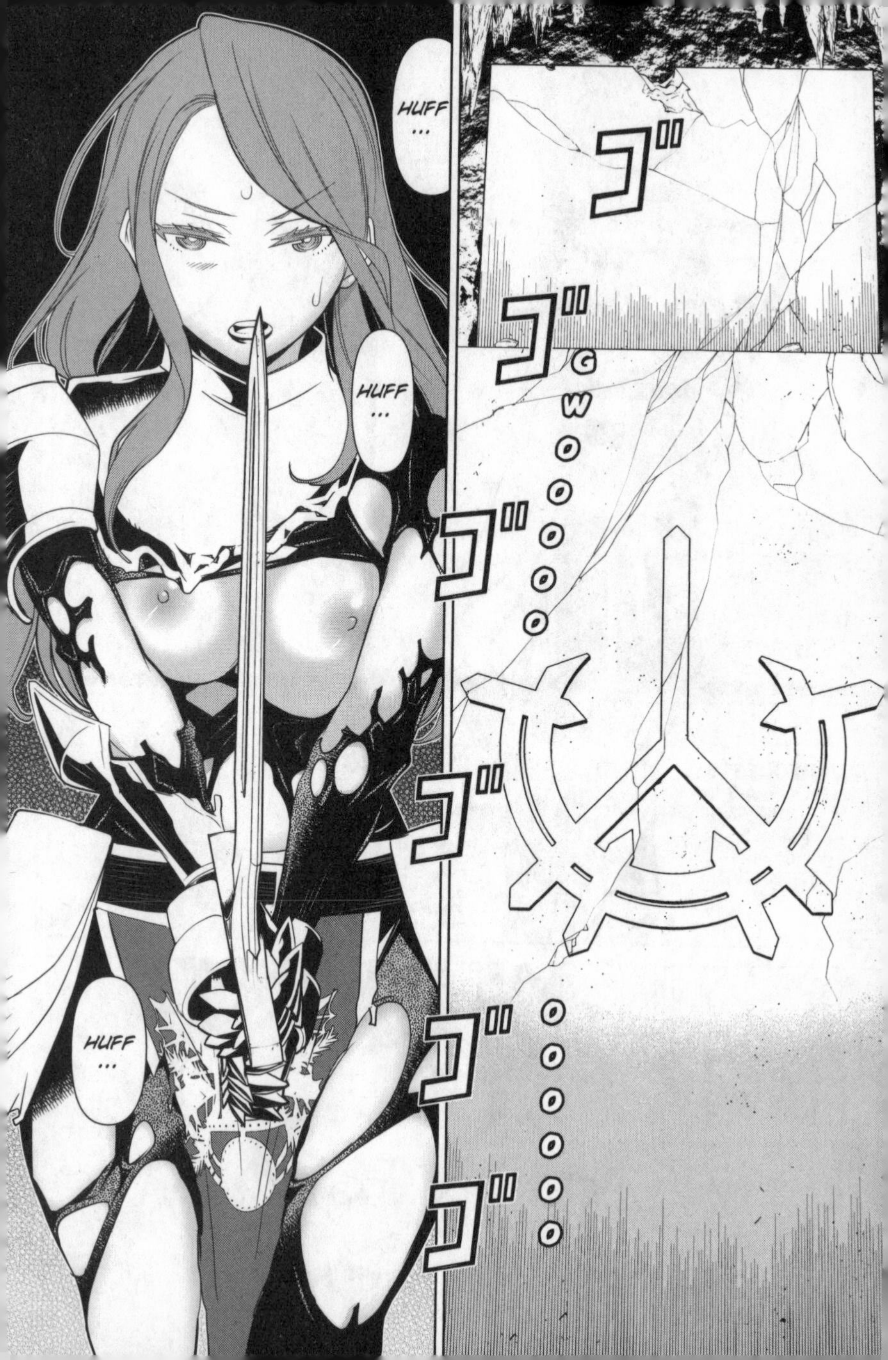
ゴ
ゴ
GWOOOOOOOOOOOOO
ゴ
ゴ
ゴ
ゴ
HUFF …
HUFF …
HUFF …

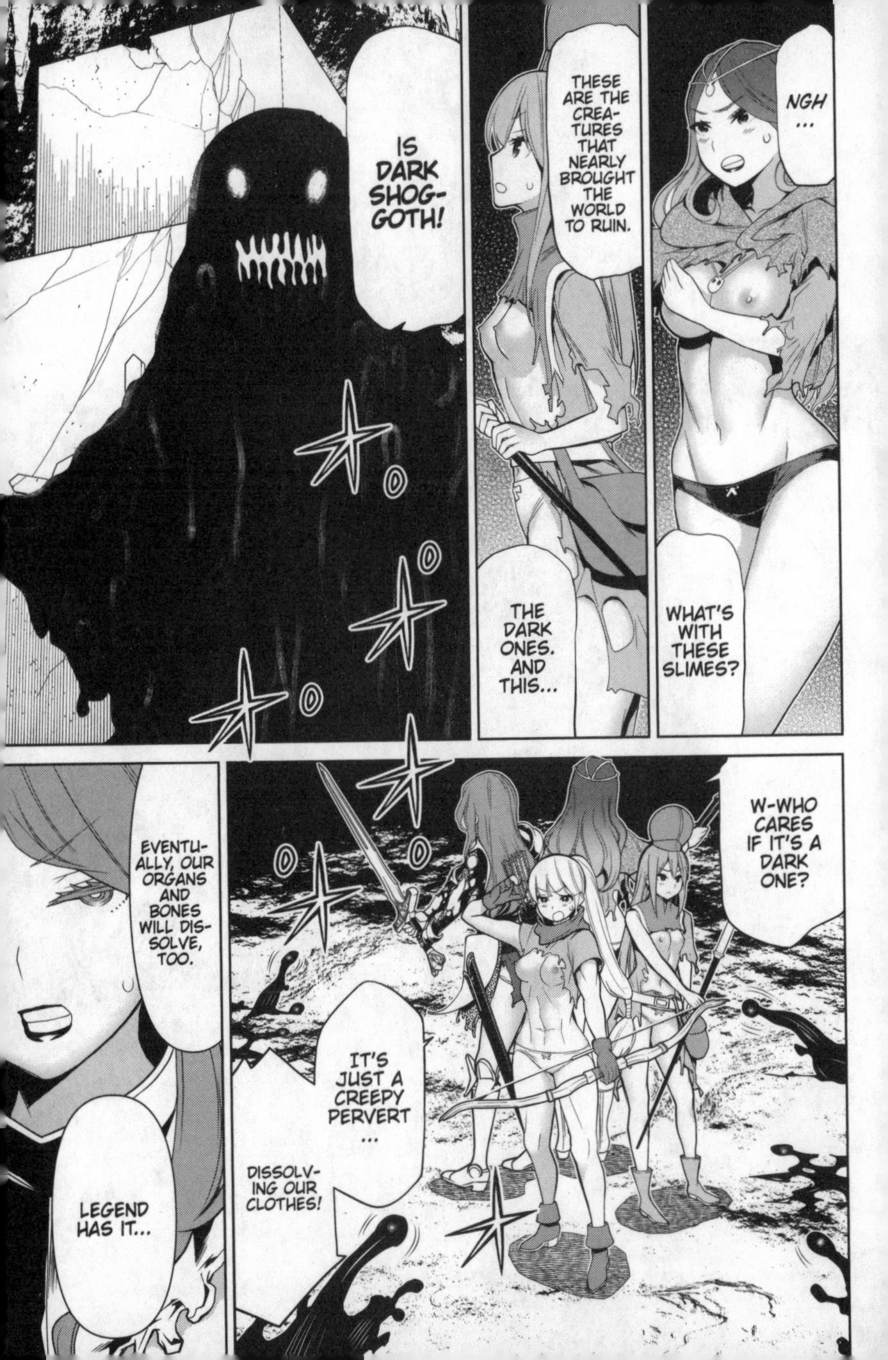
NGH ...
WHAT'S WITH THESE SLIMES?
THESE ARE THE CREATURES THAT NEARLY BROUGHT THE WORLD TO RUIN.
THE DARK ONES. AND THIS...
IS DARK SHOGGOTH!
W-WHO CARES IF IT'S A DARK ONE?
IT'S JUST A CREEPY PERVERT ...
DISSOLVING OUR CLOTHES!
EVENTUALLY, OUR ORGANS AND BONES WILL DISSOLVE, TOO.
LEGEND HAS IT...

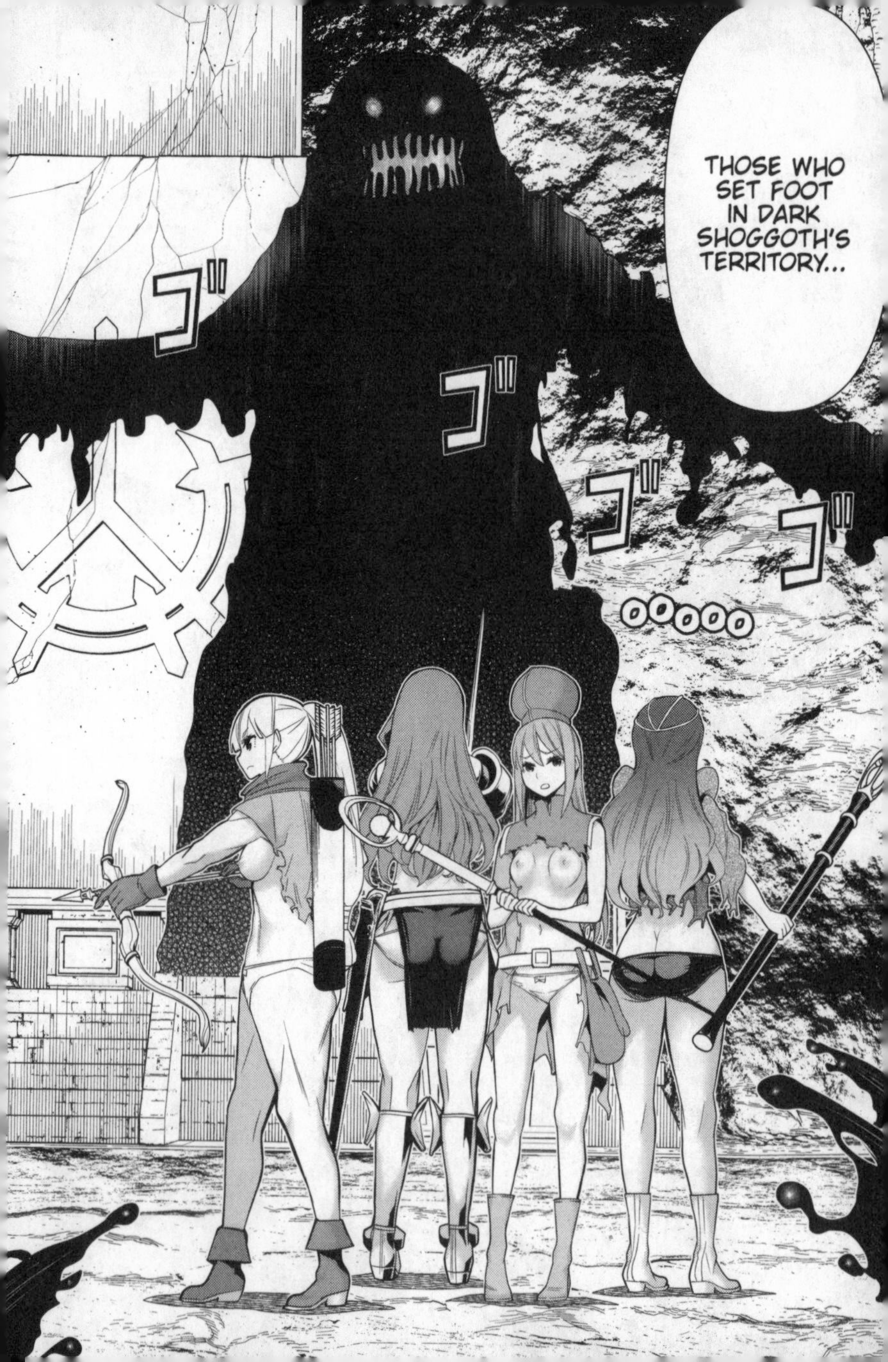
THOSE WHO SET FOOT IN DARK SHOGGOTH'S TERRITORY...
ゴ
ゴ
ゴ
ゴ
OOOOO

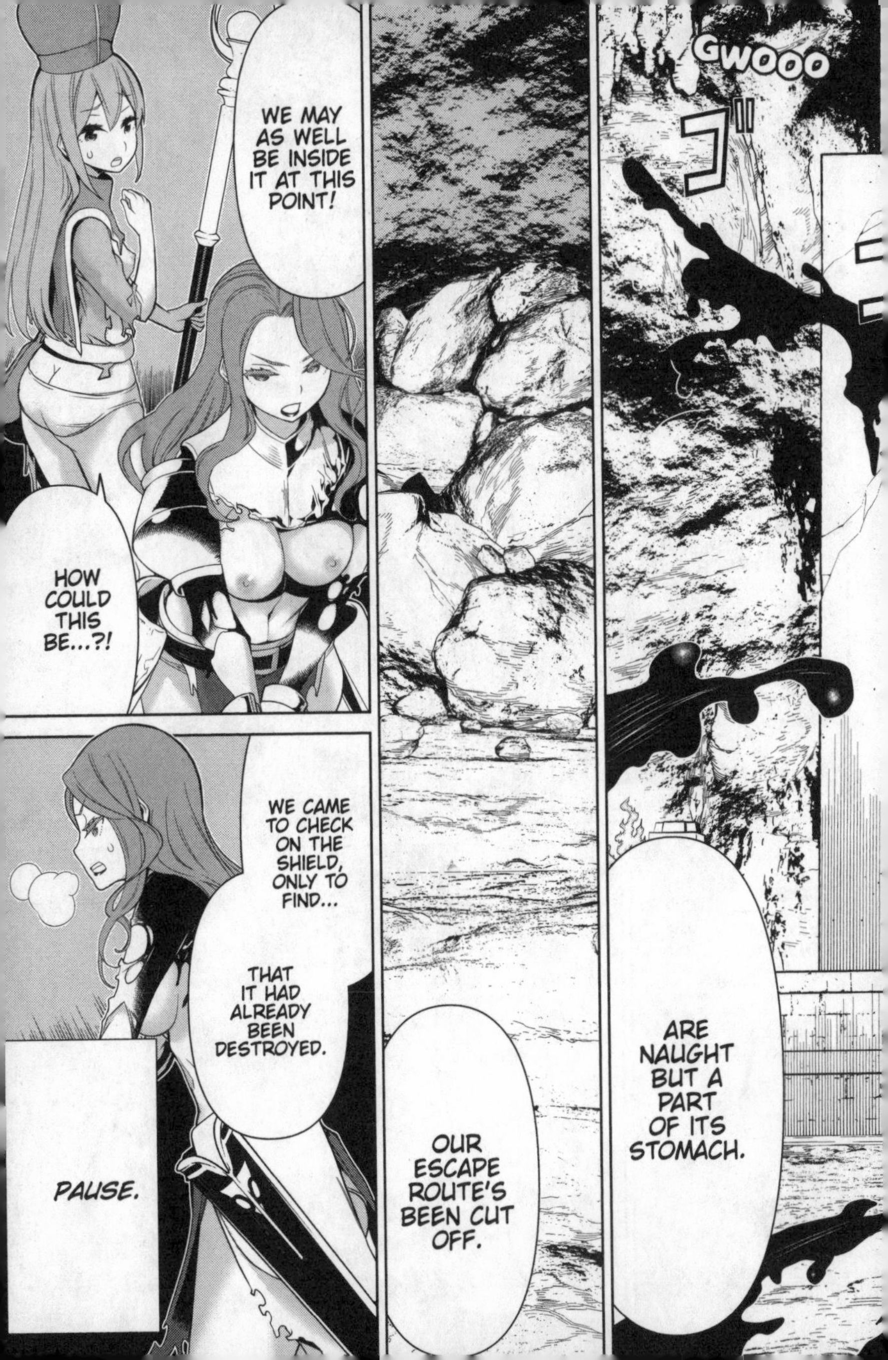
GWOOO
ゴ
ARE NAUGHT BUT A PART OF ITS STOMACH.
OUR ESCAPE ROUTE'S BEEN CUT OFF.
WE MAY AS WELL BE INSIDE IT AT THIS POINT!
HOW COULD THIS BE...?!
WE CAME TO CHECK ON THE SHIELD, ONLY TO FIND...
THAT IT HAD ALREADY BEEN DESTROYED.
PAUSE.

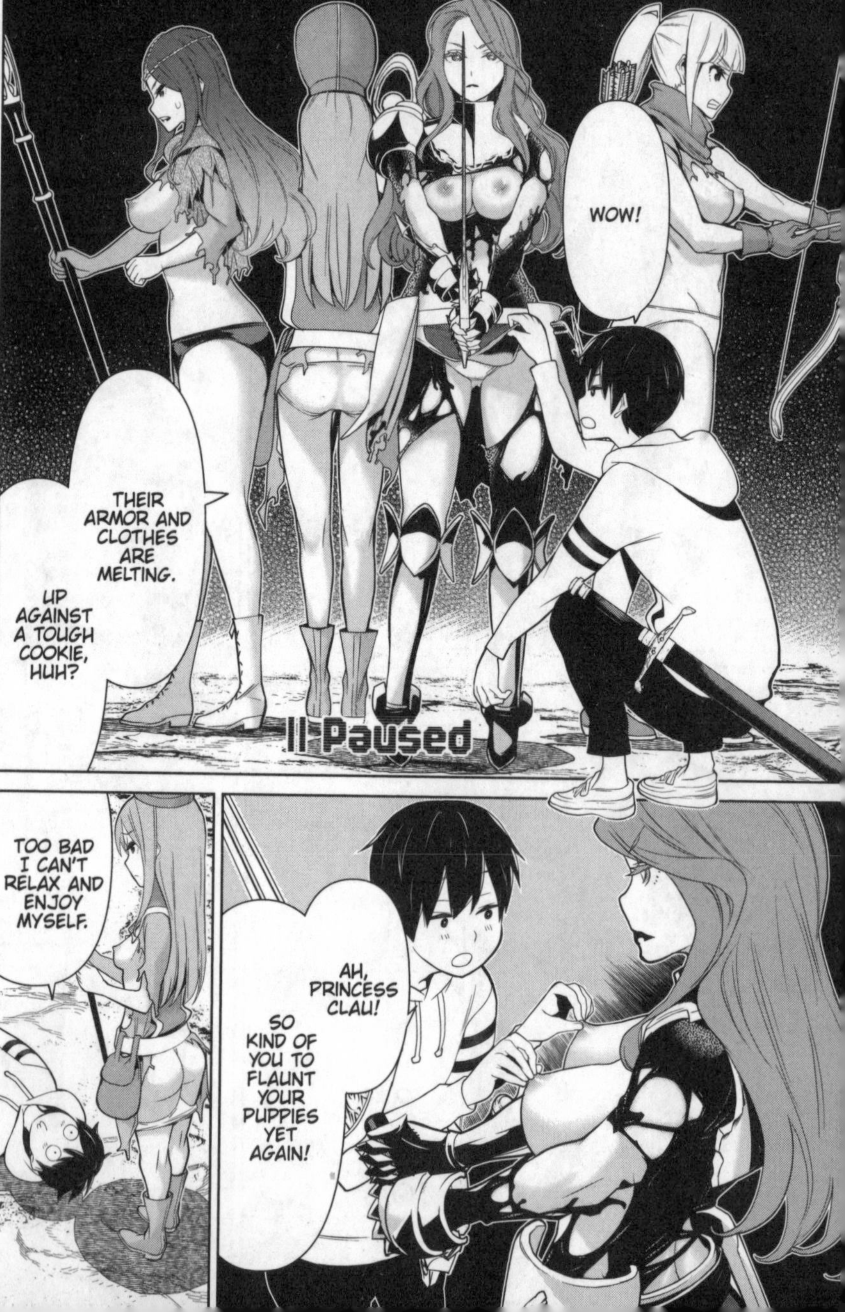
WOW!
THEIR ARMOR AND CLOTHES ARE MELTING.
UP AGAINST A TOUGH COOKIE, HUH?
Paused
AH, PRINCESS CLAU!
SO KIND OF YOU TO FLAUNT YOUR PUPPIES YET AGAIN!
TOO BAD I CAN'T RELAX AND ENJOY MYSELF.

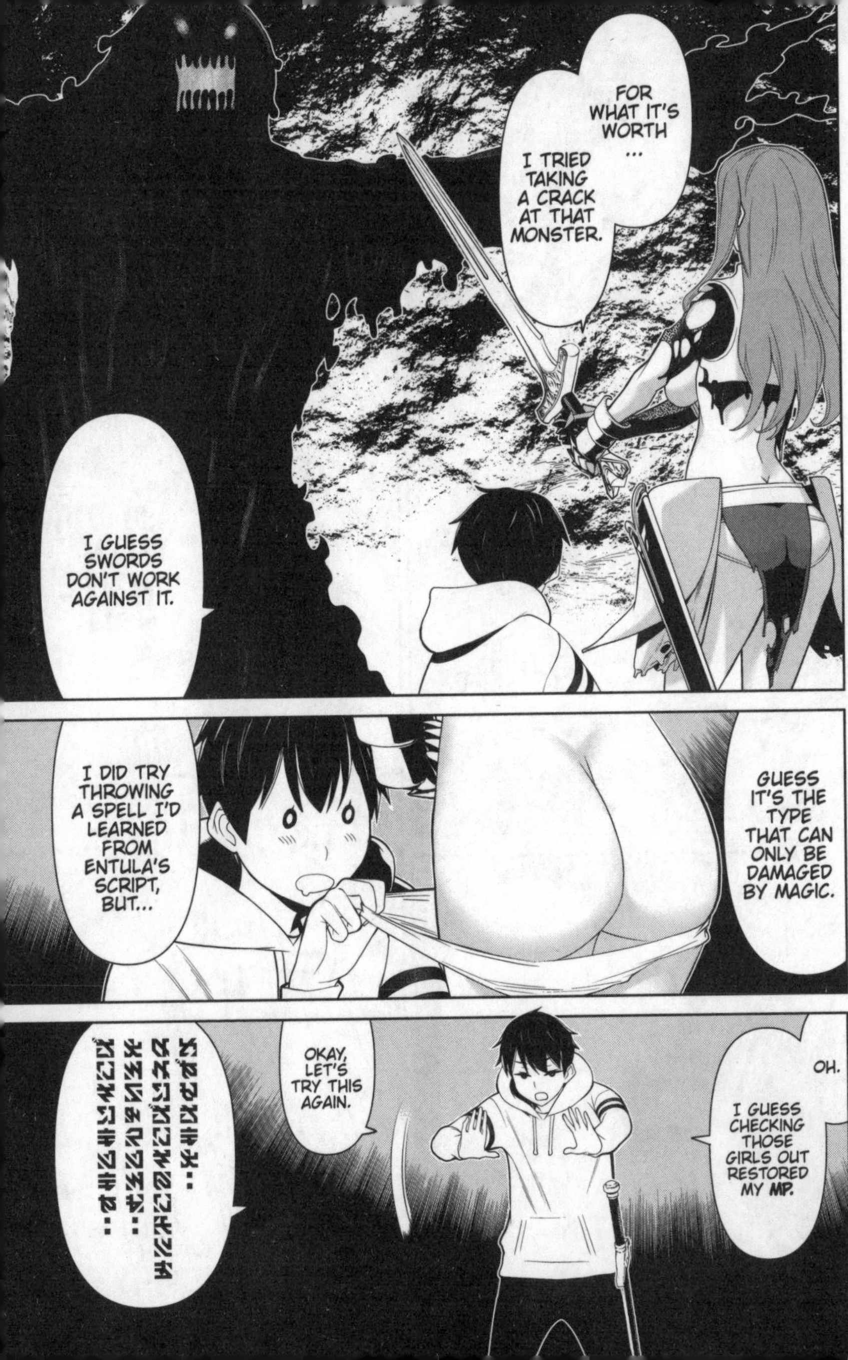
FOR WHAT IT'S WORTH ...
I TRIED TAKING A CRACK AT THAT MONSTER.
I GUESS SWORDS DON'T WORK AGAINST IT.
GUESS IT'S THE TYPE THAT CAN ONLY BE DAMAGED BY MAGIC.
I DID TRY THROWING A SPELL I'D LEARNED FROM ENTULA'S SCRIPT, BUT...
OH.
I GUESS CHECKING THOSE GIRLS OUT RESTORED MY MP.
OKAY, LET'S TRY THIS AGAIN.

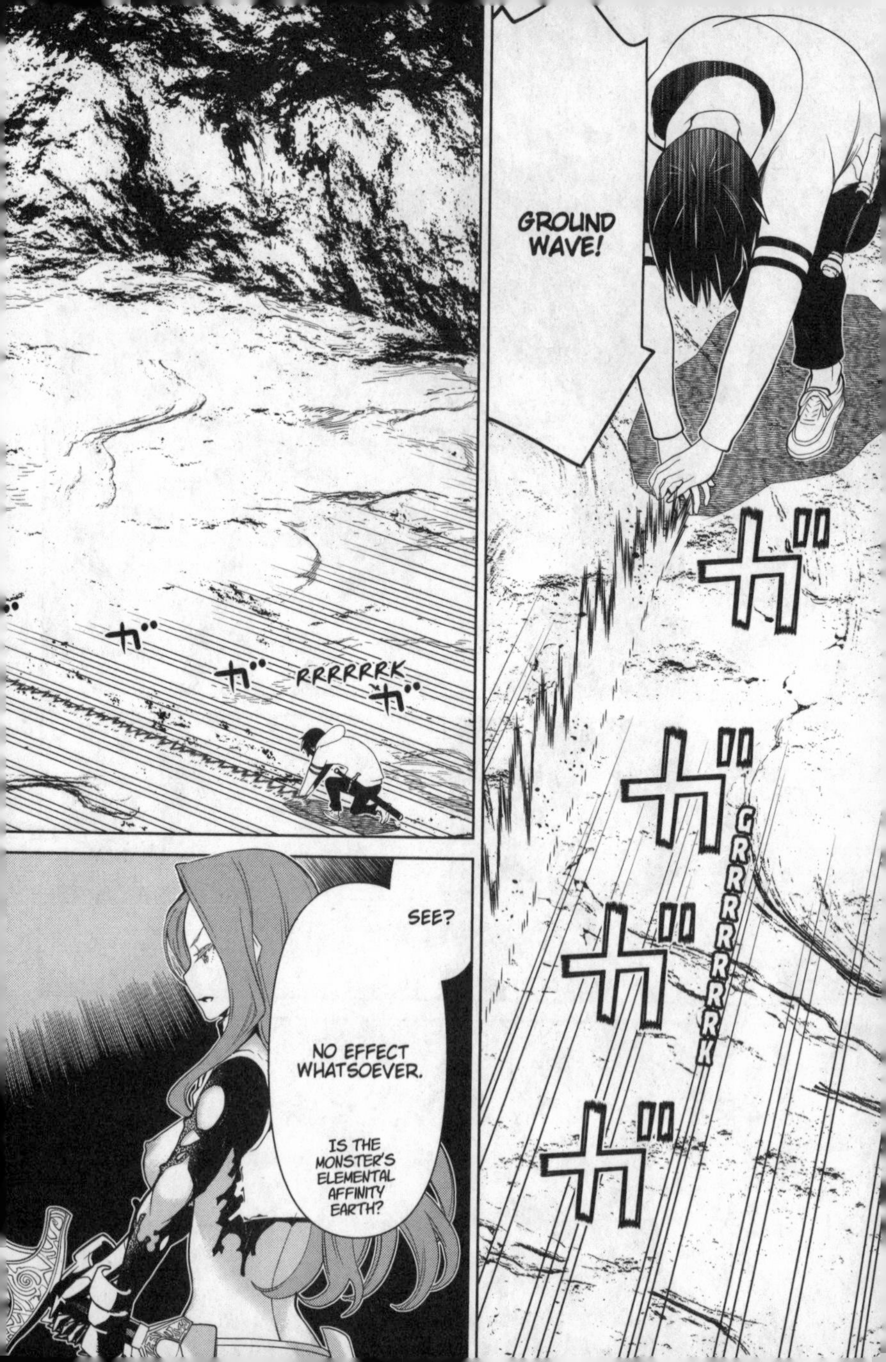
GROUND WAVE!
ガ
ガ
GRRRRRRRK
ガ
ガ
ガ
ガ
RRRRRRK
ガ
SEE?
NO EFFECT WHATSOEVER.
IS THE MONSTER'S ELEMENTAL AFFINITY EARTH?

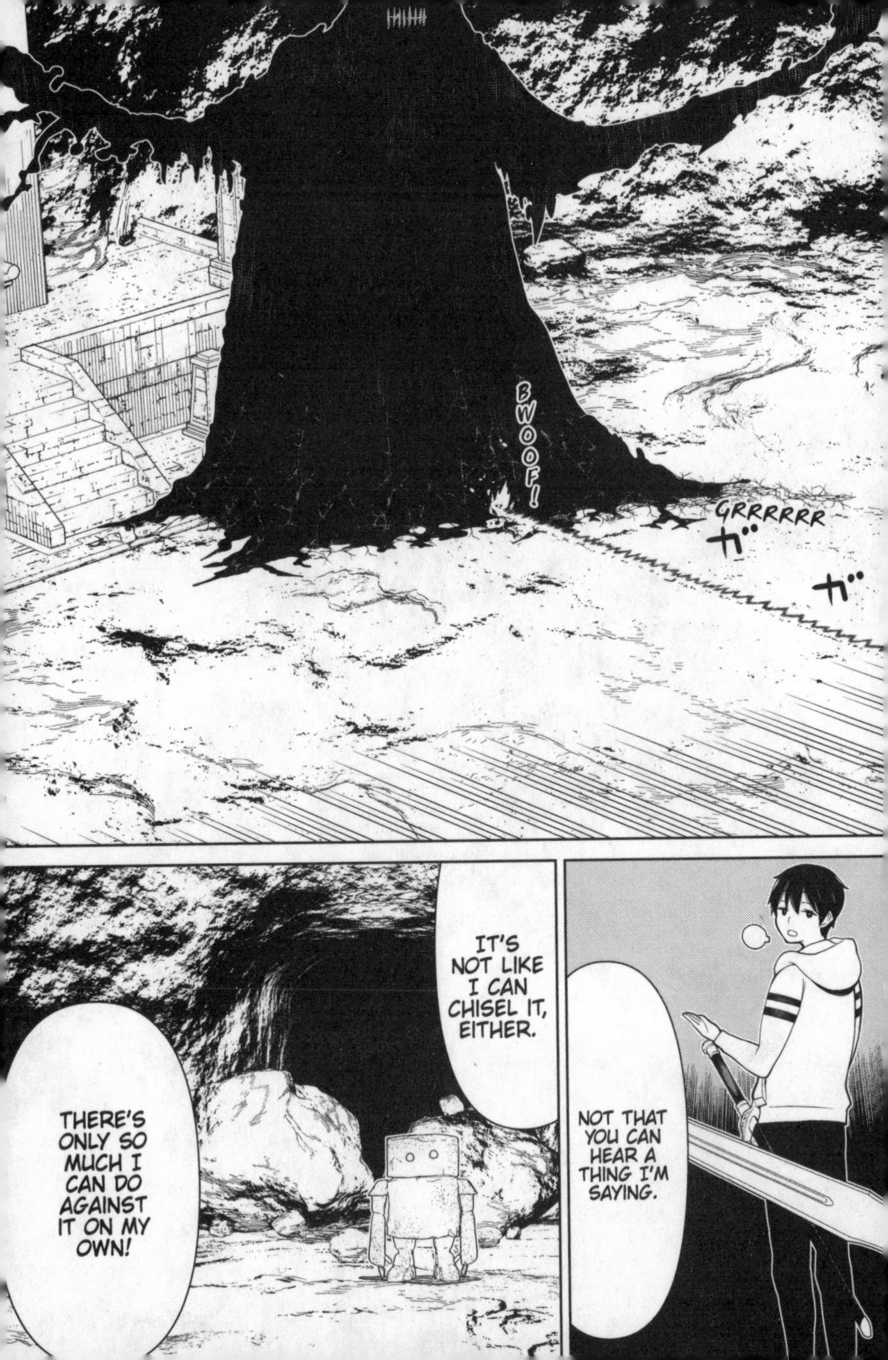
BWOOF!
GRRRRRR
ガ
ガ
NOT THAT YOU CAN HEAR A THING I'M SAYING.
IT'S NOT LIKE I CAN CHISEL IT, EITHER.
THERE'S ONLY SO MUCH I CAN DO AGAINST IT ON MY OWN!

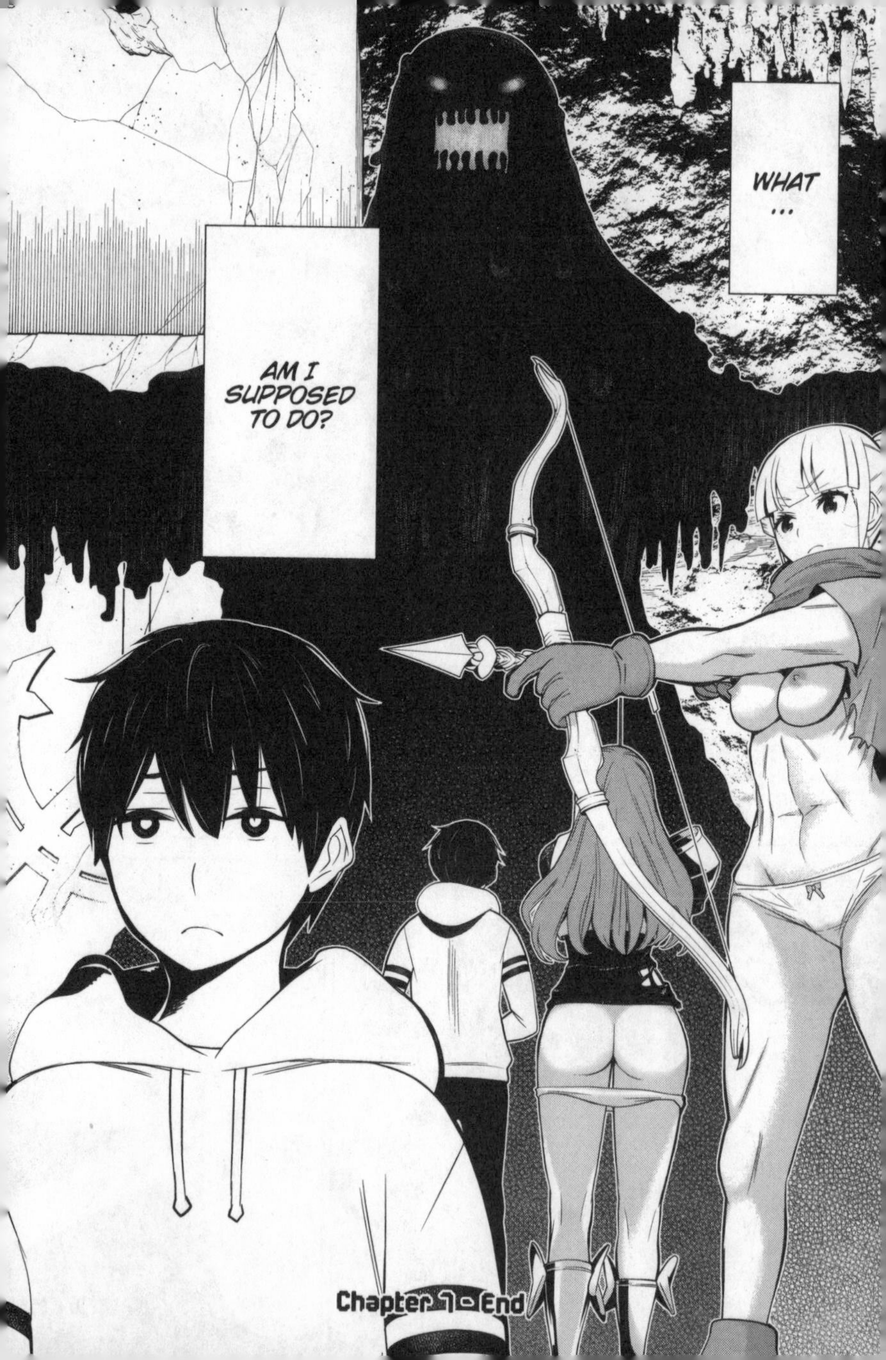
WHAT ...
AM I SUPPOSED TO DO?
Chapter 1 - End

2 3 4 5 6 7

8

START
▶ PAUSE

▶START
PAUSE

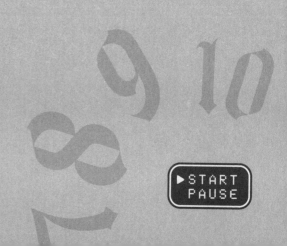

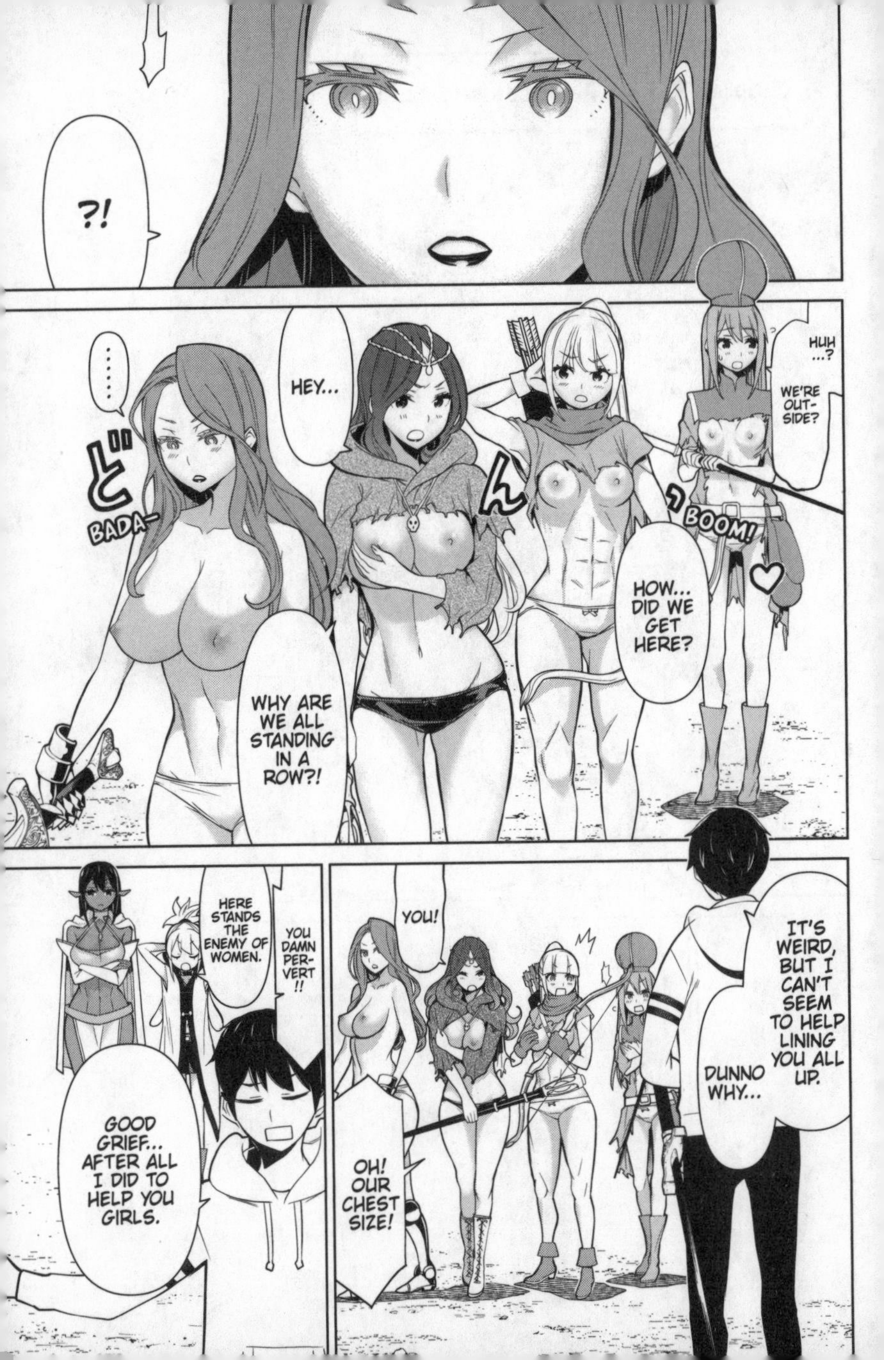
?!
HUH...? WE'RE OUT-SIDE?
どん BADA-BOOM!
HOW... DID WE GET HERE?
HEY...
......
WHY ARE WE ALL STANDING IN A ROW?!
IT'S WEIRD, BUT I CAN'T SEEM TO HELP LINING YOU ALL UP.
YOU!
DUNNO WHY...
OH! OUR CHEST SIZE!
YOU DAMN PERVERT!!
HERE STANDS THE ENEMY OF WOMEN.
GOOD GRIEF... AFTER ALL I DID TO HELP YOU GIRLS.

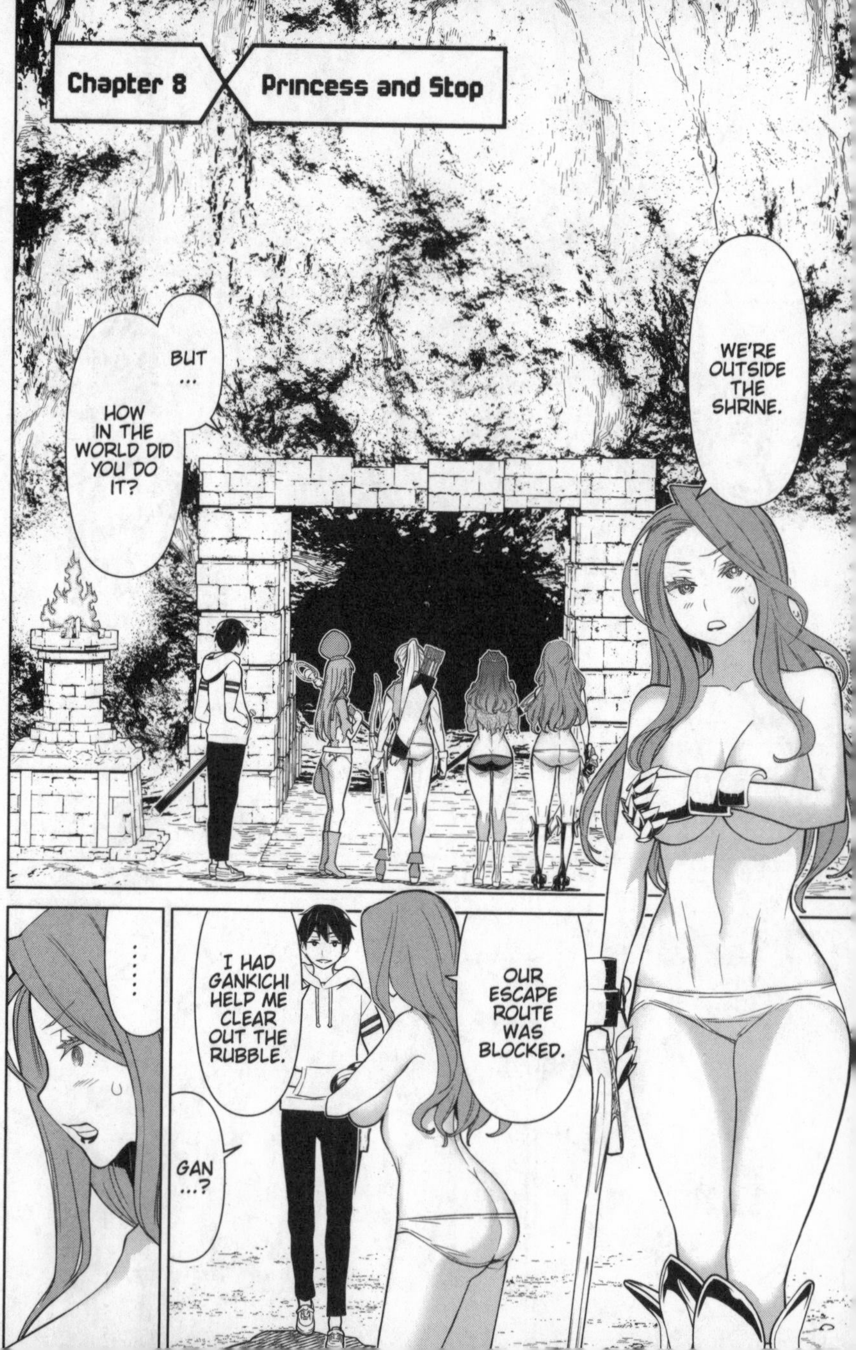
Chapter 8
Princess and Stop
WE'RE OUTSIDE THE SHRINE.
BUT ... HOW IN THE WORLD DID YOU DO IT?
OUR ESCAPE ROUTE WAS BLOCKED.
I HAD GANKICHI HELP ME CLEAR OUT THE RUBBLE.
GAN ...?
......

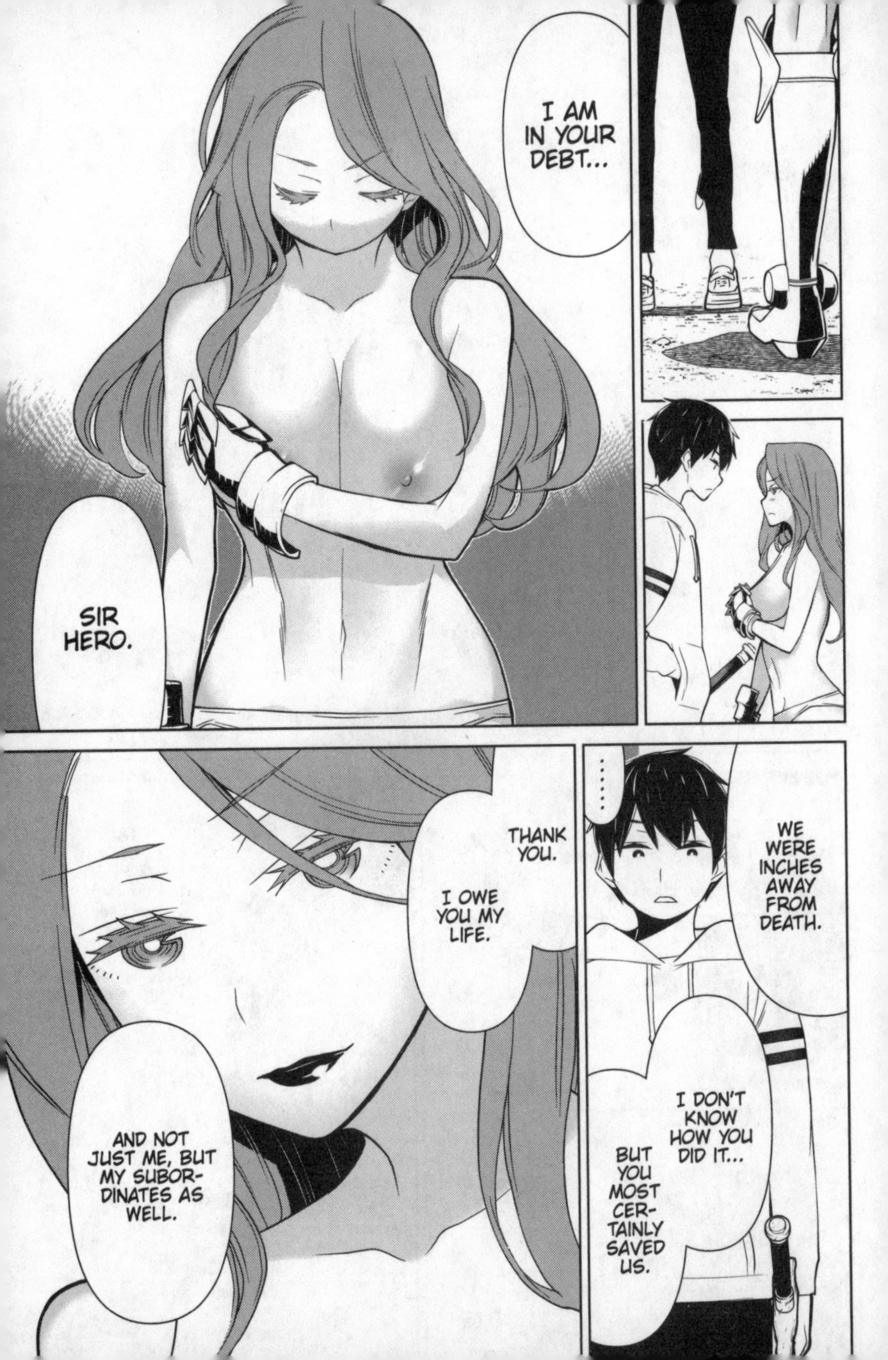
I AM IN YOUR DEBT...
SIR HERO.
WE WERE INCHES AWAY FROM DEATH.
......
I DON'T KNOW HOW YOU DID IT...
BUT YOU MOST CERTAINLY SAVED US.
THANK YOU.
I OWE YOU MY LIFE.
AND NOT JUST ME, BUT MY SUBORDINATES AS WELL.

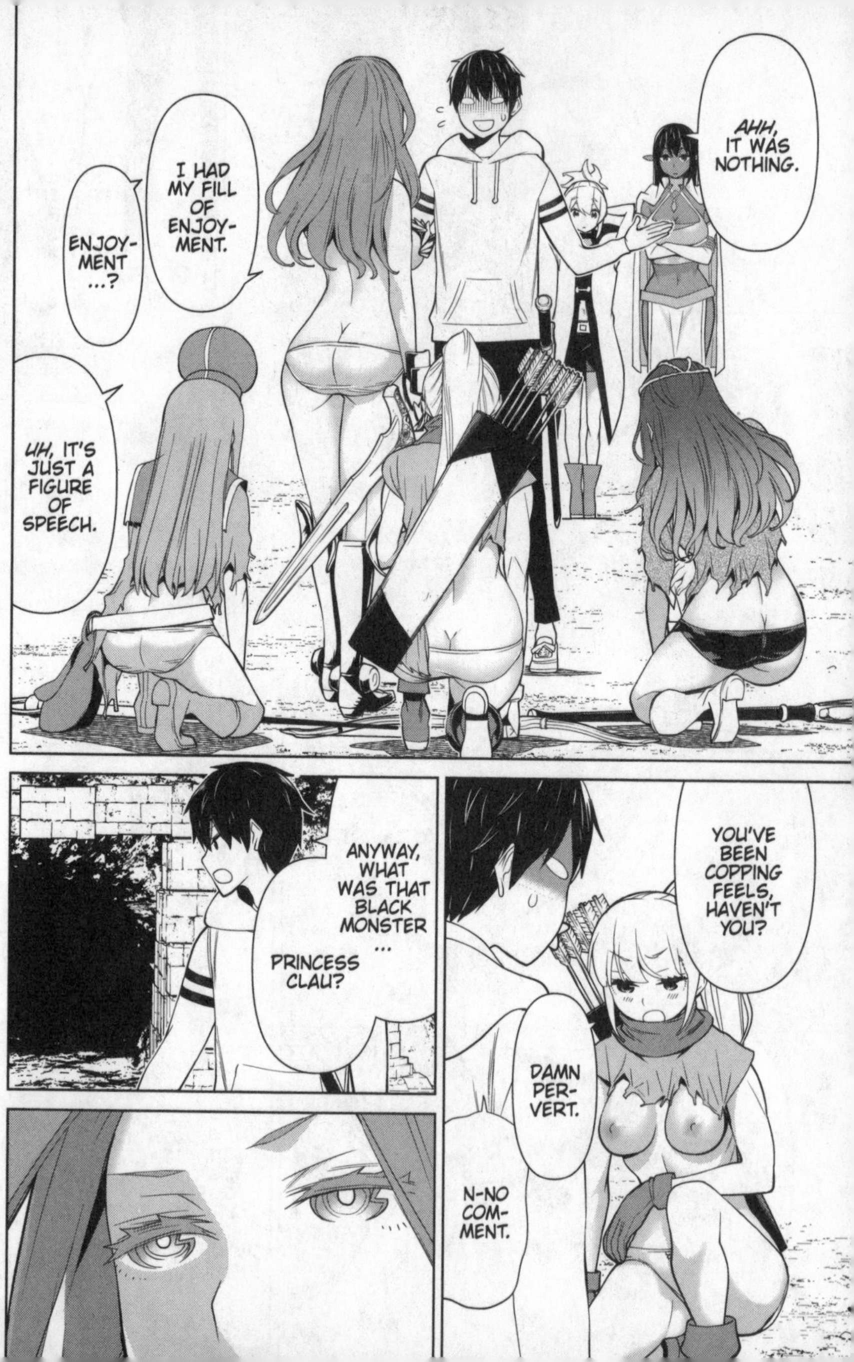
AHH, IT WAS NOTHING.
I HAD MY FILL OF ENJOY-MENT.
ENJOY-MENT ...?
UH, IT'S JUST A FIGURE OF SPEECH.
YOU'VE BEEN COPPING FEELS, HAVEN'T YOU?
DAMN PER-VERT.
N-NO COM-MENT.
ANYWAY, WHAT WAS THAT BLACK MONSTER ...
PRINCESS CLAU?

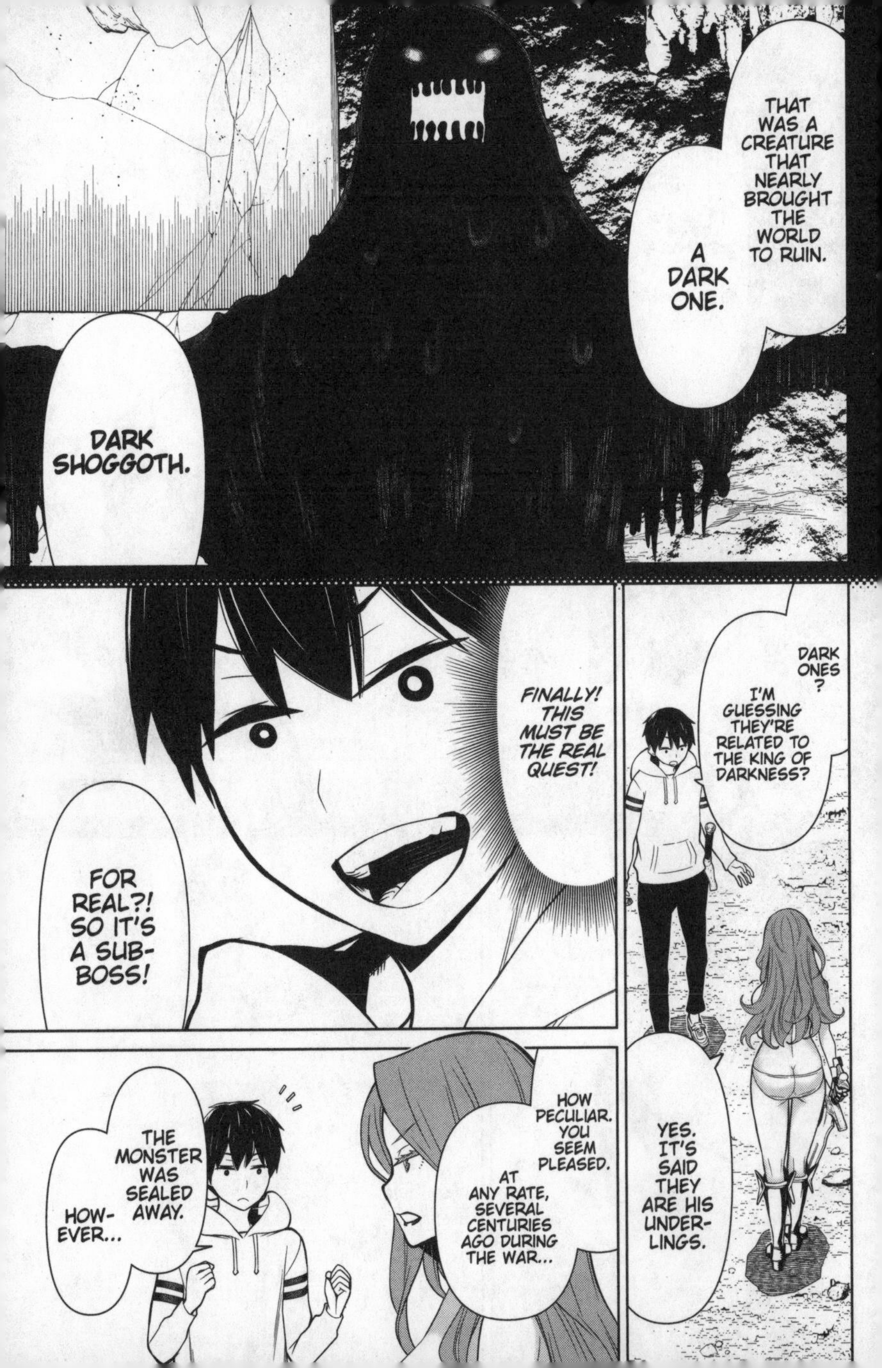
THAT WAS A CREATURE THAT NEARLY BROUGHT THE WORLD TO RUIN.
A DARK ONE.
DARK SHOGGOTH.
DARK ONES?
I'M GUESSING THEY'RE RELATED TO THE KING OF DARKNESS?
YES. IT'S SAID THEY ARE HIS UNDER-LINGS.
FINALLY! THIS MUST BE THE REAL QUEST!
FOR REAL?! SO IT'S A SUB-BOSS!
HOW PECULIAR. YOU SEEM PLEASED.
AT ANY RATE, SEVERAL CENTURIES AGO DURING THE WAR...
THE MONSTER WAS SEALED AWAY.
HOW-EVER...

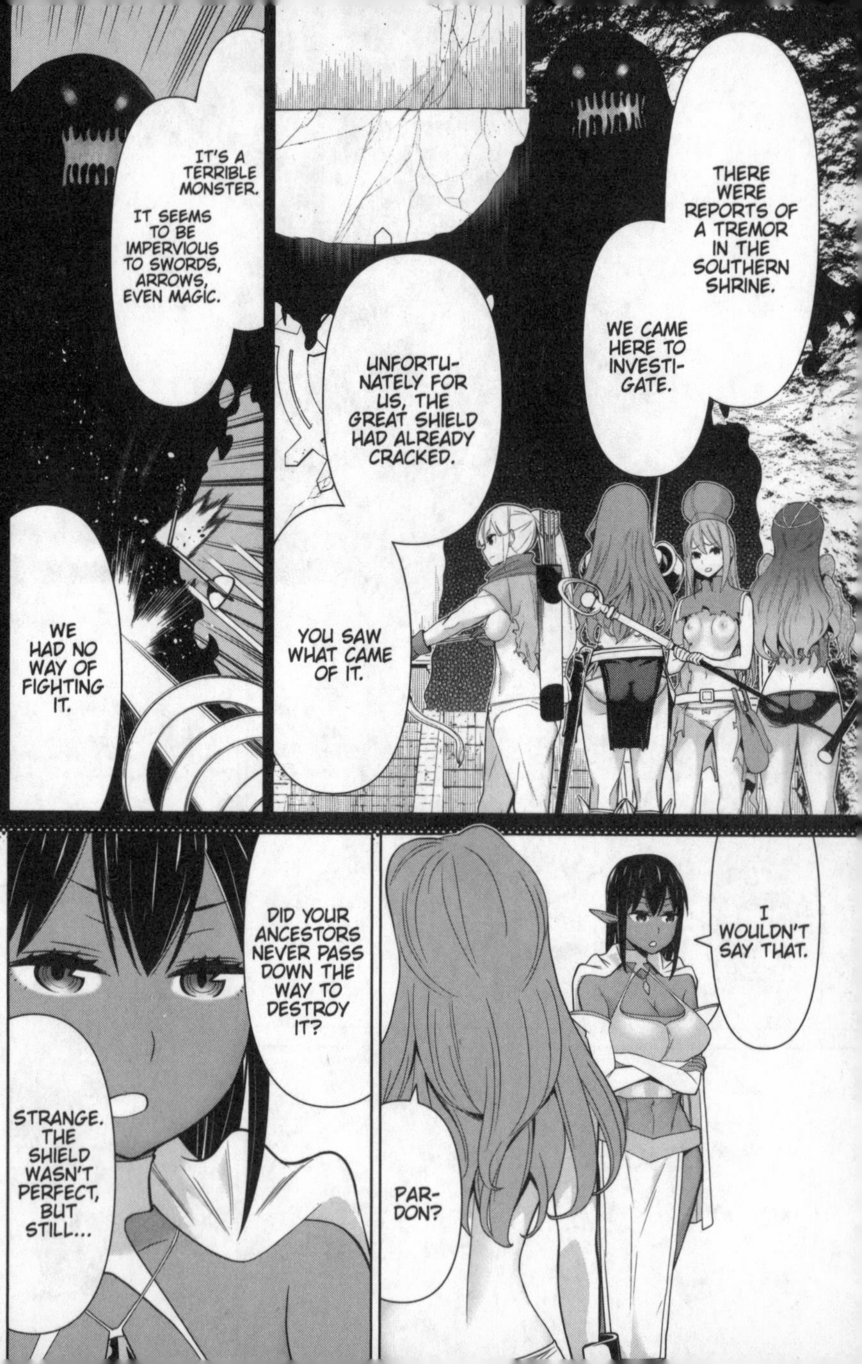
THERE WERE REPORTS OF A TREMOR IN THE SOUTHERN SHRINE.
WE CAME HERE TO INVESTIGATE.
UNFORTUNATELY FOR US, THE GREAT SHIELD HAD ALREADY CRACKED.
YOU SAW WHAT CAME OF IT.
IT'S A TERRIBLE MONSTER.
IT SEEMS TO BE IMPERVIOUS TO SWORDS, ARROWS, EVEN MAGIC.
WE HAD NO WAY OF FIGHTING IT.
I WOULDN'T SAY THAT.
PARDON?
DID YOUR ANCESTORS NEVER PASS DOWN THE WAY TO DESTROY IT?
STRANGE. THE SHIELD WASN'T PERFECT, BUT STILL...

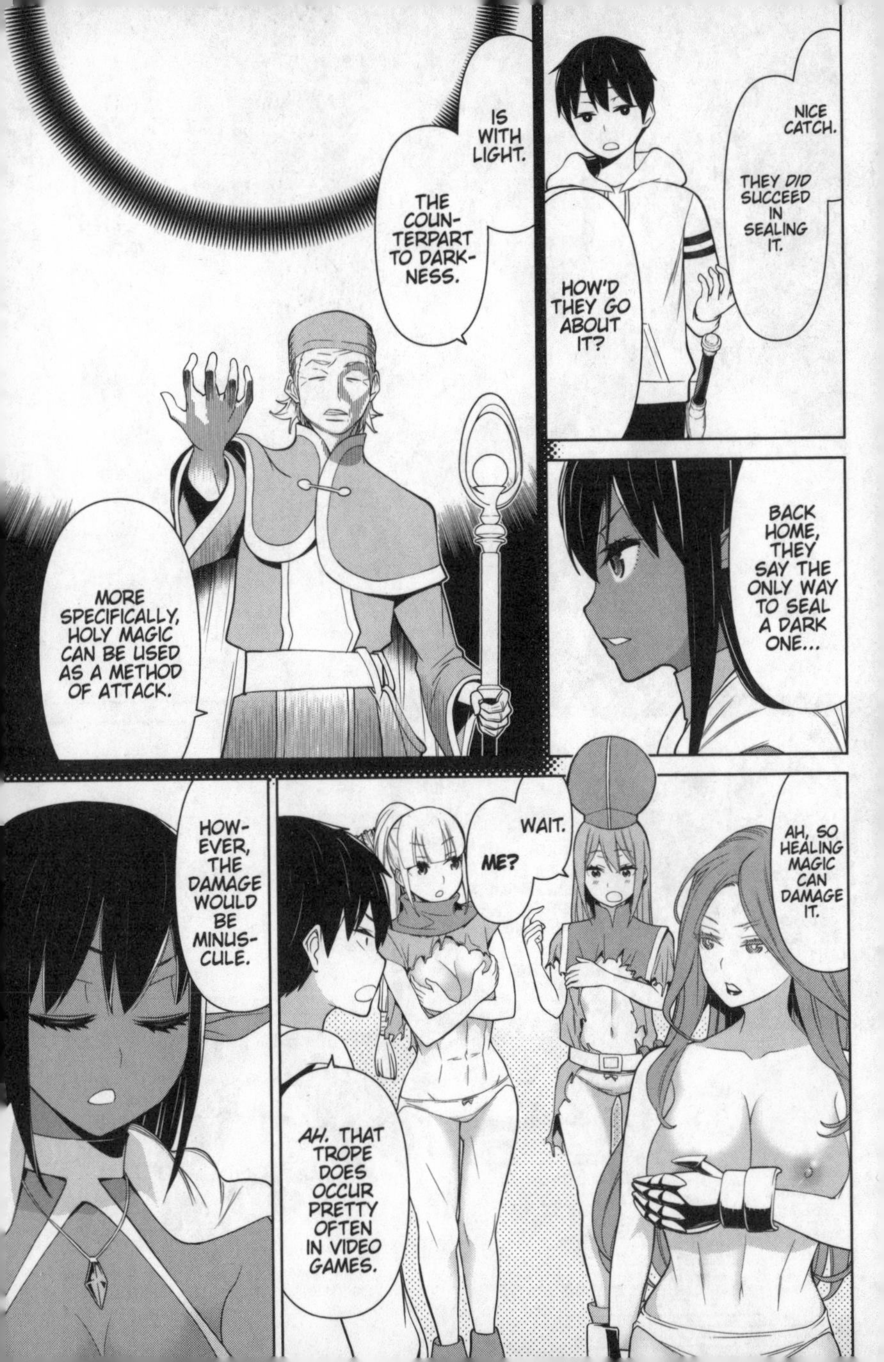
NICE CATCH.
THEY *DID* SUCCEED IN SEALING IT.
HOW'D THEY GO ABOUT IT?
BACK HOME, THEY SAY THE ONLY WAY TO SEAL A DARK ONE...
IS WITH LIGHT.
THE COUNTERPART TO DARKNESS.
MORE SPECIFICALLY, HOLY MAGIC CAN BE USED AS A METHOD OF ATTACK.
AH, SO HEALING MAGIC CAN DAMAGE IT.
WAIT.
ME?
AH. THAT TROPE DOES OCCUR PRETTY OFTEN IN VIDEO GAMES.
HOWEVER, THE DAMAGE WOULD BE MINUSCULE.

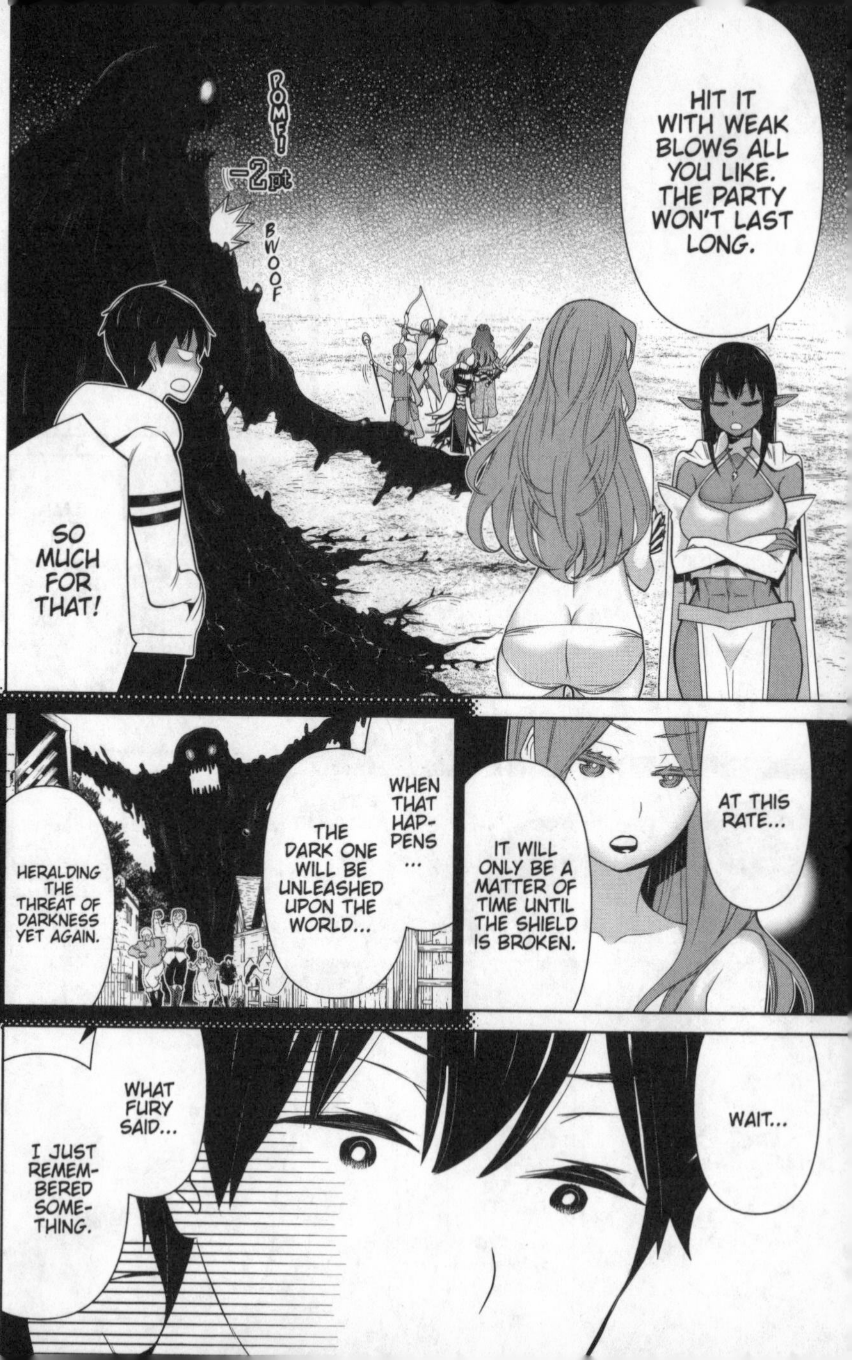
HIT IT WITH WEAK BLOWS ALL YOU LIKE. THE PARTY WON'T LAST LONG.
POMF!
-2pt
BWOOF
SO MUCH FOR THAT!
AT THIS RATE...
IT WILL ONLY BE A MATTER OF TIME UNTIL THE SHIELD IS BROKEN.
WHEN THAT HAP-PENS...
THE DARK ONE WILL BE UNLEASHED UPON THE WORLD...
HERALDING THE THREAT OF DARKNESS YET AGAIN.
WAIT...
WHAT FURY SAID...
I JUST REMEM-BERED SOME-THING.

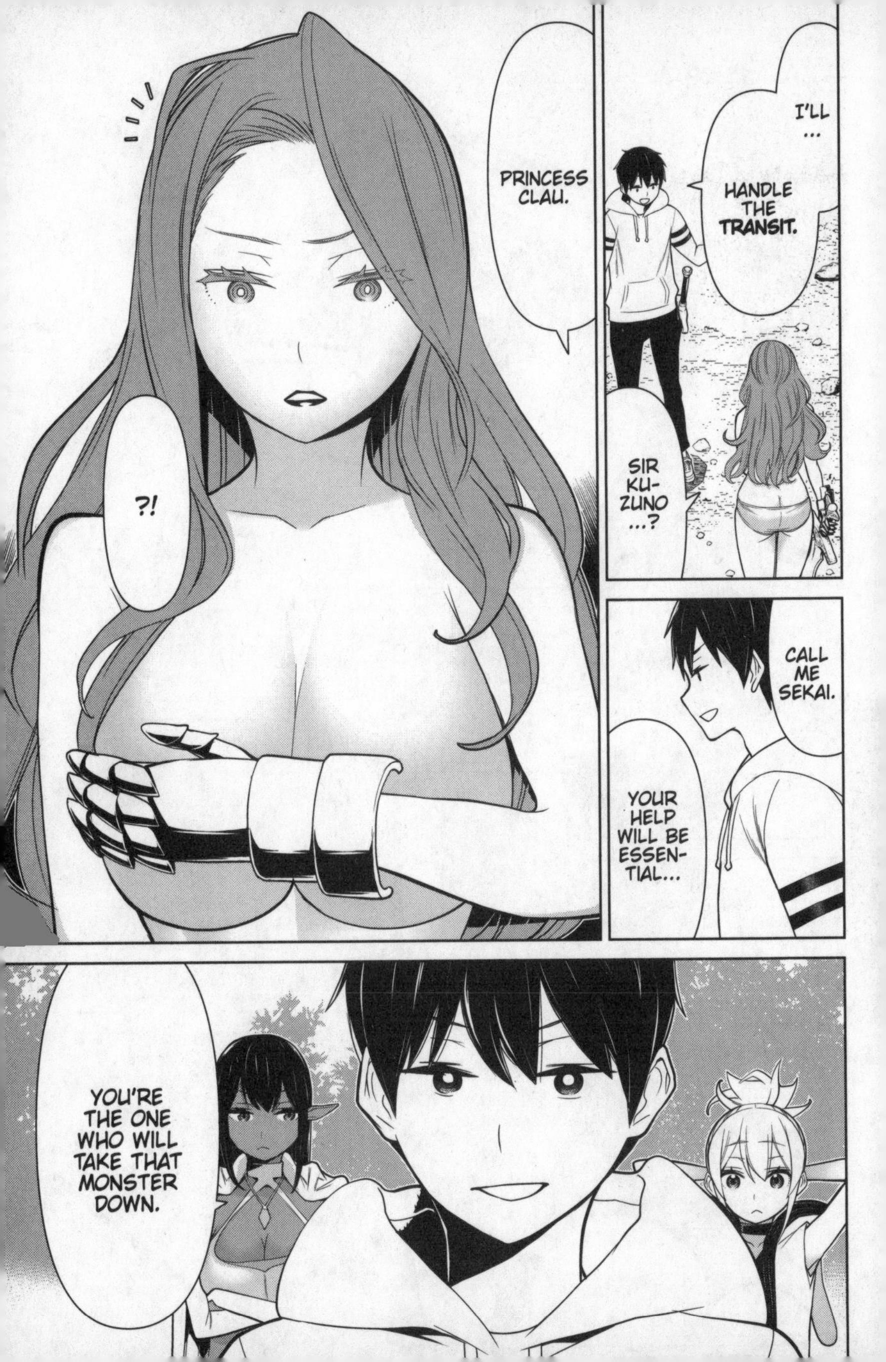
I'LL ...
HANDLE THE TRANSIT.
SIR KU-ZUNO ...?
CALL ME SEKAI.
YOUR HELP WILL BE ESSEN-TIAL...
PRINCESS CLAU.
?!
YOU'RE THE ONE WHO WILL TAKE THAT MONSTER DOWN.

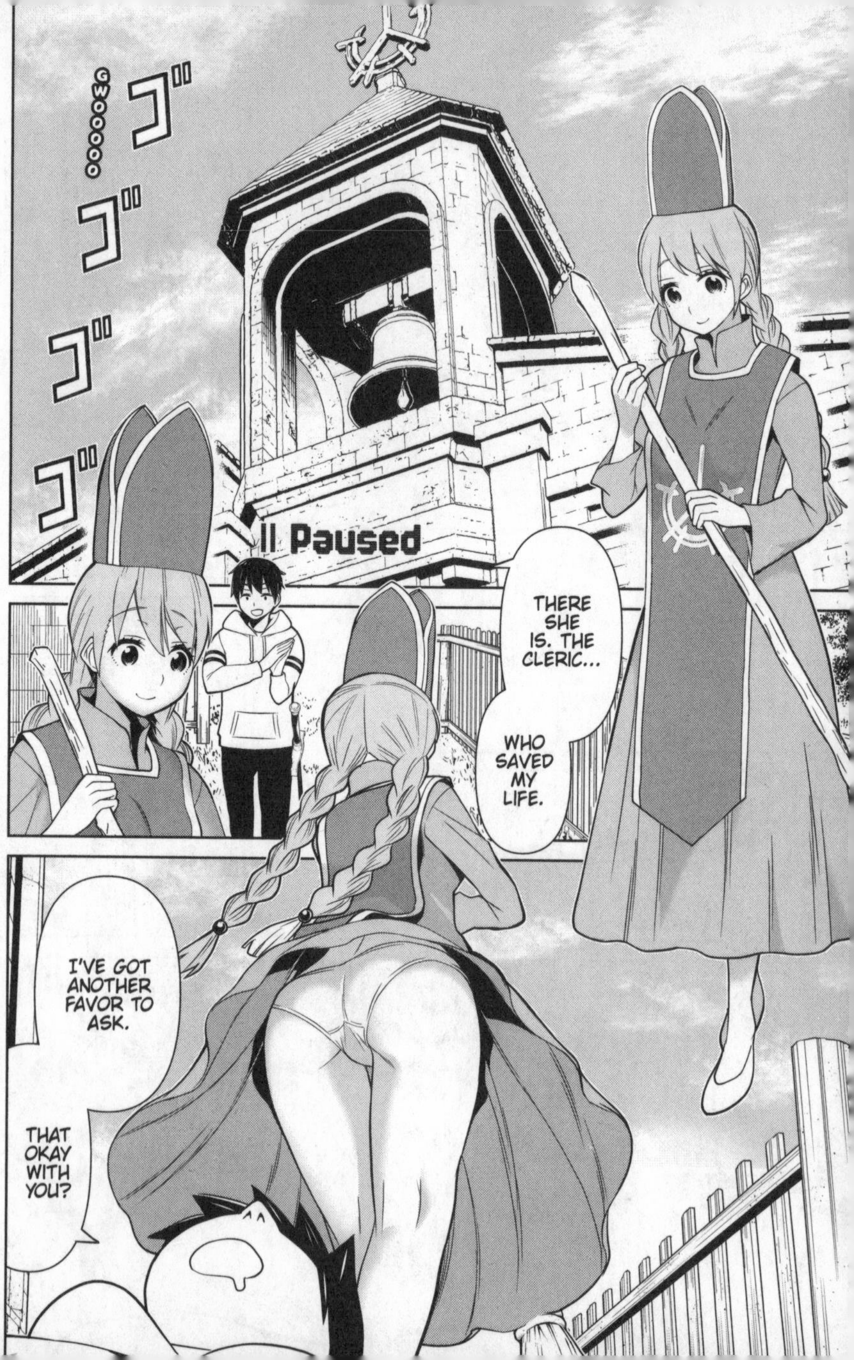
GWOOOOO
ゴゴゴゴ
Paused
THERE SHE IS. THE CLERIC...
WHO SAVED MY LIFE.
I'VE GOT ANOTHER FAVOR TO ASK.
THAT OKAY WITH YOU?

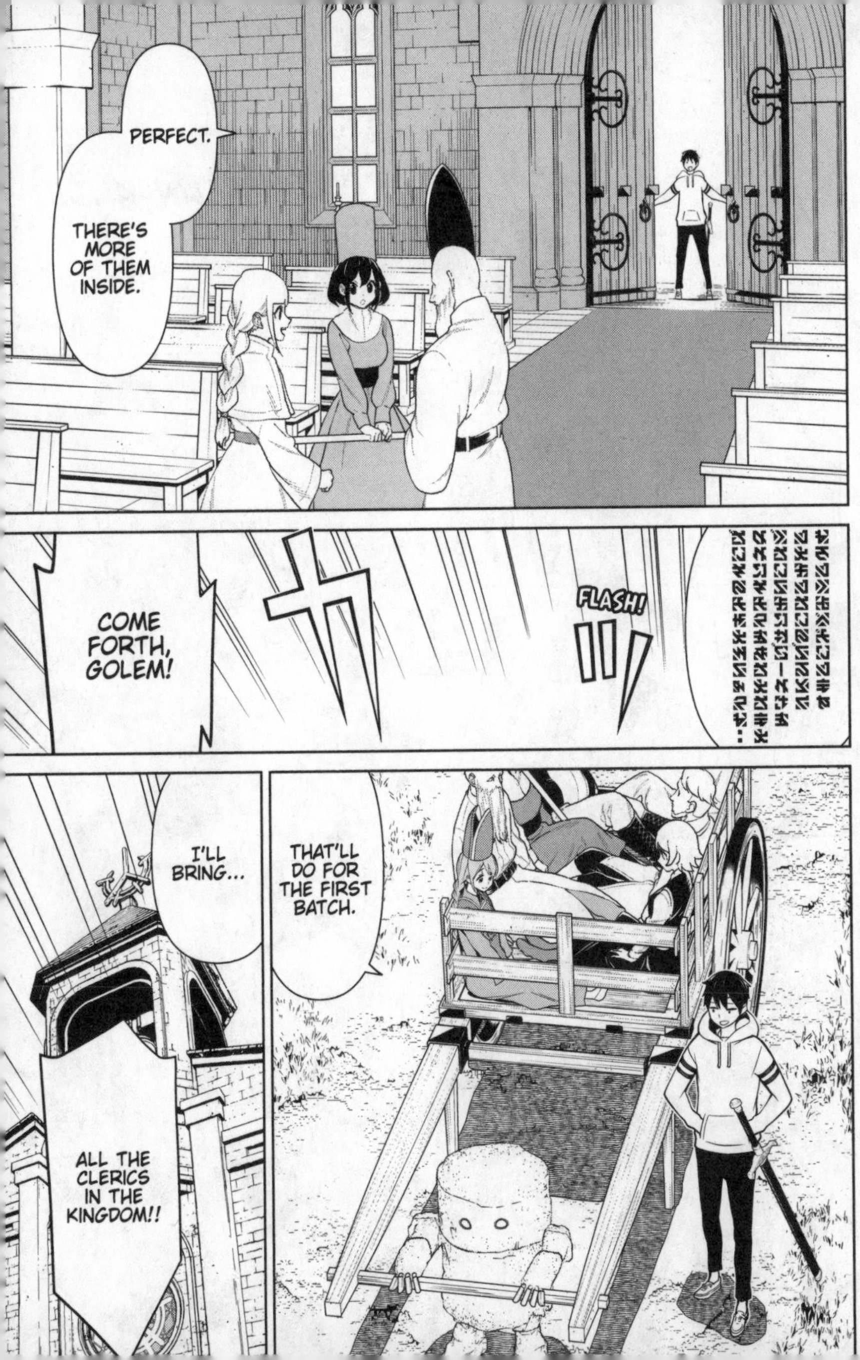

PERFECT.
THERE'S MORE OF THEM INSIDE.
FLASH!
COME FORTH, GOLEM!
THAT'LL DO FOR THE FIRST BATCH.
I'LL BRING...
ALL THE CLERICS IN THE KINGDOM!!

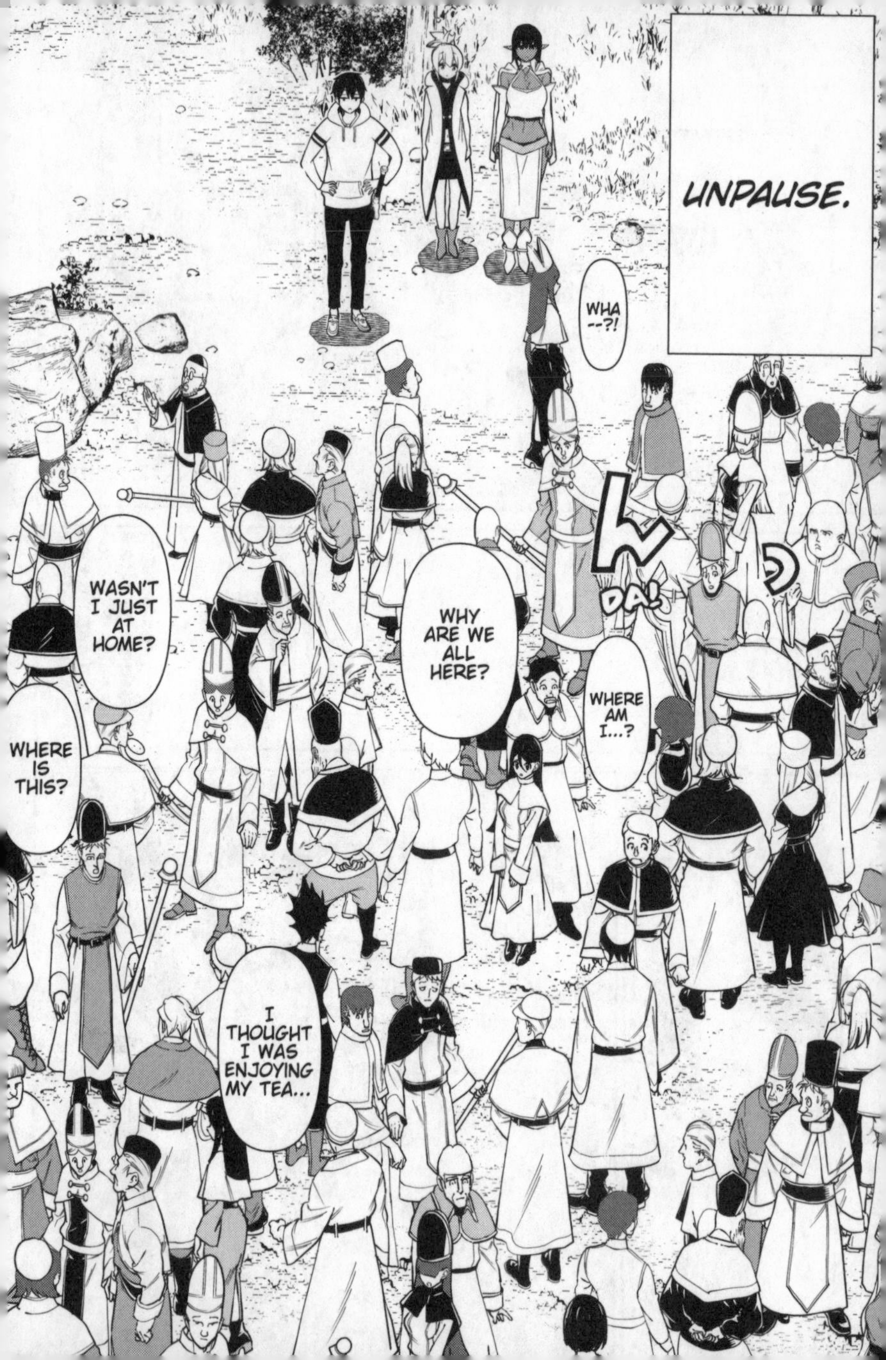
UNPAUSE.
WHA--?!
DA!
WHERE AM I...?
WHY ARE WE ALL HERE?
WASN'T I JUST AT HOME?
WHERE IS THIS?
I THOUGHT I WAS ENJOYING MY TEA...

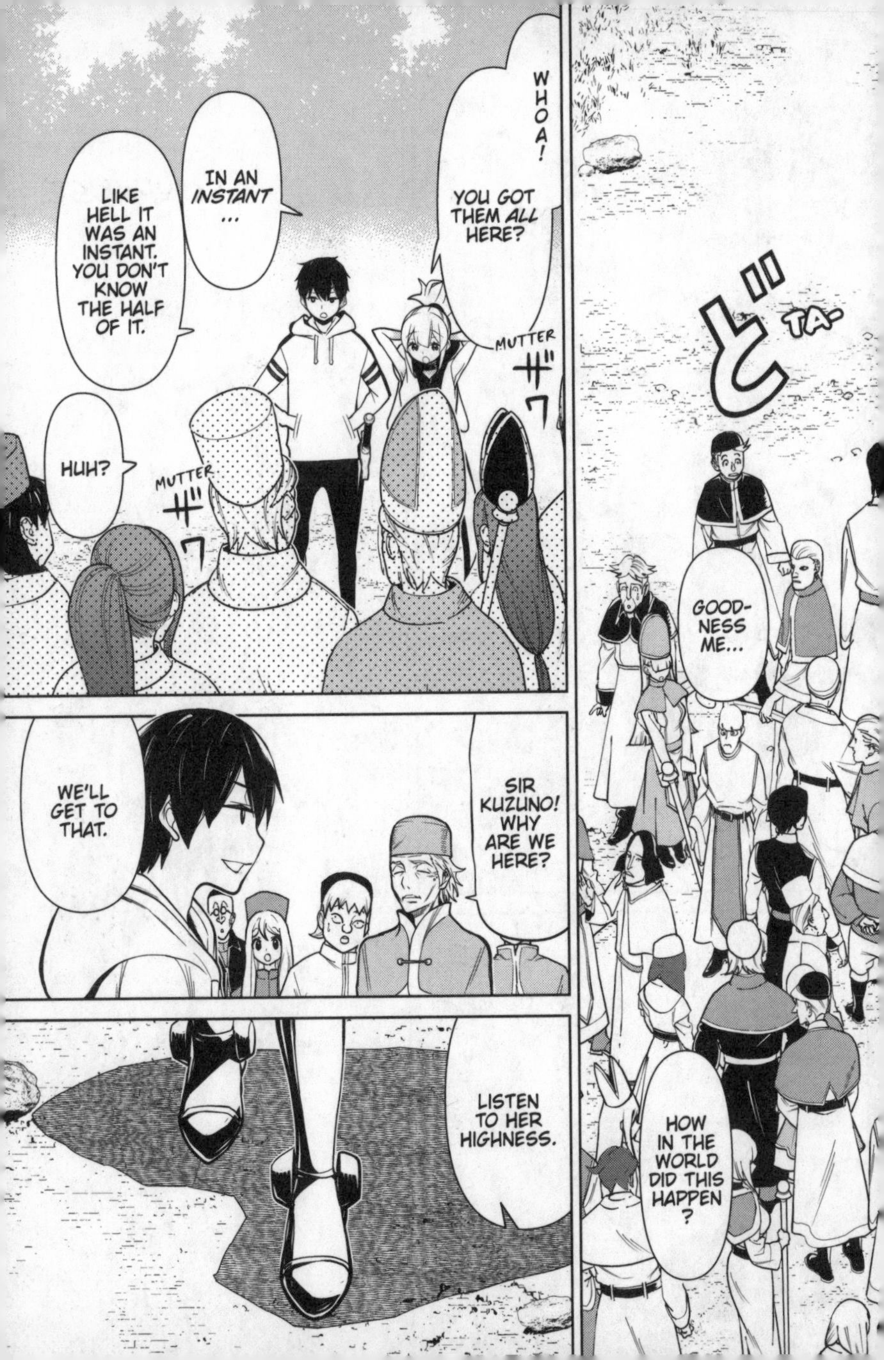
ど
TA-
GOODNESS ME...
HOW IN THE WORLD DID THIS HAPPEN?
WHOA! YOU GOT THEM ALL HERE?
MUTTER
ザワ
IN AN INSTANT...
LIKE HELL IT WAS AN INSTANT. YOU DON'T KNOW THE HALF OF IT.
MUTTER
ザワ
HUH?
SIR KUZUNO! WHY ARE WE HERE?
WE'LL GET TO THAT.
LISTEN TO HER HIGHNESS.

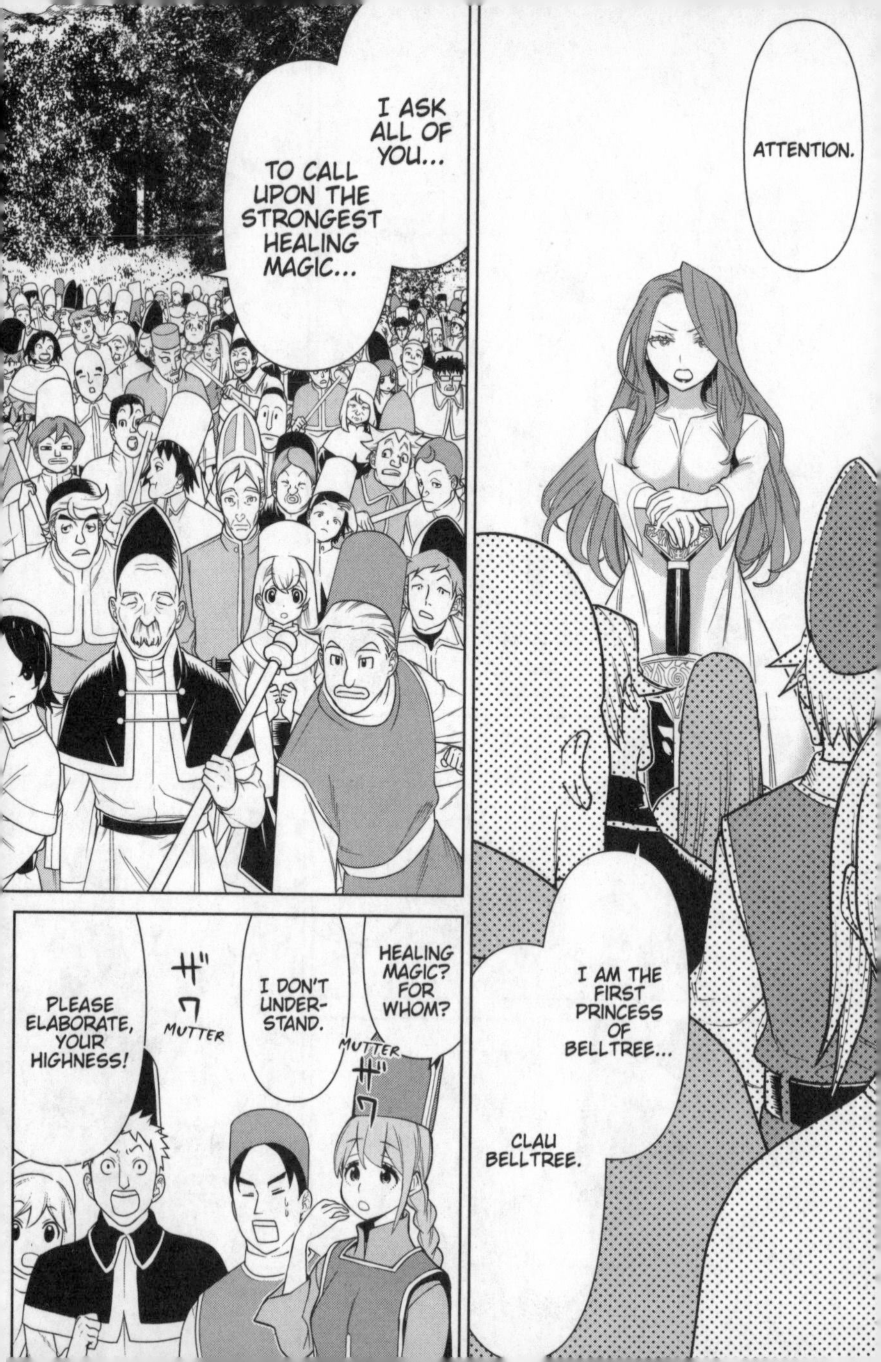
ATTENTION.
I AM THE FIRST PRINCESS OF BELLTREE...
CLAU BELLTREE.
I ASK ALL OF YOU...
TO CALL UPON THE STRONGEST HEALING MAGIC...
HEALING MAGIC? FOR WHOM?
ザワ MUTTER
I DON'T UNDER-STAND.
ザワ MUTTER
PLEASE ELABORATE, YOUR HIGHNESS!

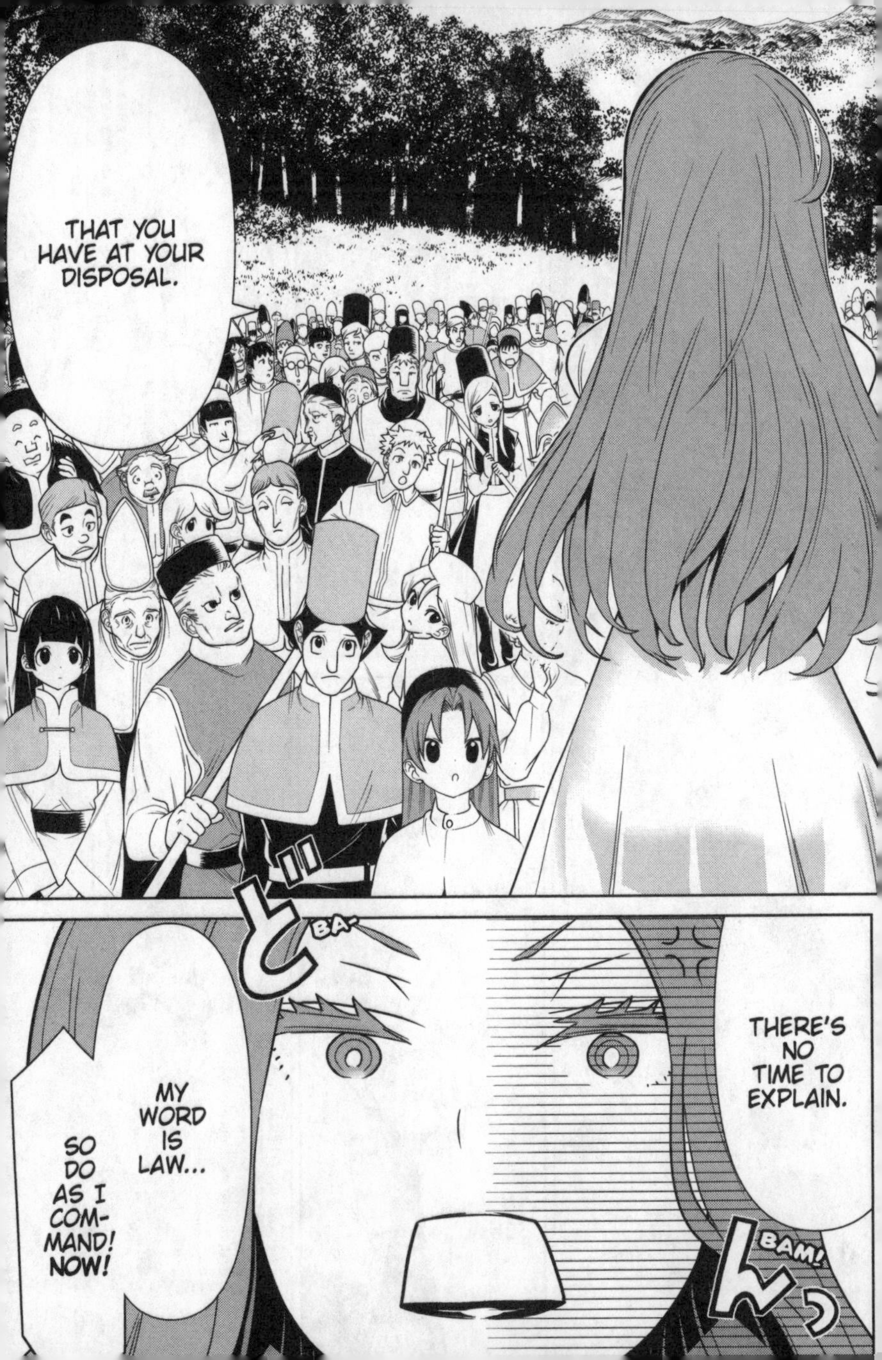
THAT YOU HAVE AT YOUR DISPOSAL.
BA-
THERE'S NO TIME TO EXPLAIN.
BAM!
MY WORD IS LAW...
SO DO AS I COM-MAND! NOW!

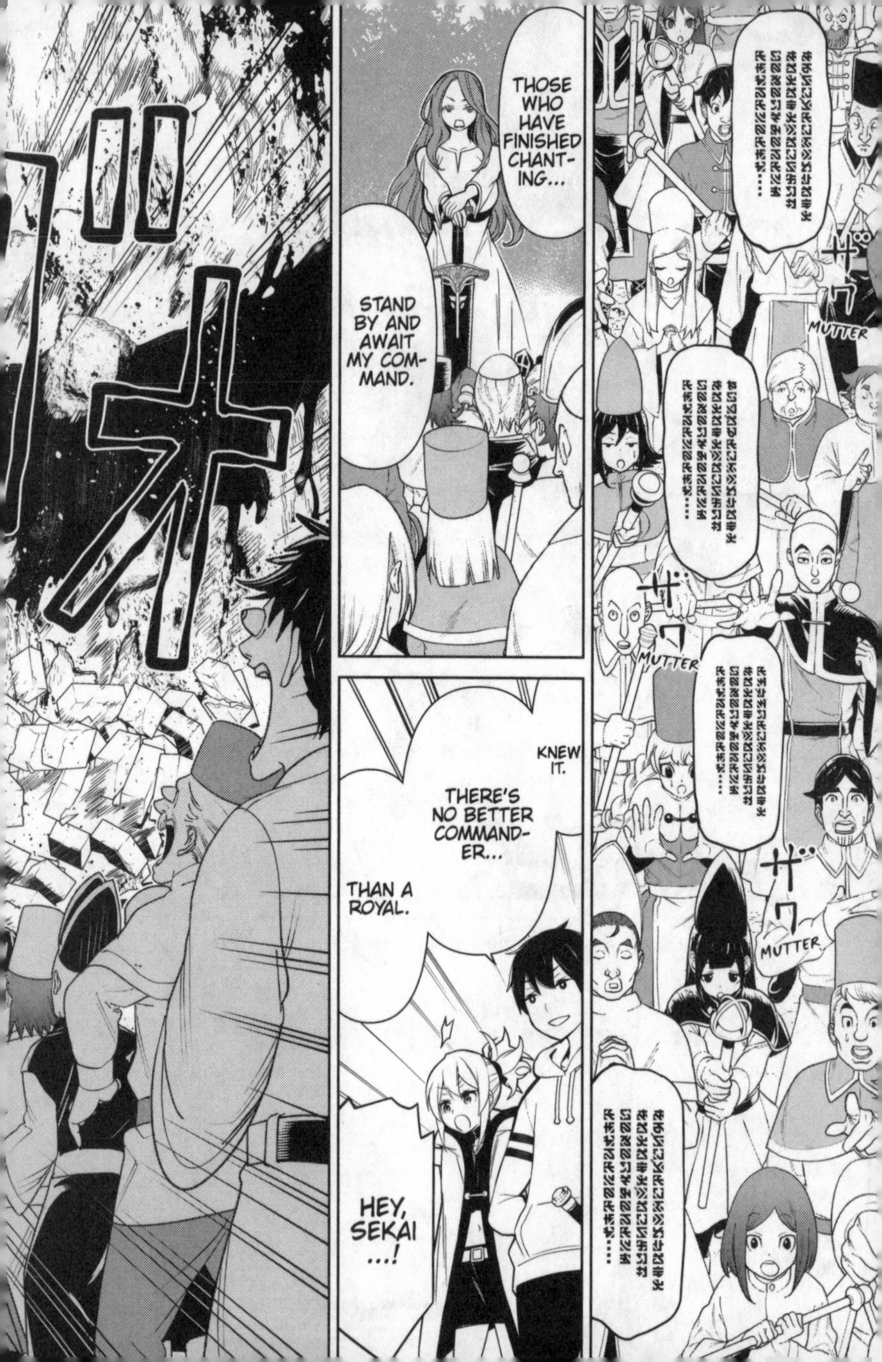
MUTTER
MUTTER
MUTTER
THOSE WHO HAVE FINISHED CHANTING...
STAND BY AND AWAIT MY COMMAND.
KNEW IT.
THERE'S NO BETTER COMMANDER...
THAN A ROYAL.
HEY, SEKAI...!

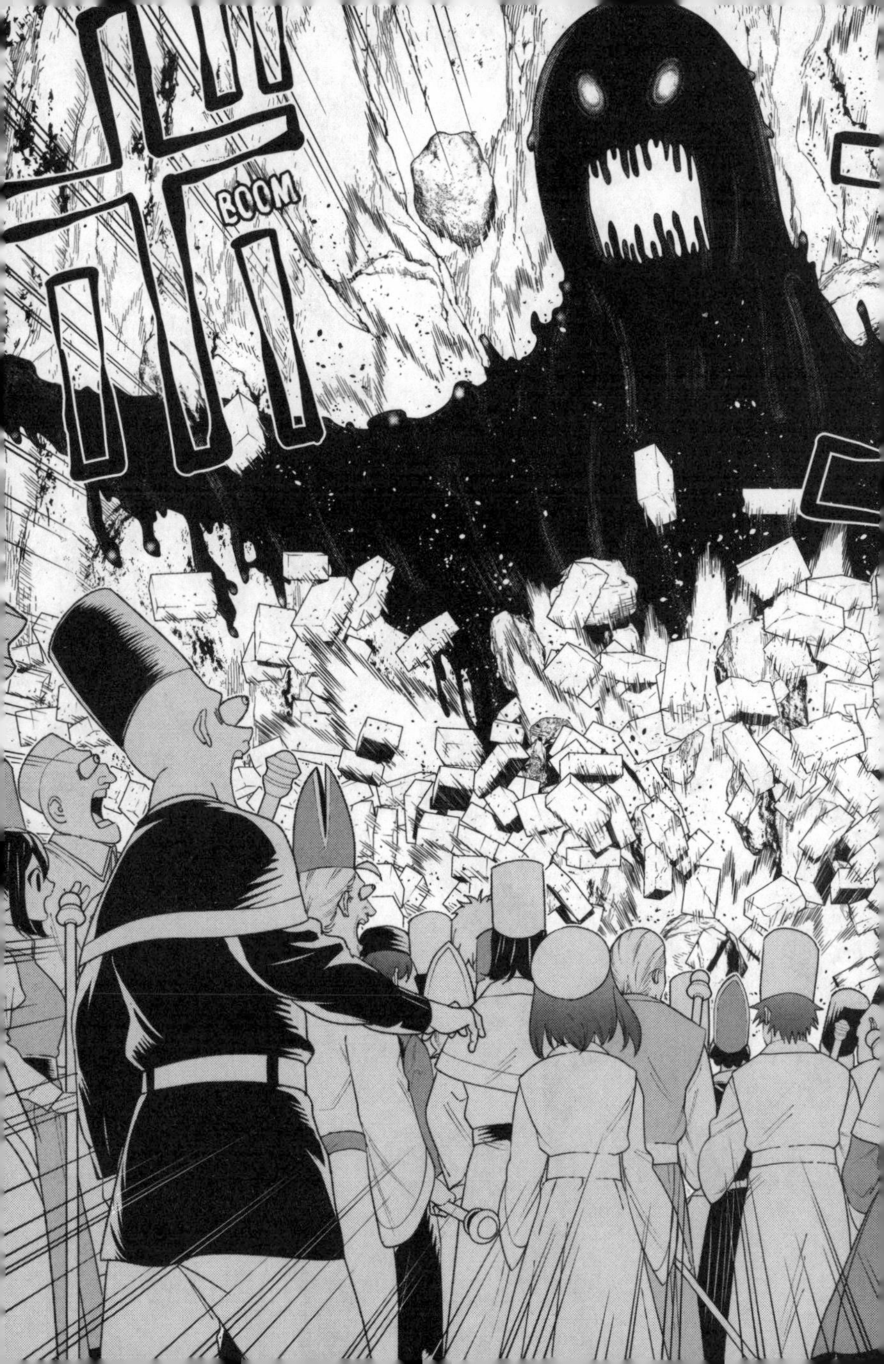
BOOM

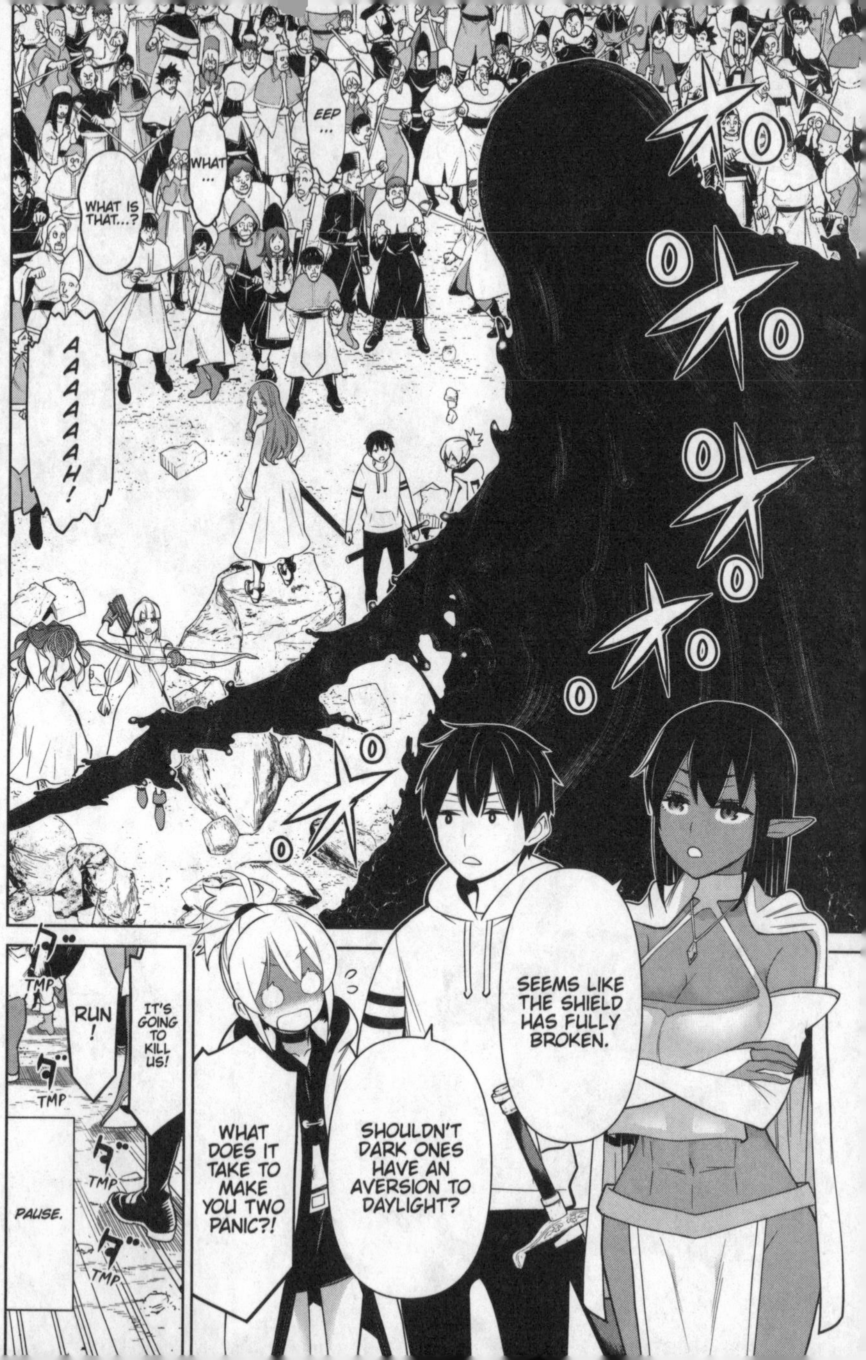
EEP ...
WHAT ...
WHAT IS THAT...?
AAAAAAH!
SEEMS LIKE THE SHIELD HAS FULLY BROKEN.
SHOULDN'T DARK ONES HAVE AN AVERSION TO DAYLIGHT?
WHAT DOES IT TAKE TO MAKE YOU TWO PANIC?!
IT'S GOING TO KILL US!
RUN!
TMP
TMP
TMP
TMP
PAUSE.

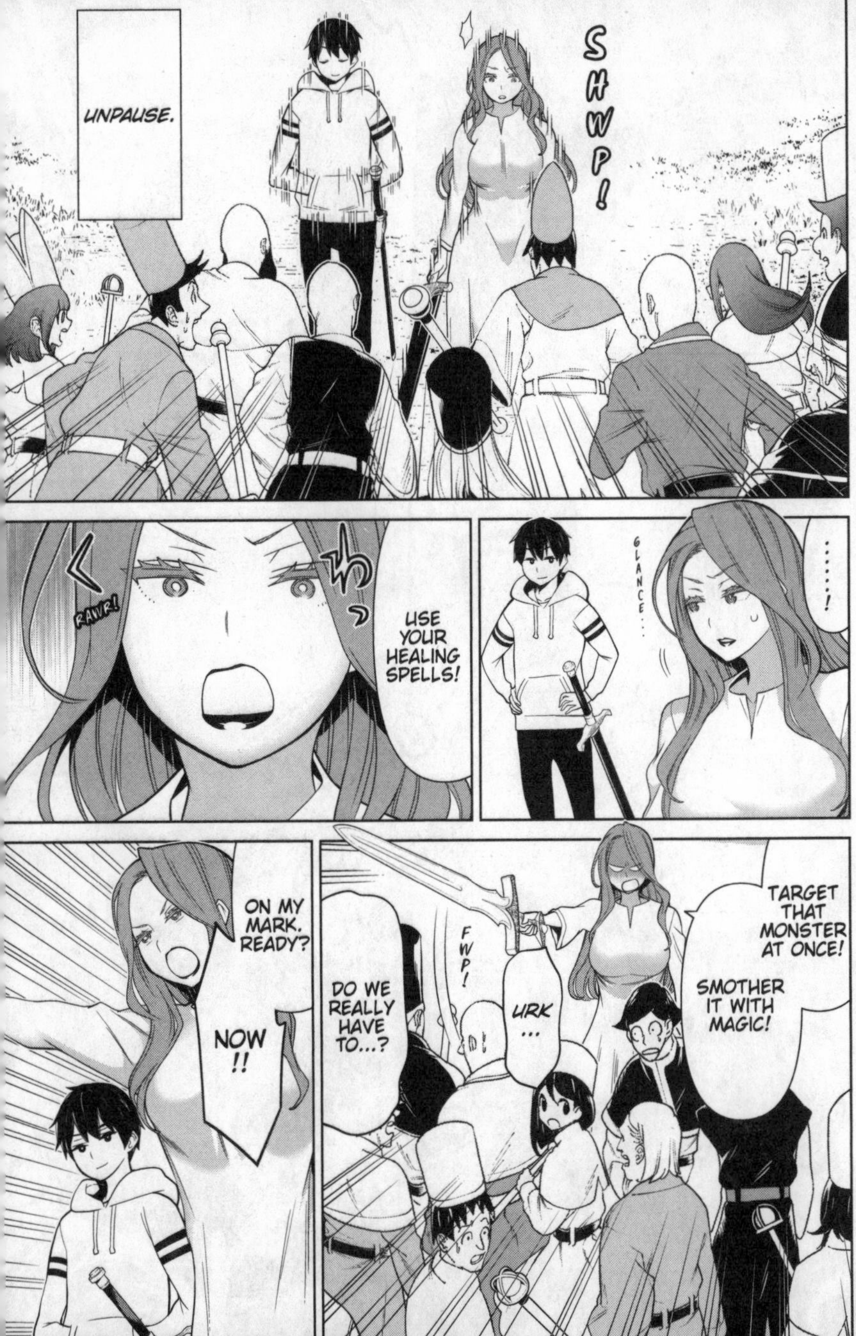
SHWP!
UNPAUSE.
......!
GLANCE...
USE YOUR HEALING SPELLS!
RAWR!
TARGET THAT MONSTER AT ONCE!
SMOTHER IT WITH MAGIC!
URK ...
FWP!
DO WE REALLY HAVE TO...?
ON MY MARK. READY?
NOW !!

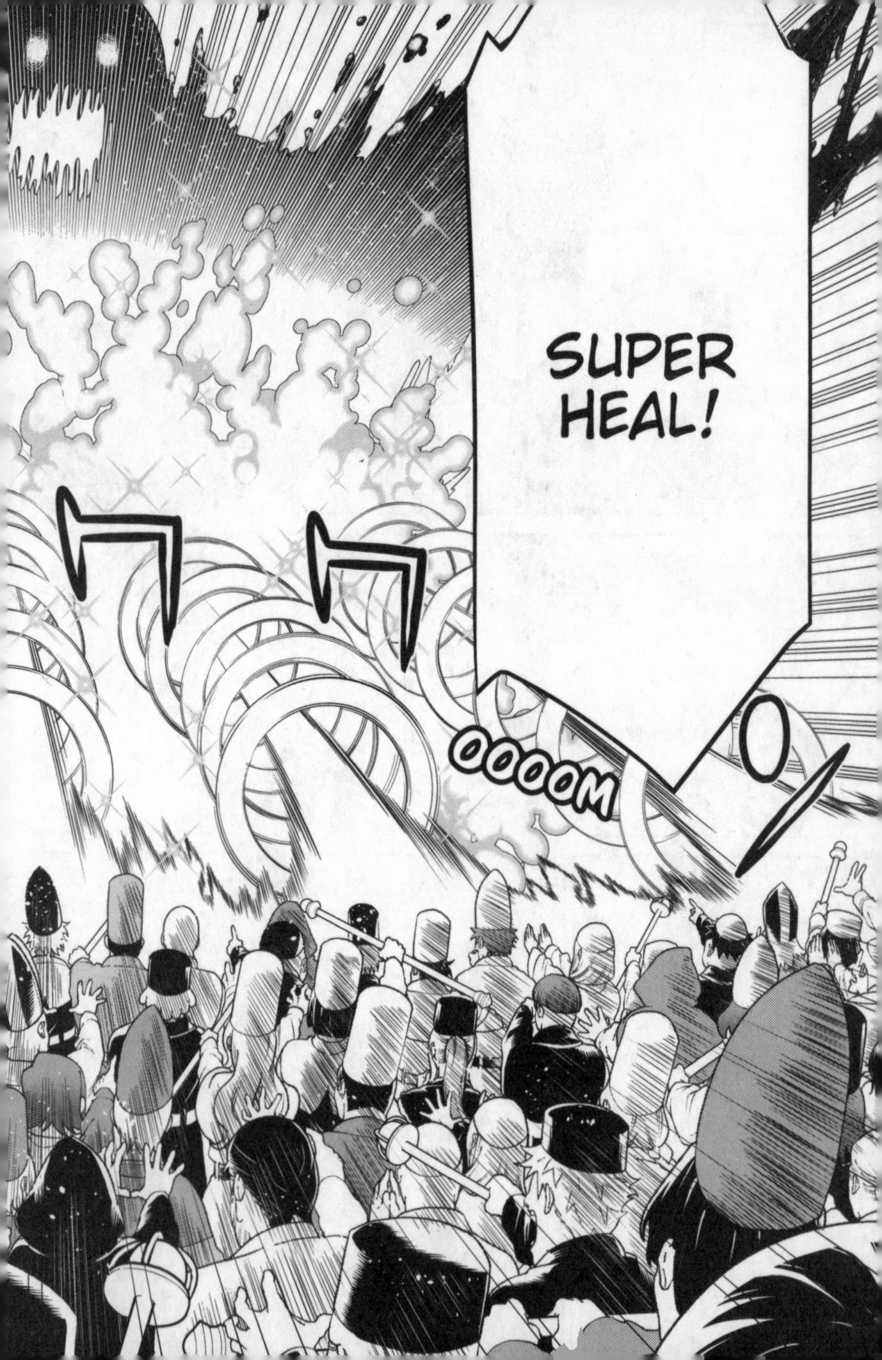
SUPER HEAL!
OOOOM

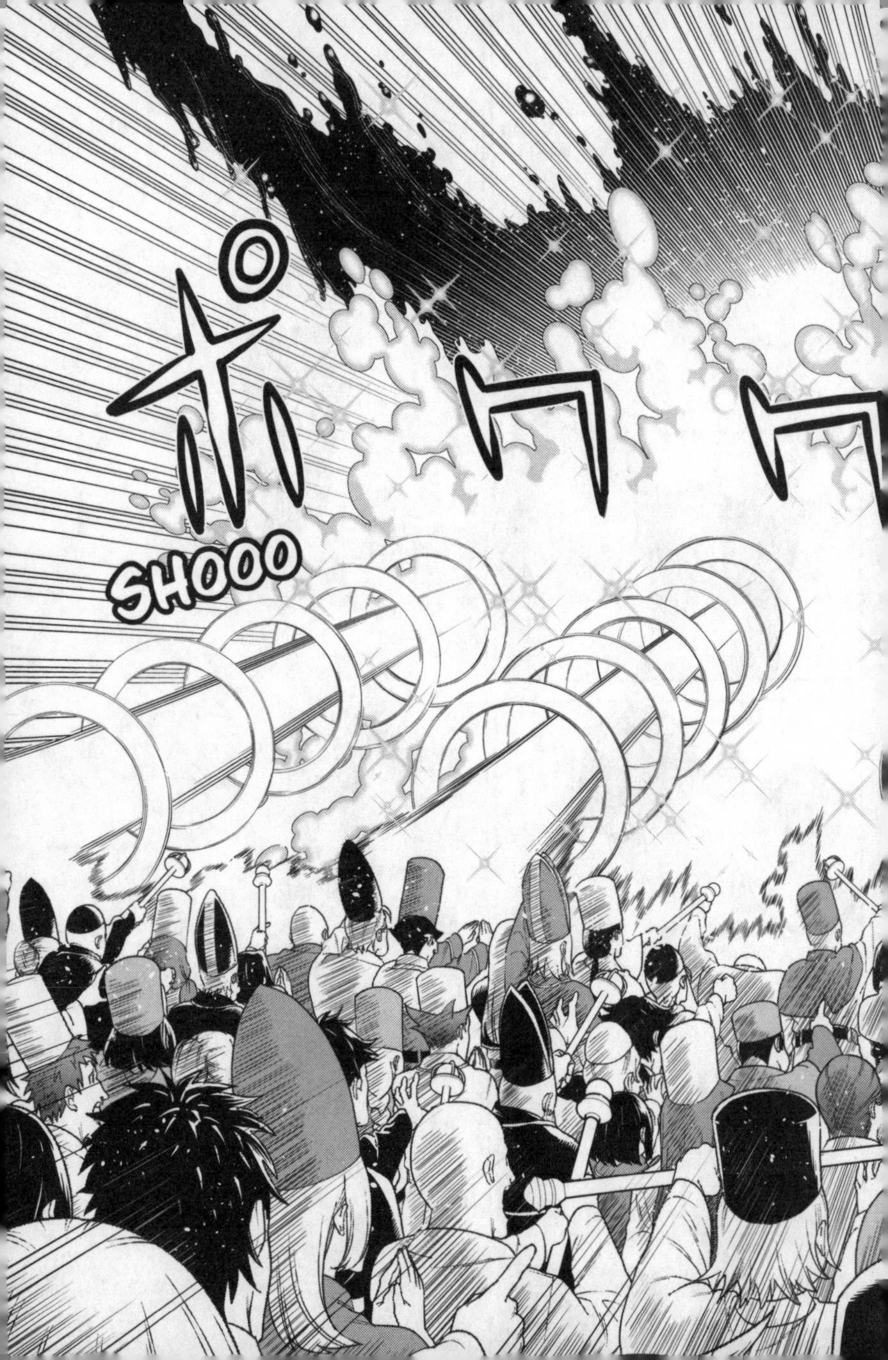

ポワワ
SHOOO

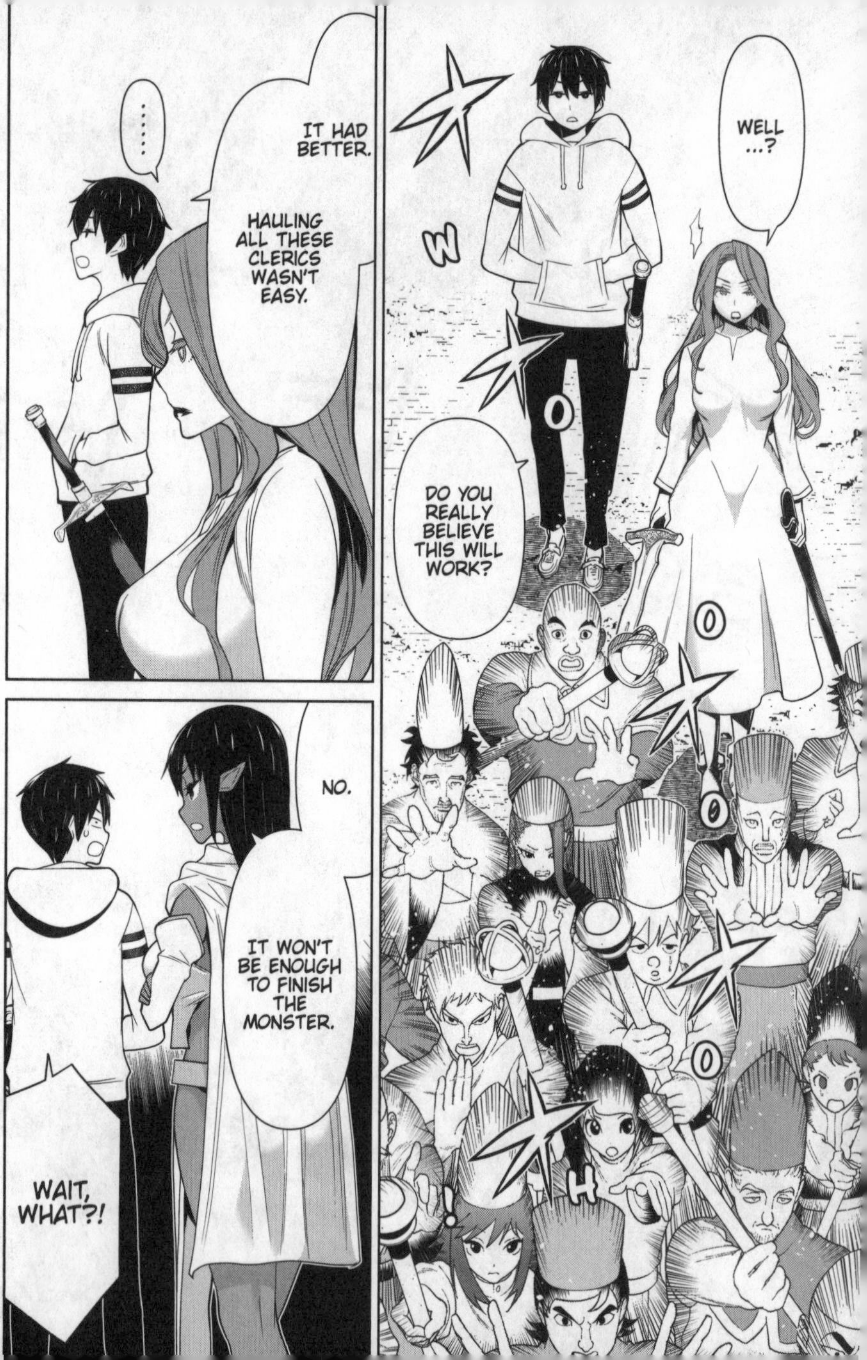
WELL ...?
WOOOOH
DO YOU REALLY BELIEVE THIS WILL WORK?
IT HAD BETTER.
HAULING ALL THESE CLERICS WASN'T EASY.
......
NO.
IT WON'T BE ENOUGH TO FINISH THE MONSTER.
WAIT, WHAT?!

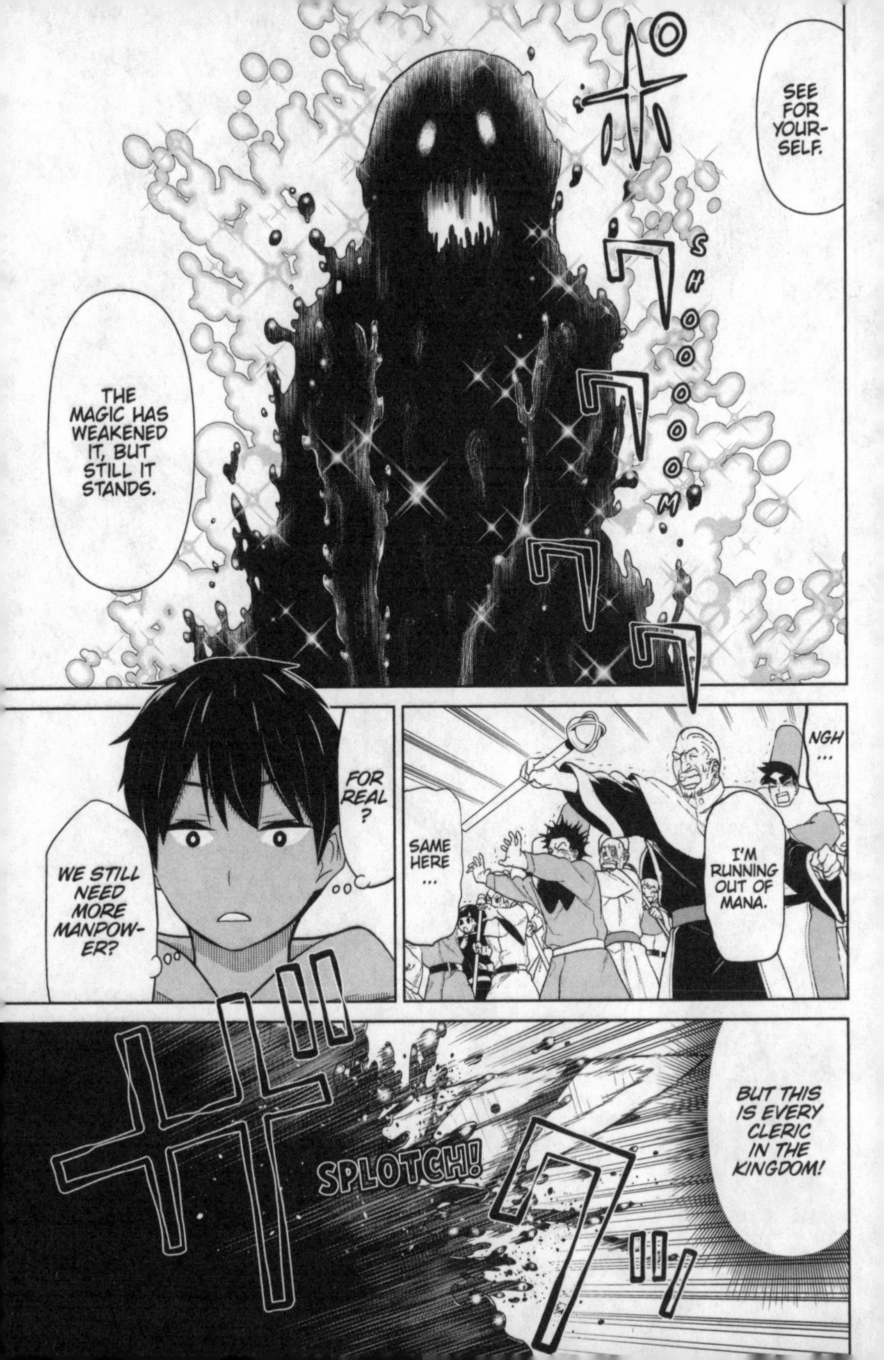
SEE FOR YOUR-SELF.
SHOOOOOOOM
THE MAGIC HAS WEAKENED IT, BUT STILL IT STANDS.
NGH ...
I'M RUNNING OUT OF MANA.
SAME HERE ...
FOR REAL?
WE STILL NEED MORE MANPOW-ER?
BUT THIS IS EVERY CLERIC IN THE KINGDOM!
SPLOTCH!

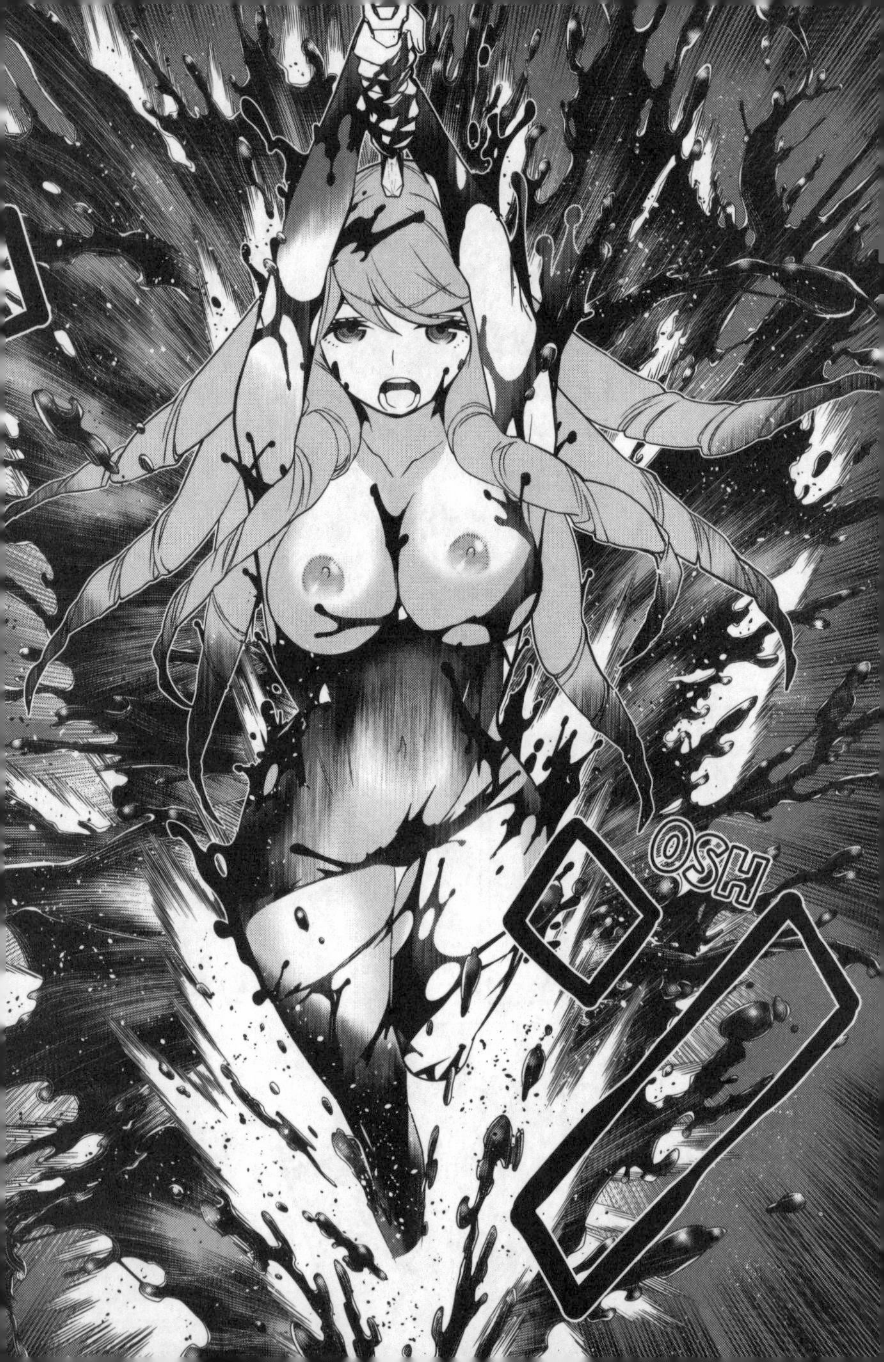
OSH

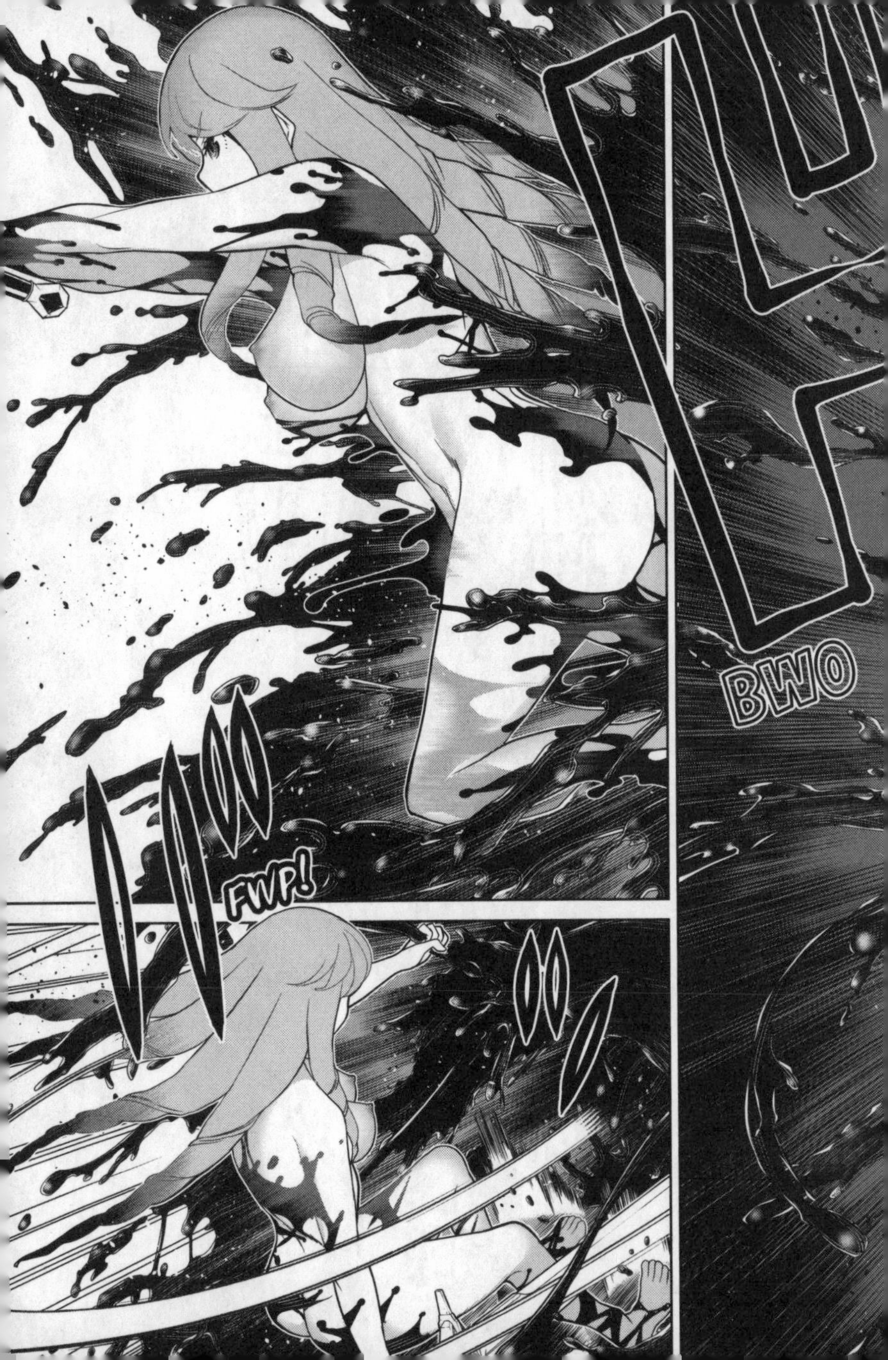
BWO
FWP!

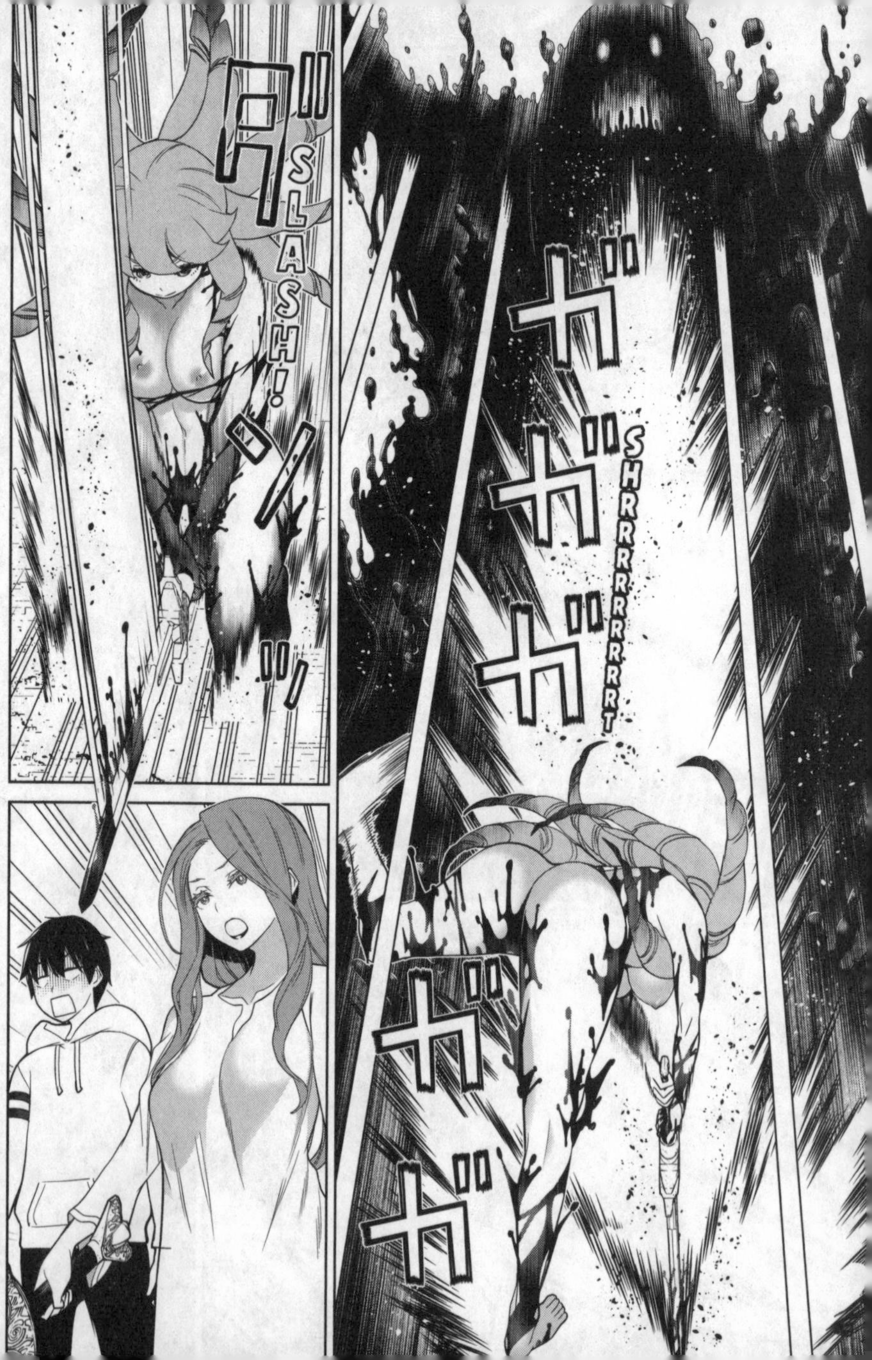
SHRRRRRRRRRT
SLASH!

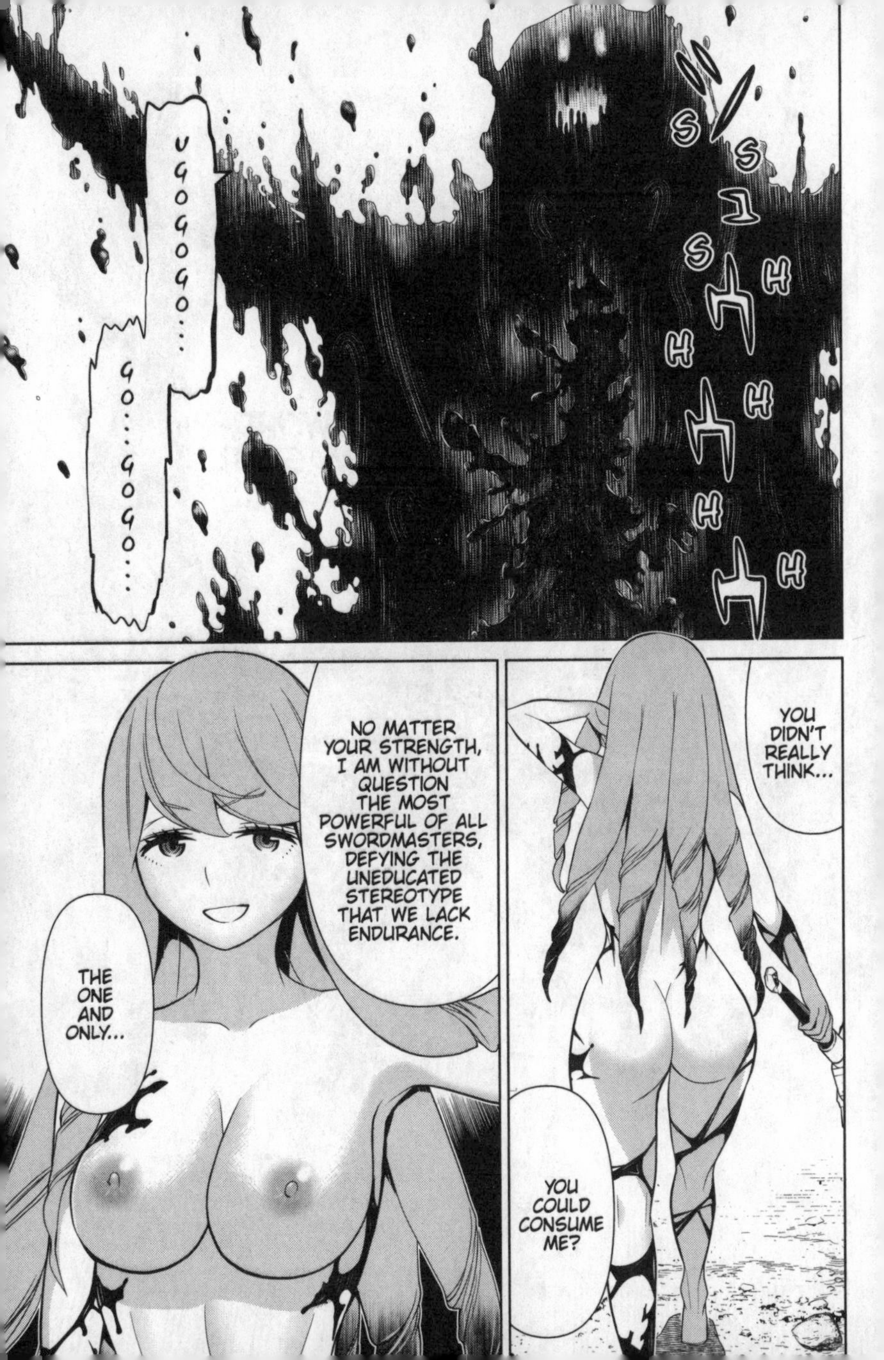

SSSSHHHHHHHH
UGOGOGO... GO...GOGOGO...
YOU DIDN'T REALLY THINK...
YOU COULD CONSUME ME?
NO MATTER YOUR STRENGTH, I AM WITHOUT QUESTION THE MOST POWERFUL OF ALL SWORDMASTERS, DEFYING THE UNEDUCATED STEREOTYPE THAT WE LACK ENDURANCE.
THE ONE AND ONLY...

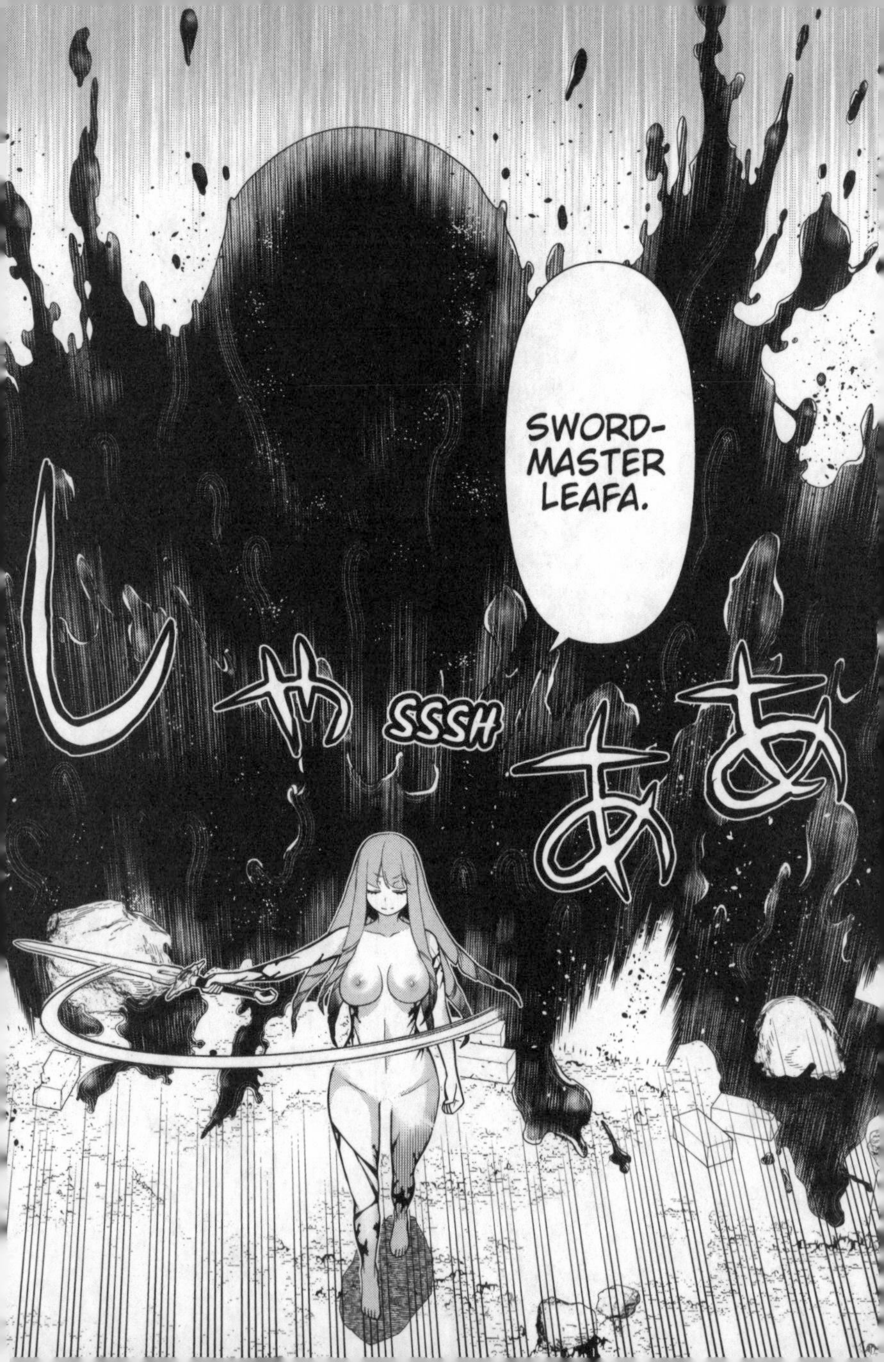
SWORD-MASTER LEAFA.
しゃああ
SSSH

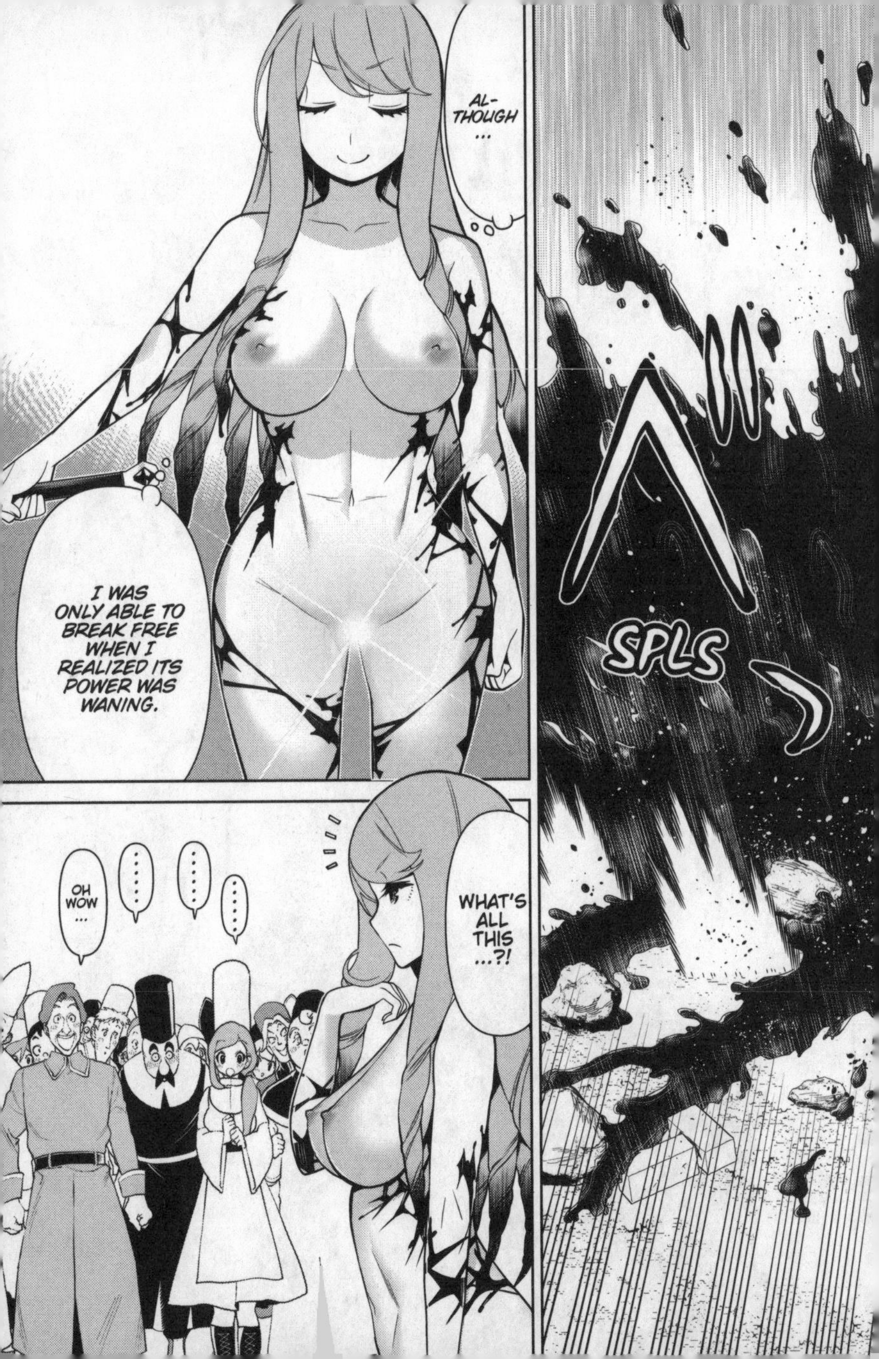
SPLS
AL-THOUGH ...
I WAS ONLY ABLE TO BREAK FREE WHEN I REALIZED ITS POWER WAS WANING.
WHAT'S ALL THIS ...?!
......
......
......
OH WOW ...

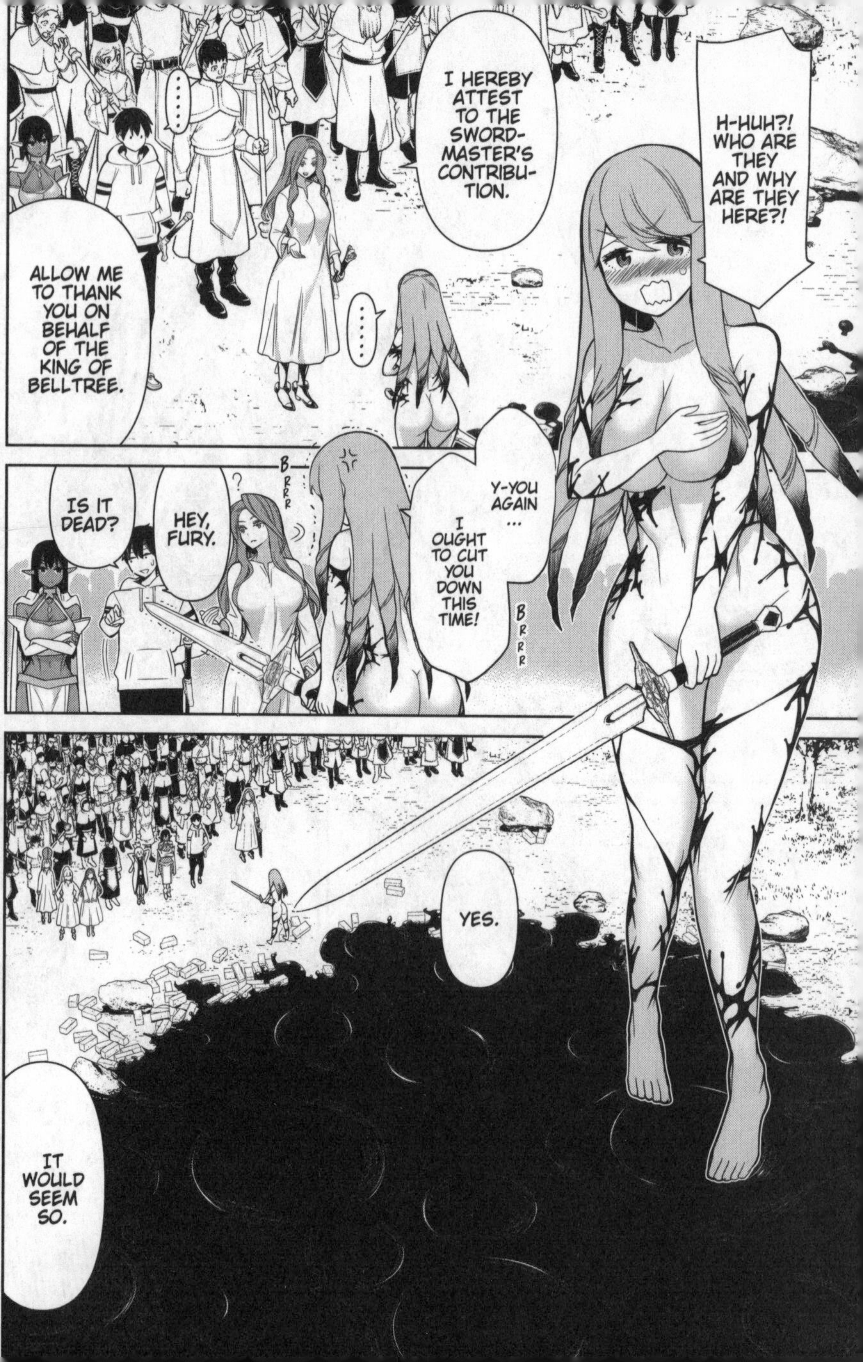
H-HUH?! WHO ARE THEY AND WHY ARE THEY HERE?!
I HEREBY ATTEST TO THE SWORD-MASTER'S CONTRIBU-TION.
......
ALLOW ME TO THANK YOU ON BEHALF OF THE KING OF BELLTREE.
......
Y-YOU AGAIN ... I OUGHT TO CUT YOU DOWN THIS TIME!
BRRR
BRRR
?
HEY, FURY.
IS IT DEAD?
YES.
IT WOULD SEEM SO.

Chapter 8 - End

2 3 4 5 6 7 8

START
▶ PAUSE

▶START
PAUSE

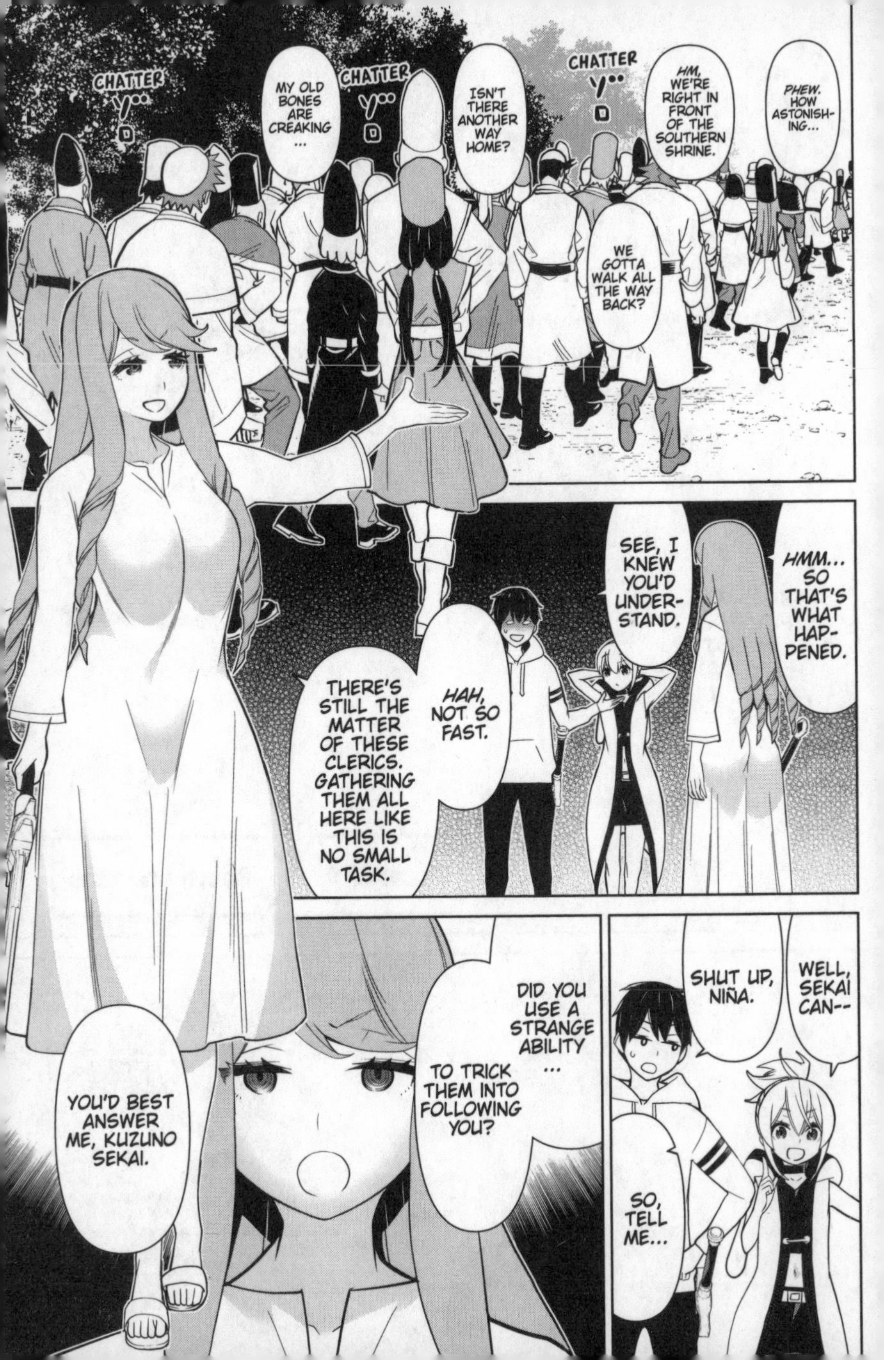
PHEW. HOW ASTONISHING...
HM, WE'RE RIGHT IN FRONT OF THE SOUTHERN SHRINE.
CHATTER
WE GOTTA WALK ALL THE WAY BACK?
ISN'T THERE ANOTHER WAY HOME?
CHATTER
MY OLD BONES ARE CREAKING ...
CHATTER
HMM... SO THAT'S WHAT HAPPENED.
SEE, I KNEW YOU'D UNDERSTAND.
HAH, NOT SO FAST.
THERE'S STILL THE MATTER OF THESE CLERICS. GATHERING THEM ALL HERE LIKE THIS IS NO SMALL TASK.
WELL, SEKAI CAN--
SHUT UP, NIÑA.
SO, TELL ME...
DID YOU USE A STRANGE ABILITY ...
TO TRICK THEM INTO FOLLOWING YOU?
YOU'D BEST ANSWER ME, KUZUNO SEKAI.

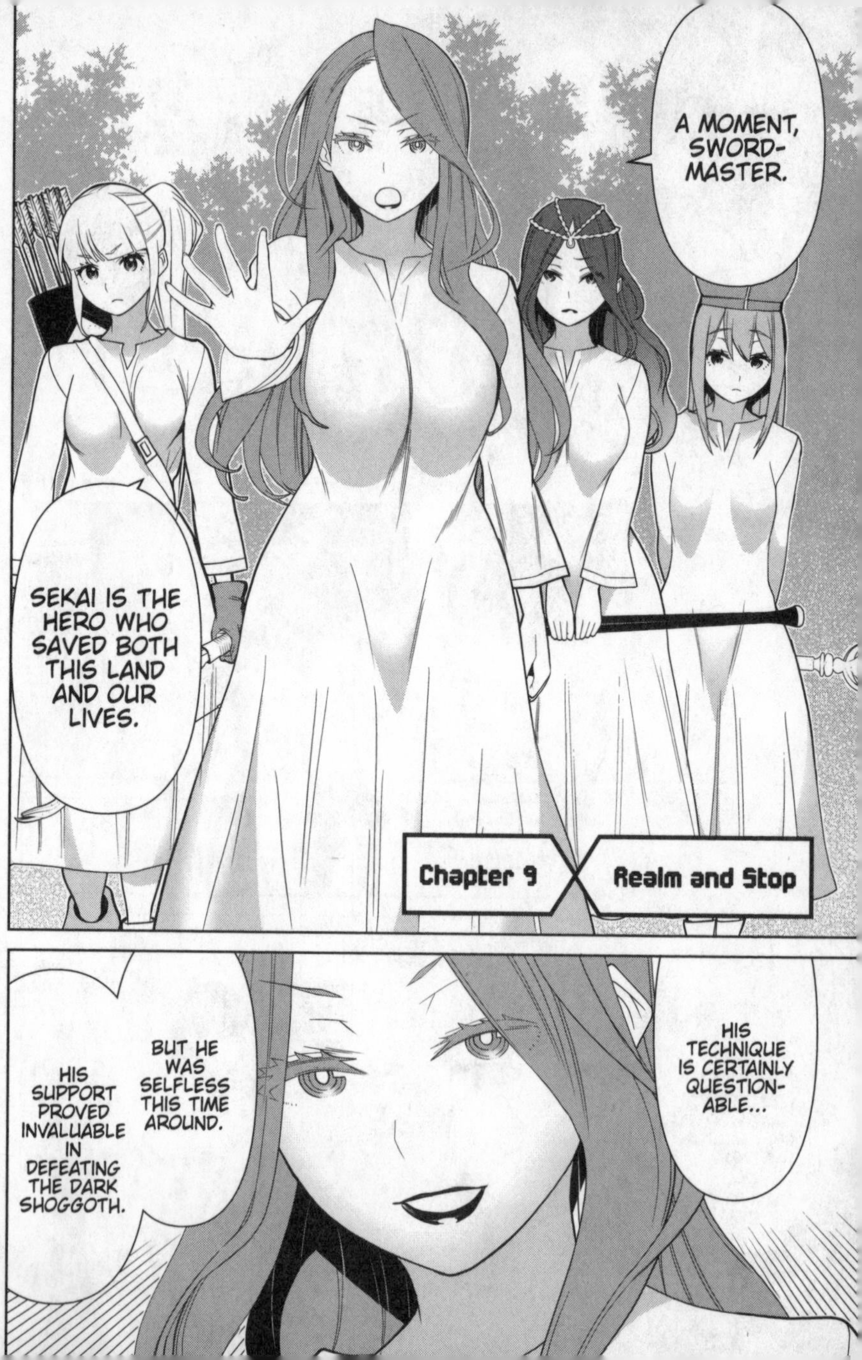
A MOMENT, SWORD-MASTER.
SEKAI IS THE HERO WHO SAVED BOTH THIS LAND AND OUR LIVES.
Chapter 9
Realm and Stop
HIS TECHNIQUE IS CERTAINLY QUESTION-ABLE...
BUT HE WAS SELFLESS THIS TIME AROUND.
HIS SUPPORT PROVED INVALUABLE IN DEFEATING THE DARK SHOGGOTH.

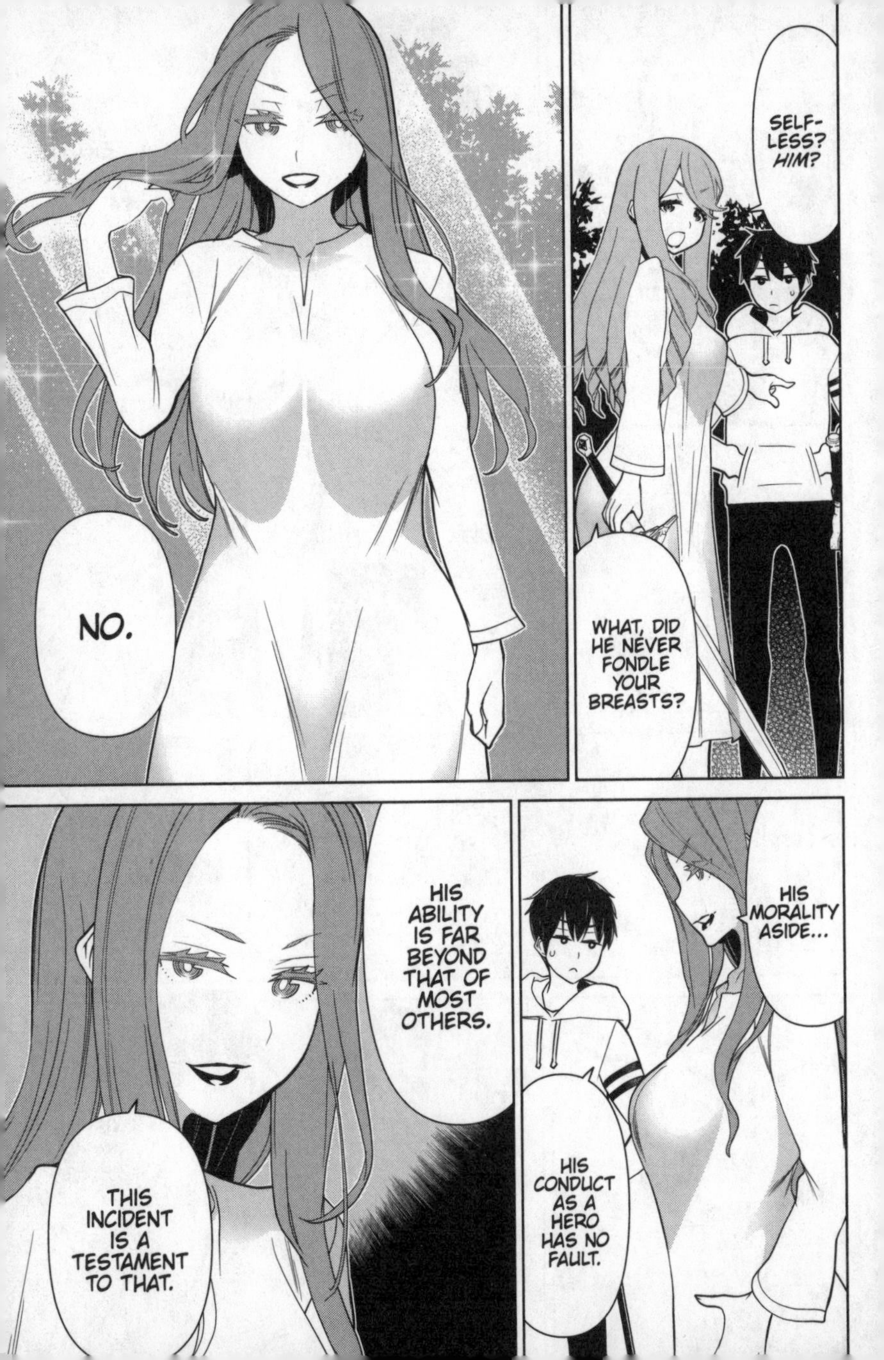
SELF-LESS? HIM?
WHAT, DID HE NEVER FONDLE YOUR BREASTS?
NO.
HIS MORALITY ASIDE...
HIS CONDUCT AS A HERO HAS NO FAULT.
HIS ABILITY IS FAR BEYOND THAT OF MOST OTHERS.
THIS INCIDENT IS A TESTAMENT TO THAT.

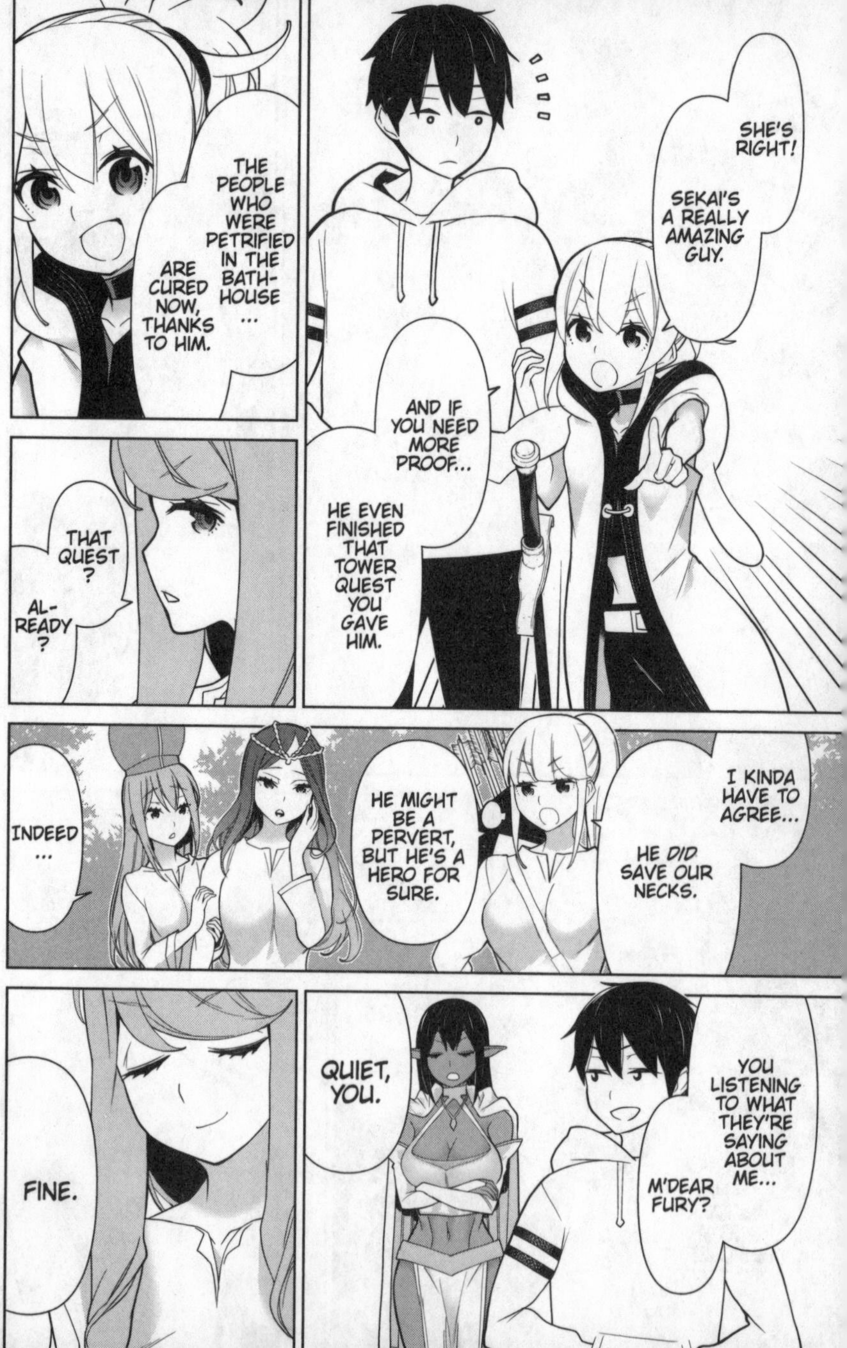
SHE'S RIGHT!
SEKAI'S A REALLY AMAZING GUY.
AND IF YOU NEED MORE PROOF...
HE EVEN FINISHED THAT TOWER QUEST YOU GAVE HIM.
THE PEOPLE WHO WERE PETRIFIED IN THE BATH-HOUSE...
ARE CURED NOW, THANKS TO HIM.
THAT QUEST?
AL-READY?
I KINDA HAVE TO AGREE...
HE *DID* SAVE OUR NECKS.
HE MIGHT BE A PERVERT, BUT HE'S A HERO FOR SURE.
INDEED...
YOU LISTENING TO WHAT THEY'RE SAYING ABOUT ME...
M'DEAR FURY?
QUIET, YOU.
FINE.

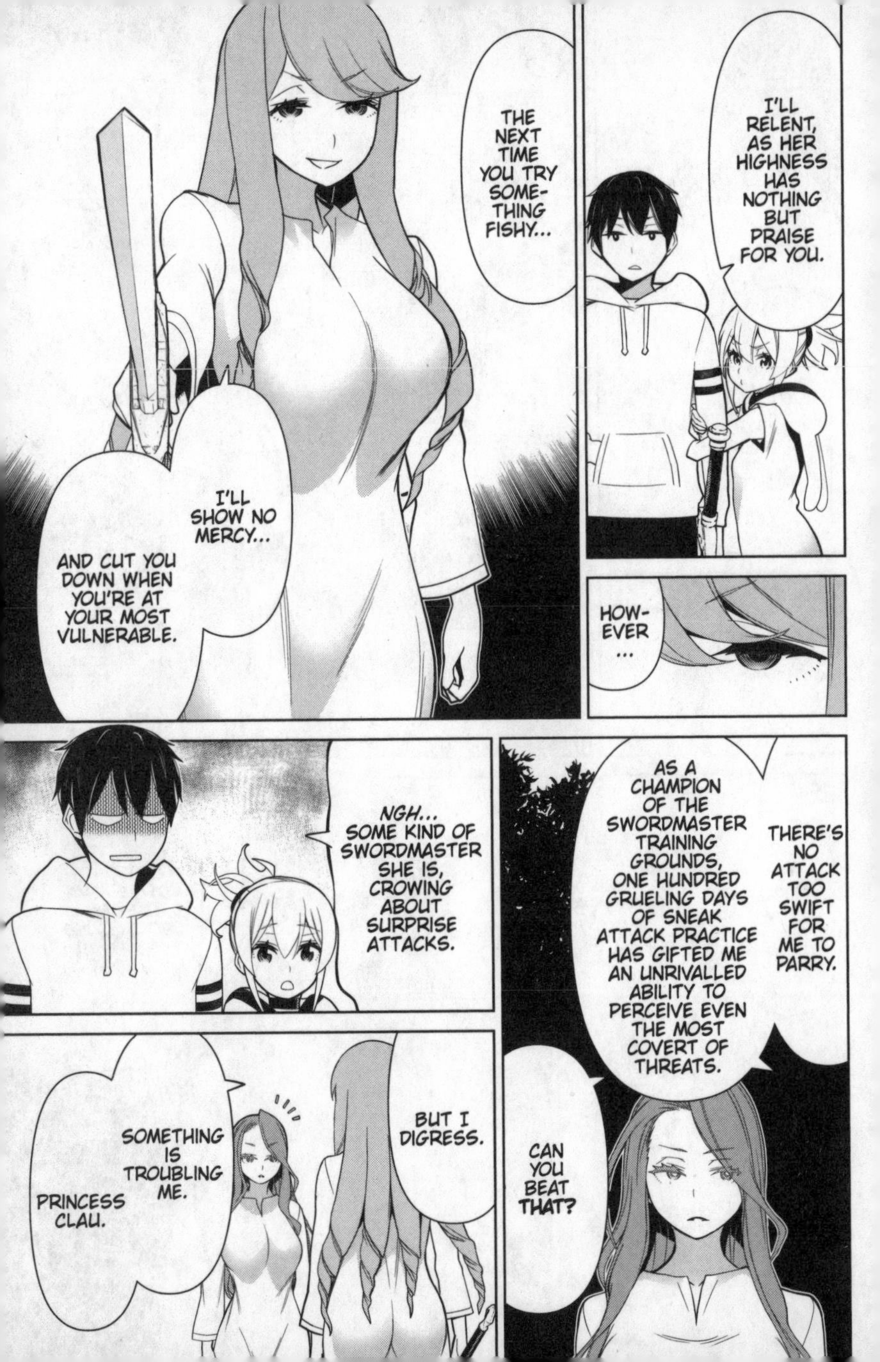
I'LL RELENT, AS HER HIGHNESS HAS NOTHING BUT PRAISE FOR YOU.
HOW-EVER ...
THE NEXT TIME YOU TRY SOME-THING FISHY...
I'LL SHOW NO MERCY...
AND CUT YOU DOWN WHEN YOU'RE AT YOUR MOST VULNERABLE.
THERE'S NO ATTACK TOO SWIFT FOR ME TO PARRY.
AS A CHAMPION OF THE SWORDMASTER TRAINING GROUNDS, ONE HUNDRED GRUELING DAYS OF SNEAK ATTACK PRACTICE HAS GIFTED ME AN UNRIVALLED ABILITY TO PERCEIVE EVEN THE MOST COVERT OF THREATS.
CAN YOU BEAT THAT?
NGH... SOME KIND OF SWORDMASTER SHE IS, CROWING ABOUT SURPRISE ATTACKS.
BUT I DIGRESS.
SOMETHING IS TROUBLING ME.
PRINCESS CLAU.

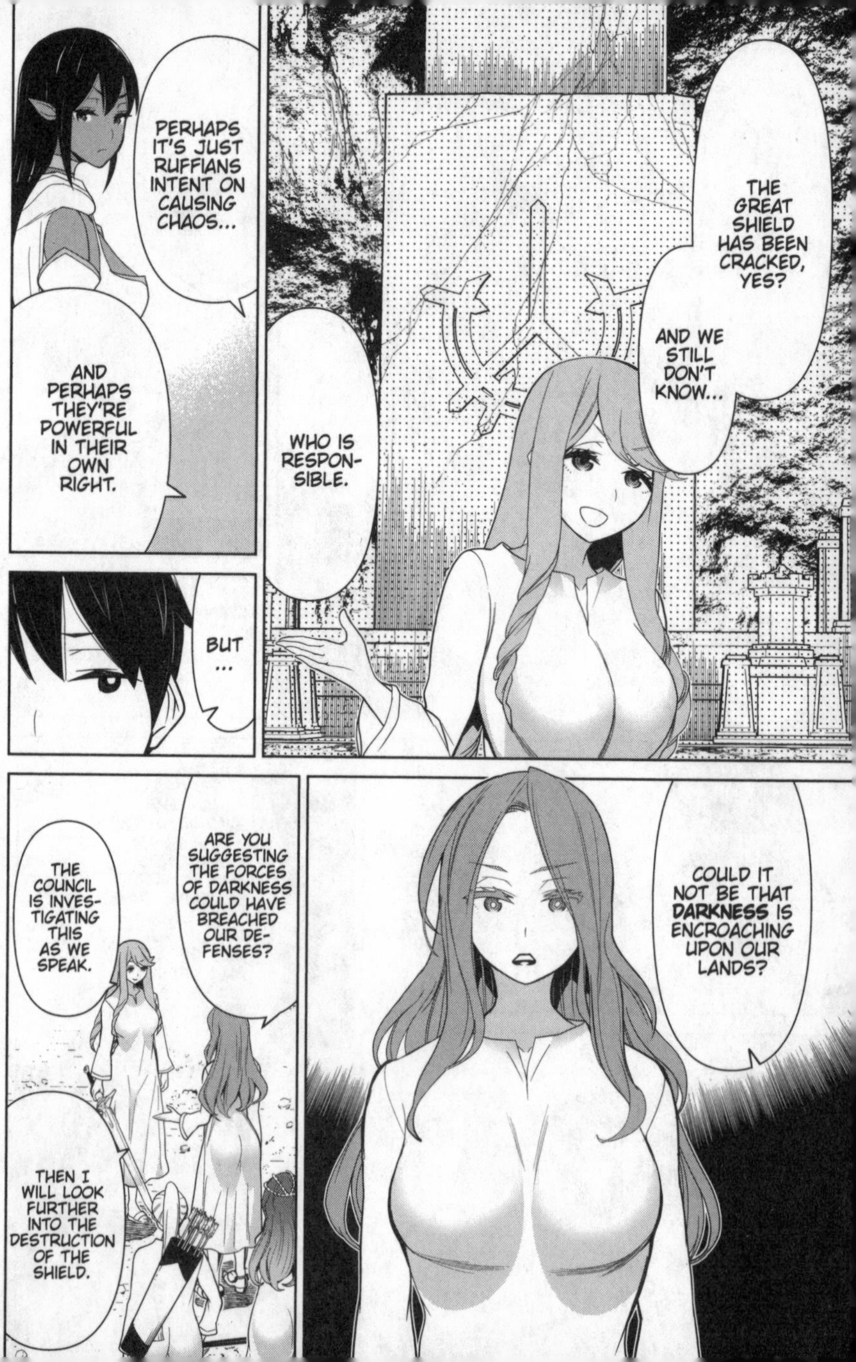
THE GREAT SHIELD HAS BEEN CRACKED, YES?
AND WE STILL DON'T KNOW...
WHO IS RESPONSIBLE.
PERHAPS IT'S JUST RUFFIANS INTENT ON CAUSING CHAOS...
AND PERHAPS THEY'RE POWERFUL IN THEIR OWN RIGHT.
BUT ...
COULD IT NOT BE THAT **DARKNESS** IS ENCROACHING UPON OUR LANDS?
ARE YOU SUGGESTING THE FORCES OF DARKNESS COULD HAVE BREACHED OUR DEFENSES?
THE COUNCIL IS INVESTIGATING THIS AS WE SPEAK.
THEN I WILL LOOK FURTHER INTO THE DESTRUCTION OF THE SHIELD.

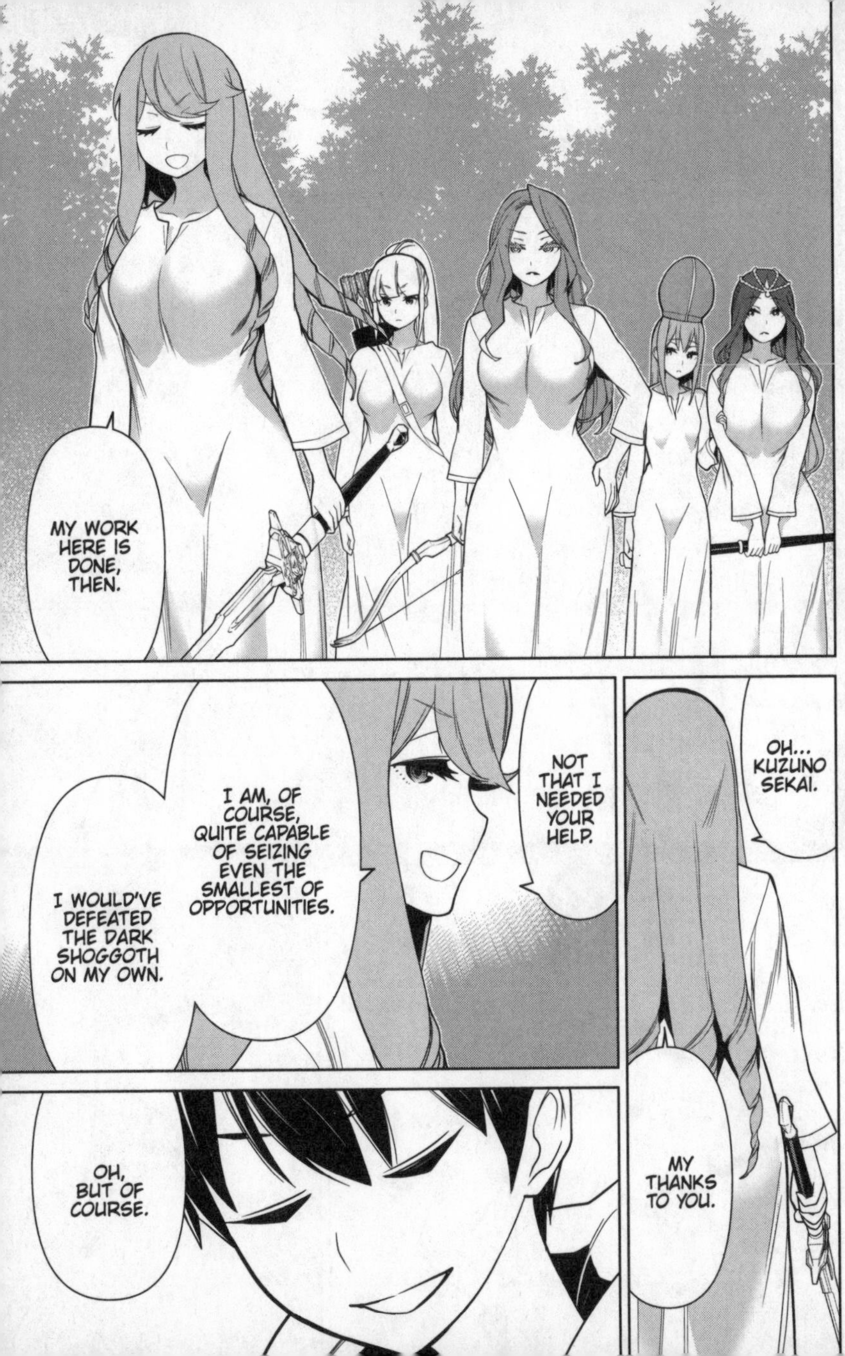
MY WORK HERE IS DONE, THEN.
OH... KUZUNO SEKAI.
MY THANKS TO YOU.
NOT THAT I NEEDED YOUR HELP.
I AM, OF COURSE, QUITE CAPABLE OF SEIZING EVEN THE SMALLEST OF OPPORTUNITIES.
I WOULD'VE DEFEATED THE DARK SHOGGOTH ON MY OWN.
OH, BUT OF COURSE.

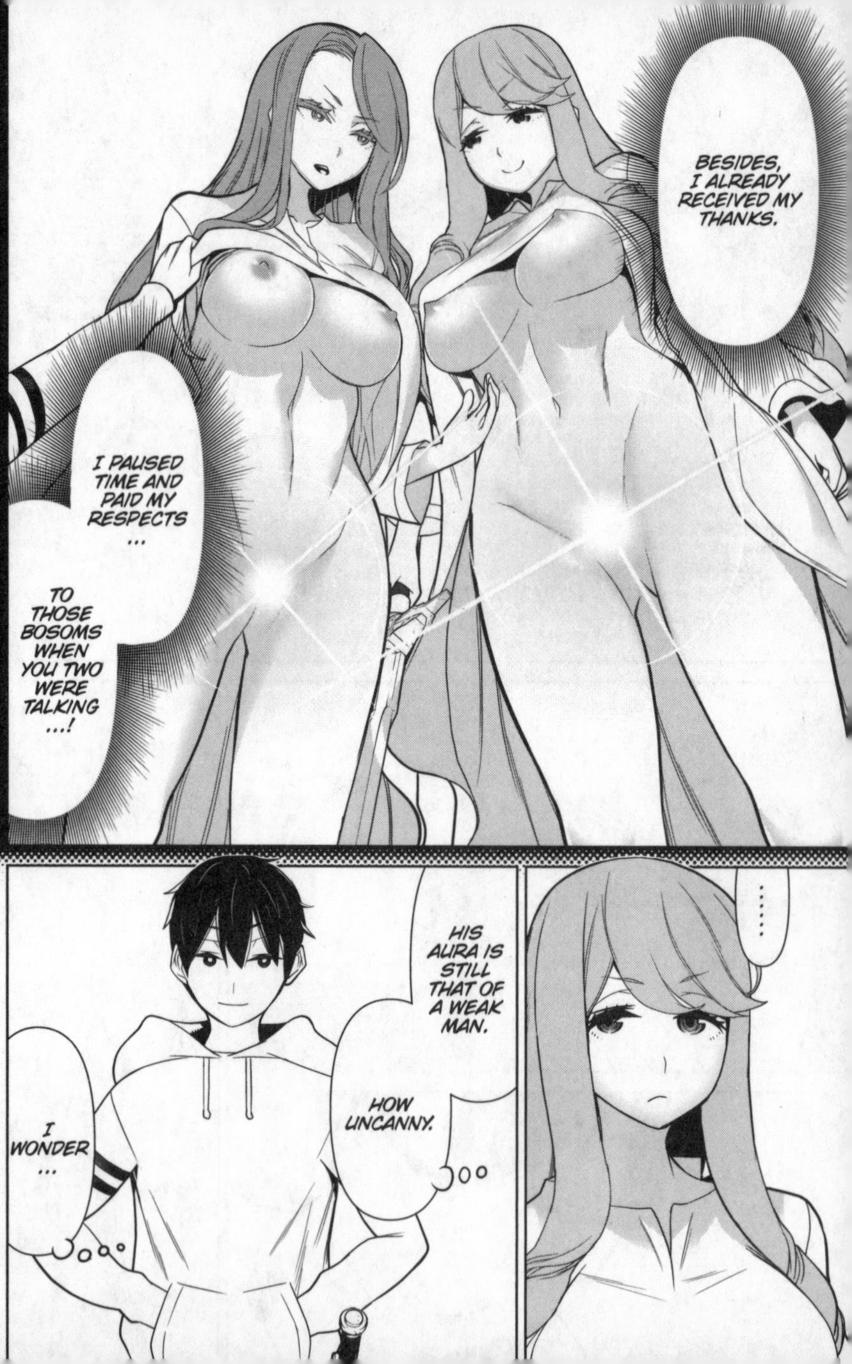
BESIDES, I ALREADY RECEIVED MY THANKS.
I PAUSED TIME AND PAID MY RESPECTS ...
TO THOSE BOSOMS WHEN YOU TWO WERE TALKING ...!
......
HIS AURA IS STILL THAT OF A WEAK MAN.
HOW UNCANNY.
I WONDER ...

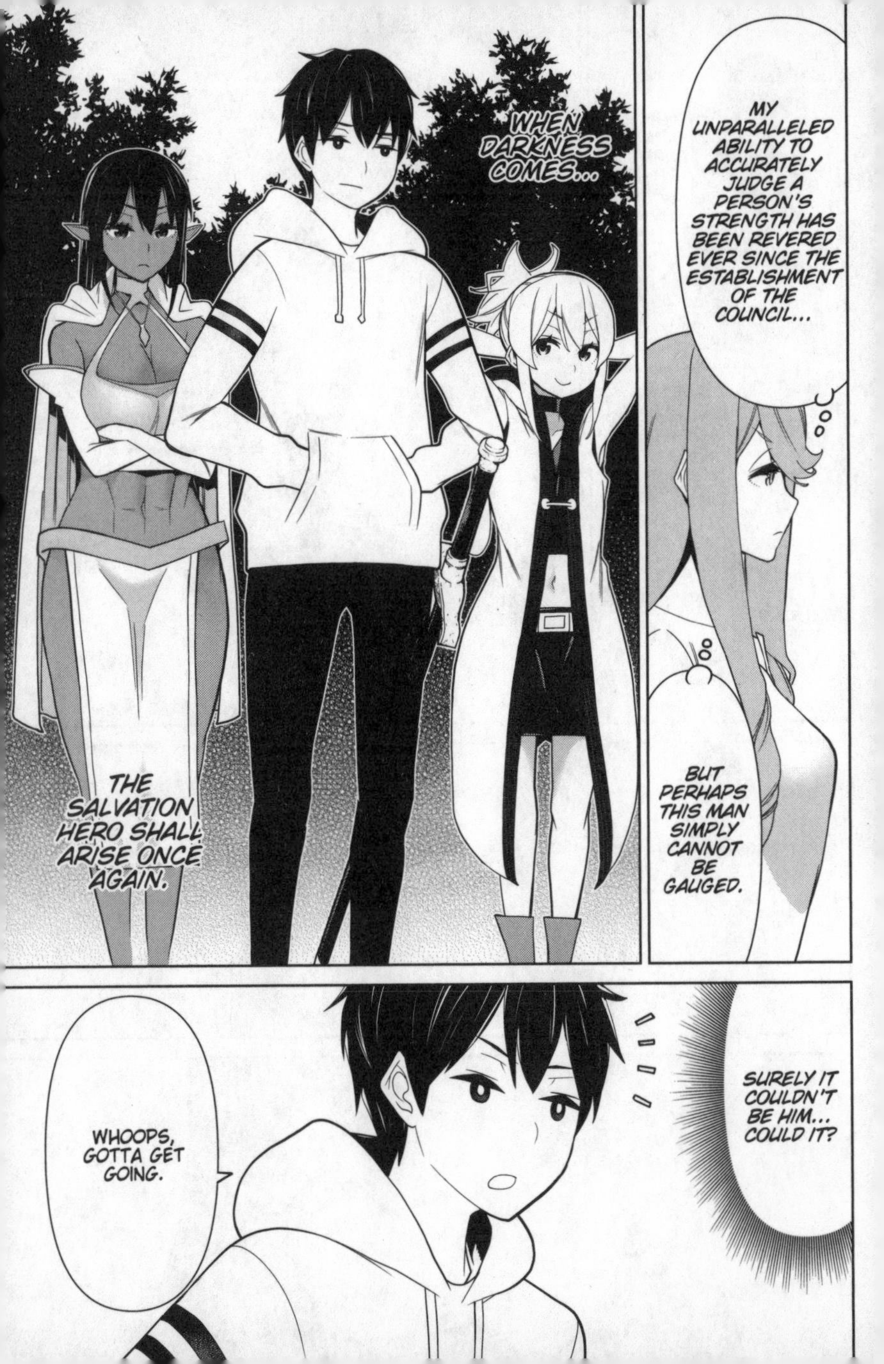
MY UNPARALLELED ABILITY TO ACCURATELY JUDGE A PERSON'S STRENGTH HAS BEEN REVERED EVER SINCE THE ESTABLISHMENT OF THE COUNCIL...
BUT PERHAPS THIS MAN SIMPLY CANNOT BE GAUGED.
WHEN DARKNESS COMES...
THE SALVATION HERO SHALL ARISE ONCE AGAIN.
SURELY IT COULDN'T BE HIM... COULD IT?
WHOOPS, GOTTA GET GOING.

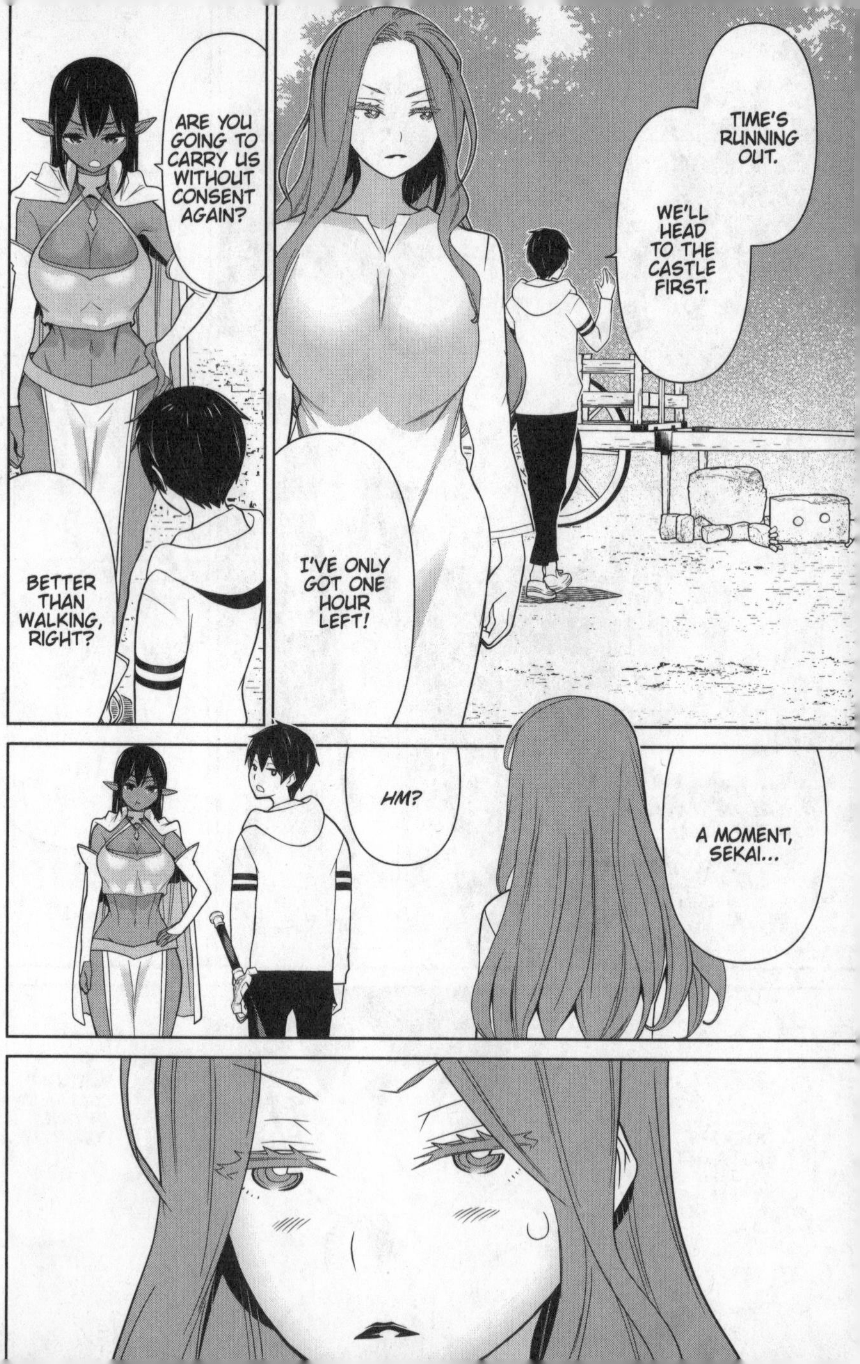
TIME'S RUNNING OUT.
WE'LL HEAD TO THE CASTLE FIRST.
I'VE ONLY GOT ONE HOUR LEFT!
ARE YOU GOING TO CARRY US WITHOUT CONSENT AGAIN?
BETTER THAN WALKING, RIGHT?
A MOMENT, SEKAI...
HM?

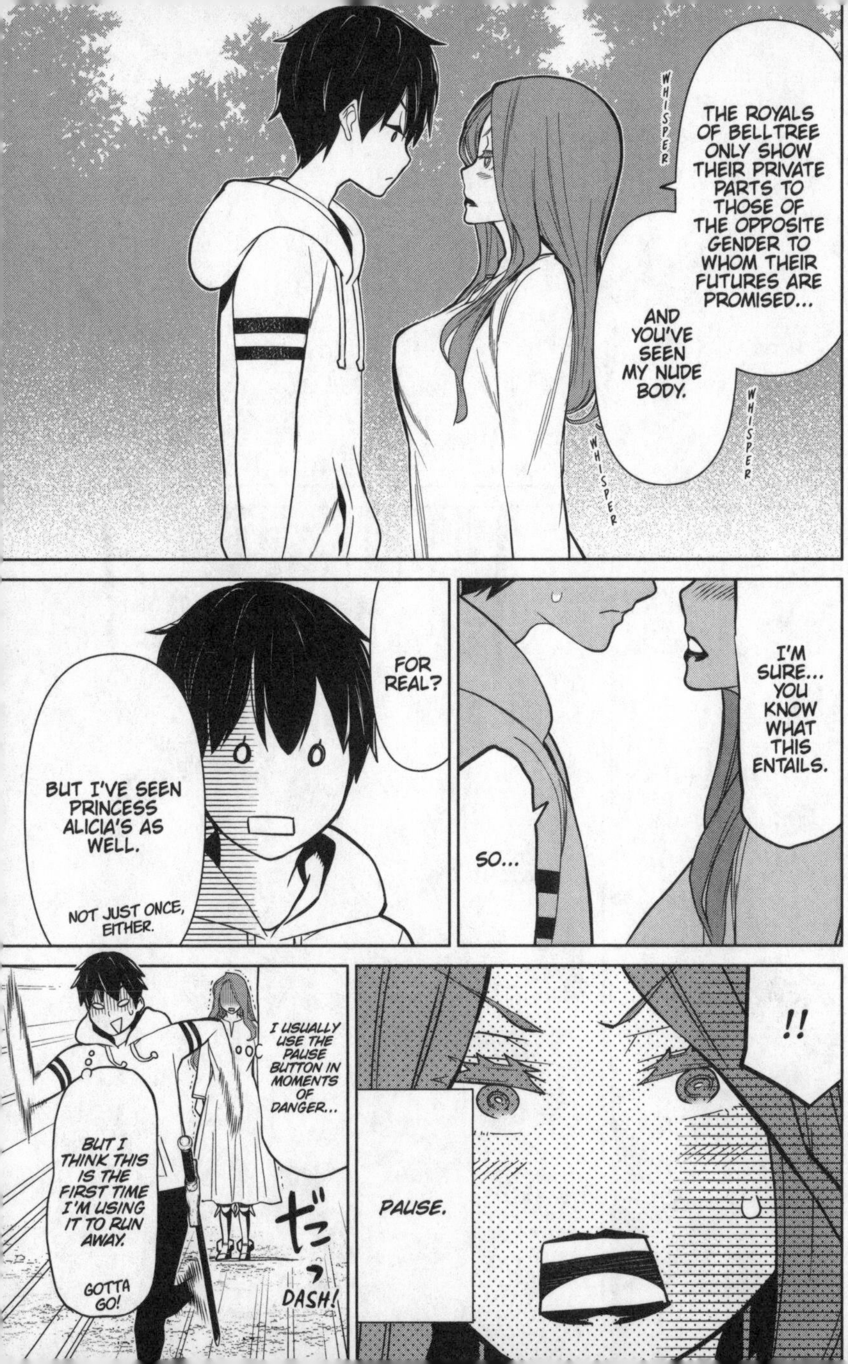
WHISPER
THE ROYALS OF BELLTREE ONLY SHOW THEIR PRIVATE PARTS TO THOSE OF THE OPPOSITE GENDER TO WHOM THEIR FUTURES ARE PROMISED...
AND YOU'VE SEEN MY NUDE BODY.
WHISPER
WHISPER
I'M SURE... YOU KNOW WHAT THIS ENTAILS.
SO...
FOR REAL?
BUT I'VE SEEN PRINCESS ALICIA'S AS WELL.
NOT JUST ONCE, EITHER.
!!
PAUSE.
I USUALLY USE THE PAUSE BUTTON IN MOMENTS OF DANGER...
BUT I THINK THIS IS THE FIRST TIME I'M USING IT TO RUN AWAY.
GOTTA GO!
DASH!

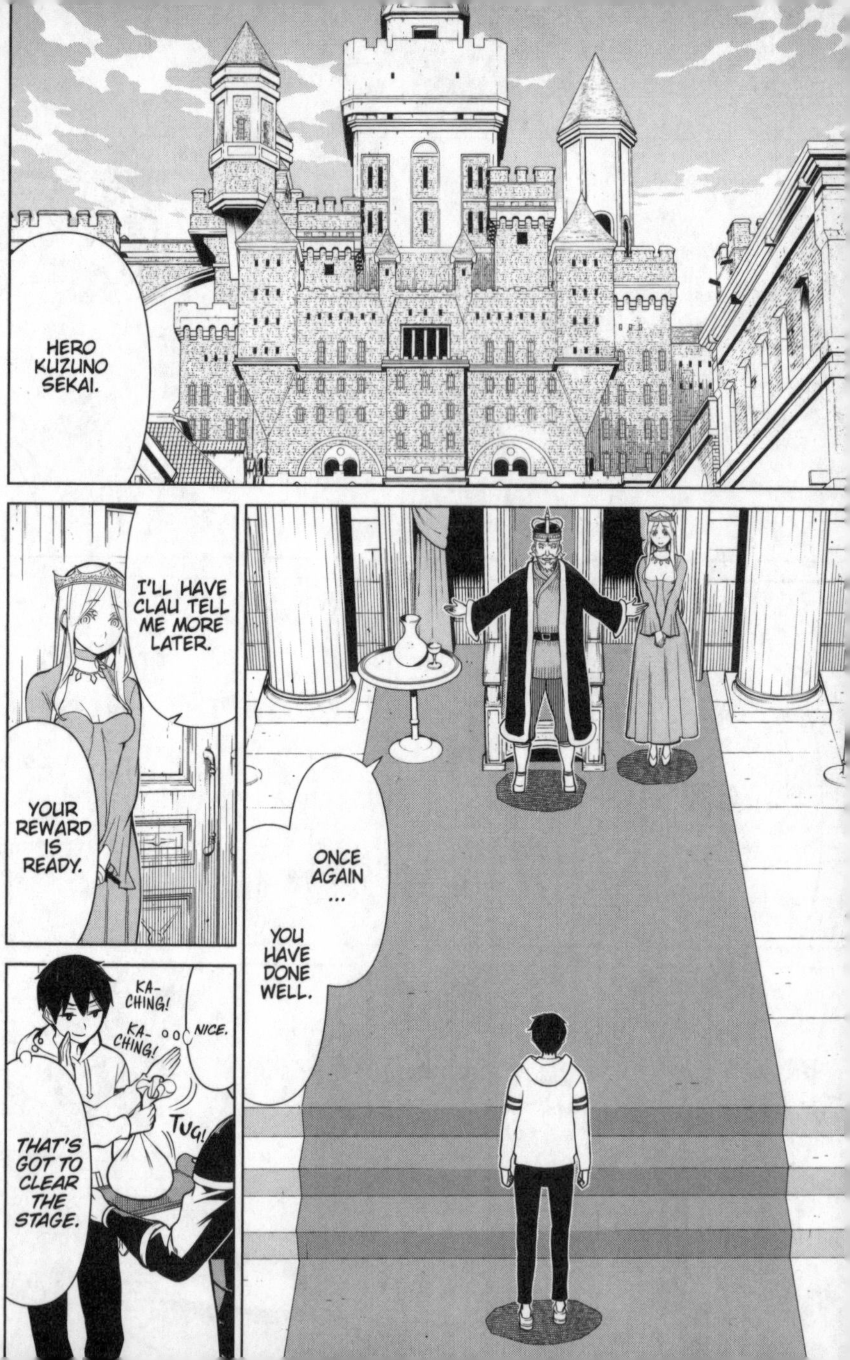
HERO KUZUNO SEKAI.
ONCE AGAIN ...
YOU HAVE DONE WELL.
I'LL HAVE CLAU TELL ME MORE LATER.
YOUR REWARD IS READY.
KA-CHING!
KA-CHING!
NICE.
TUG!
THAT'S GOT TO CLEAR THE STAGE.

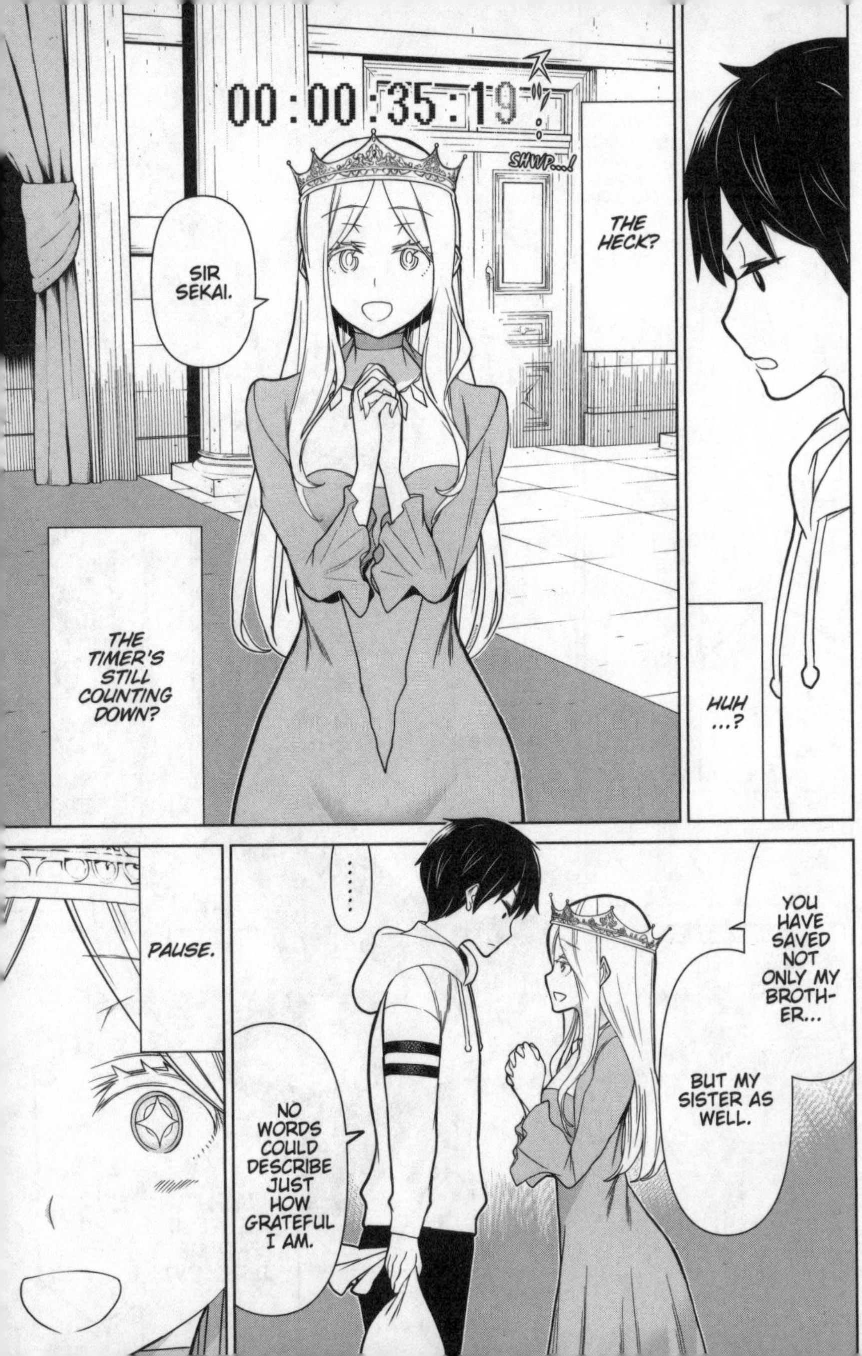
THE HECK?
HUH ...?
00:00:35:19
ス
SHWP...!
SIR SEKAI.
THE TIMER'S STILL COUNTING DOWN?
YOU HAVE SAVED NOT ONLY MY BROTH-ER...
BUT MY SISTER AS WELL.
......
NO WORDS COULD DESCRIBE JUST HOW GRATEFUL I AM.
PAUSE.

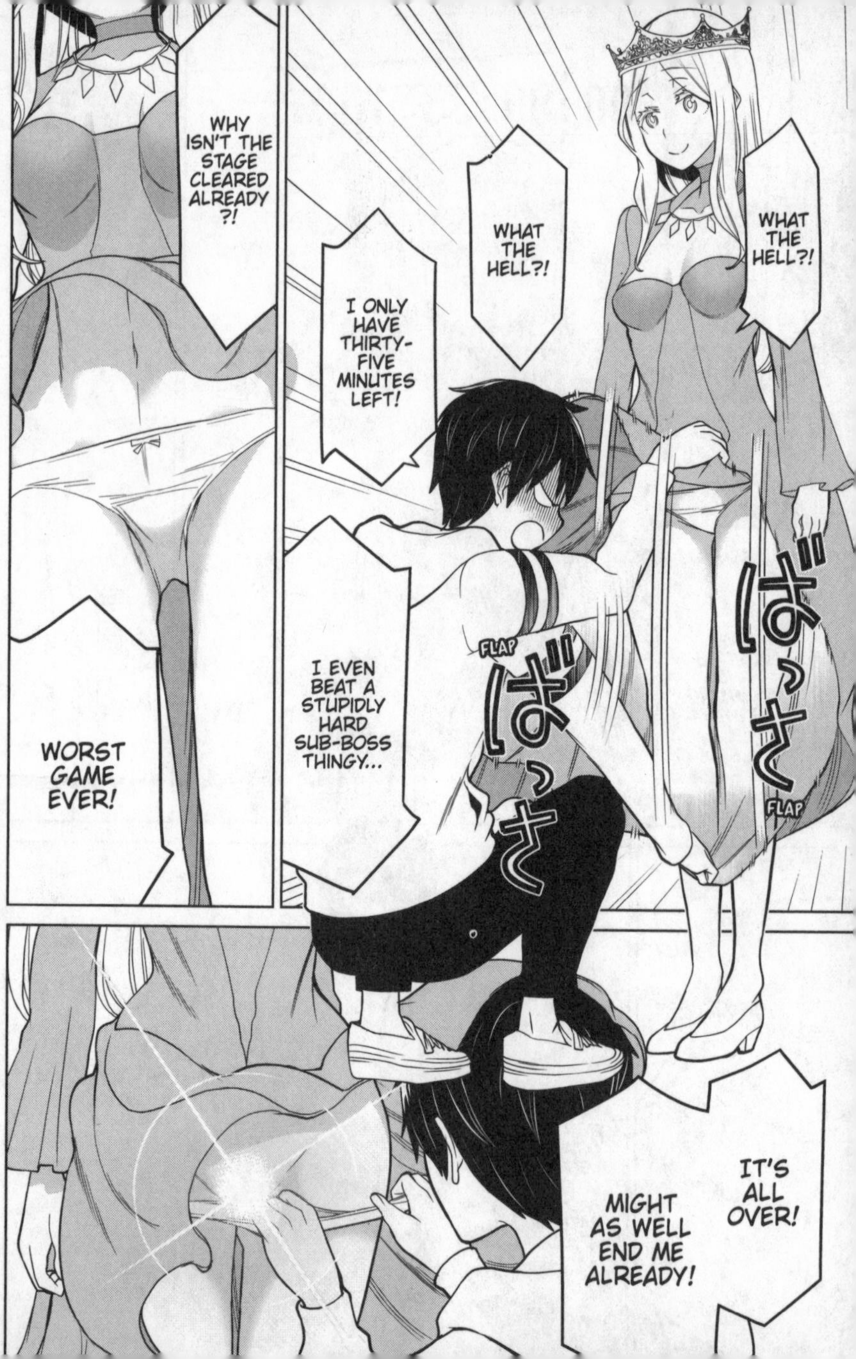

WHAT THE HELL?!
WHAT THE HELL?!
I ONLY HAVE THIRTY-FIVE MINUTES LEFT!
ばっさ
FLAP
I EVEN BEAT A STUPIDLY HARD SUB-BOSS THINGY...
ばっさ
FLAP
WHY ISN'T THE STAGE CLEARED ALREADY?!
WORST GAME EVER!
IT'S ALL OVER!
MIGHT AS WELL END ME ALREADY!

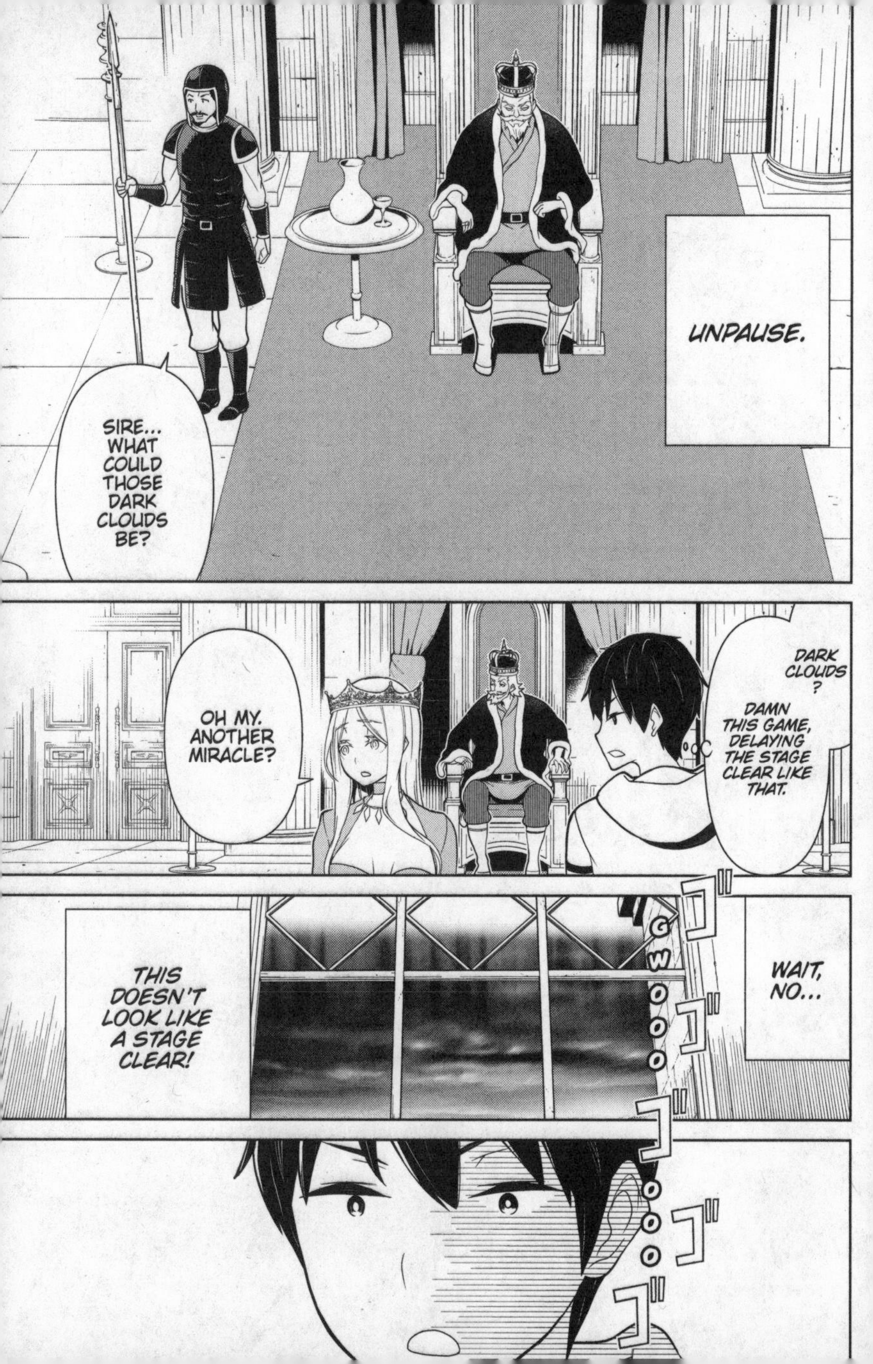
UNPAUSE.
SIRE... WHAT COULD THOSE DARK CLOUDS BE?
DARK CLOUDS? DAMN THIS GAME, DELAYING THE STAGE CLEAR LIKE THAT.
OH MY. ANOTHER MIRACLE?
WAIT, NO...
GWOOOO
THIS DOESN'T LOOK LIKE A STAGE CLEAR!
OOOO

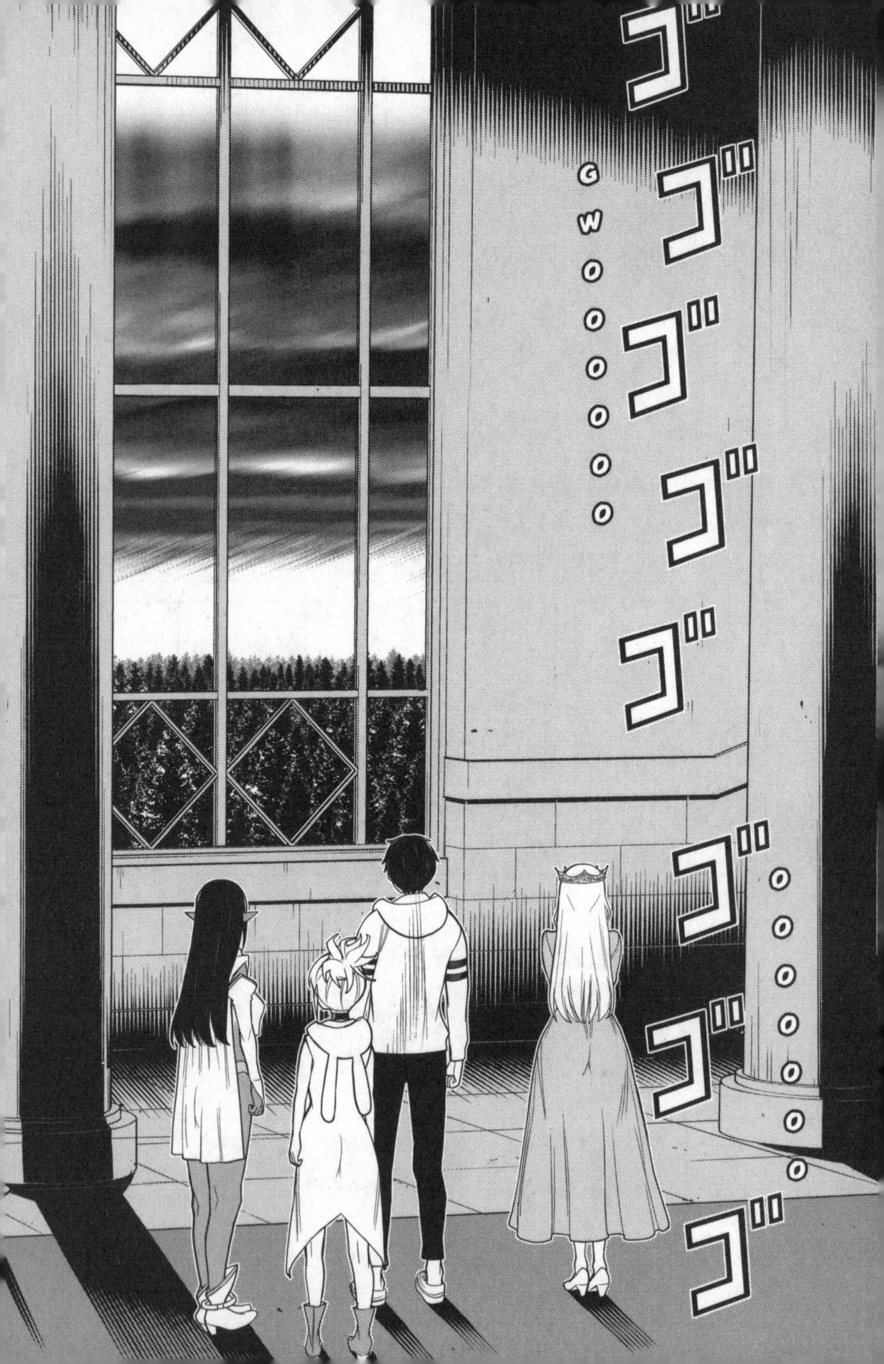
ゴゴゴゴゴゴゴゴ
GWOOOOOO
OOOOOOO

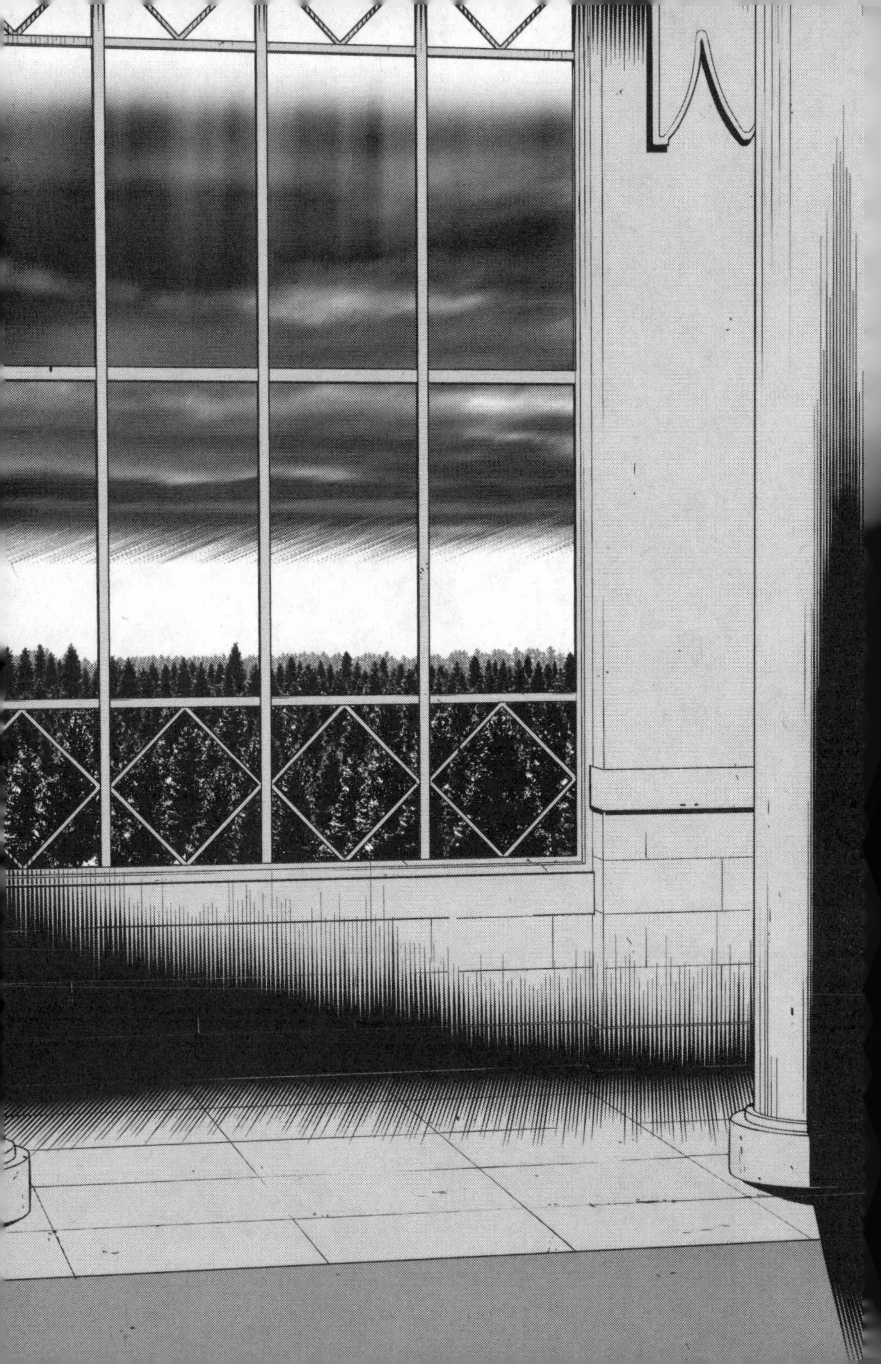

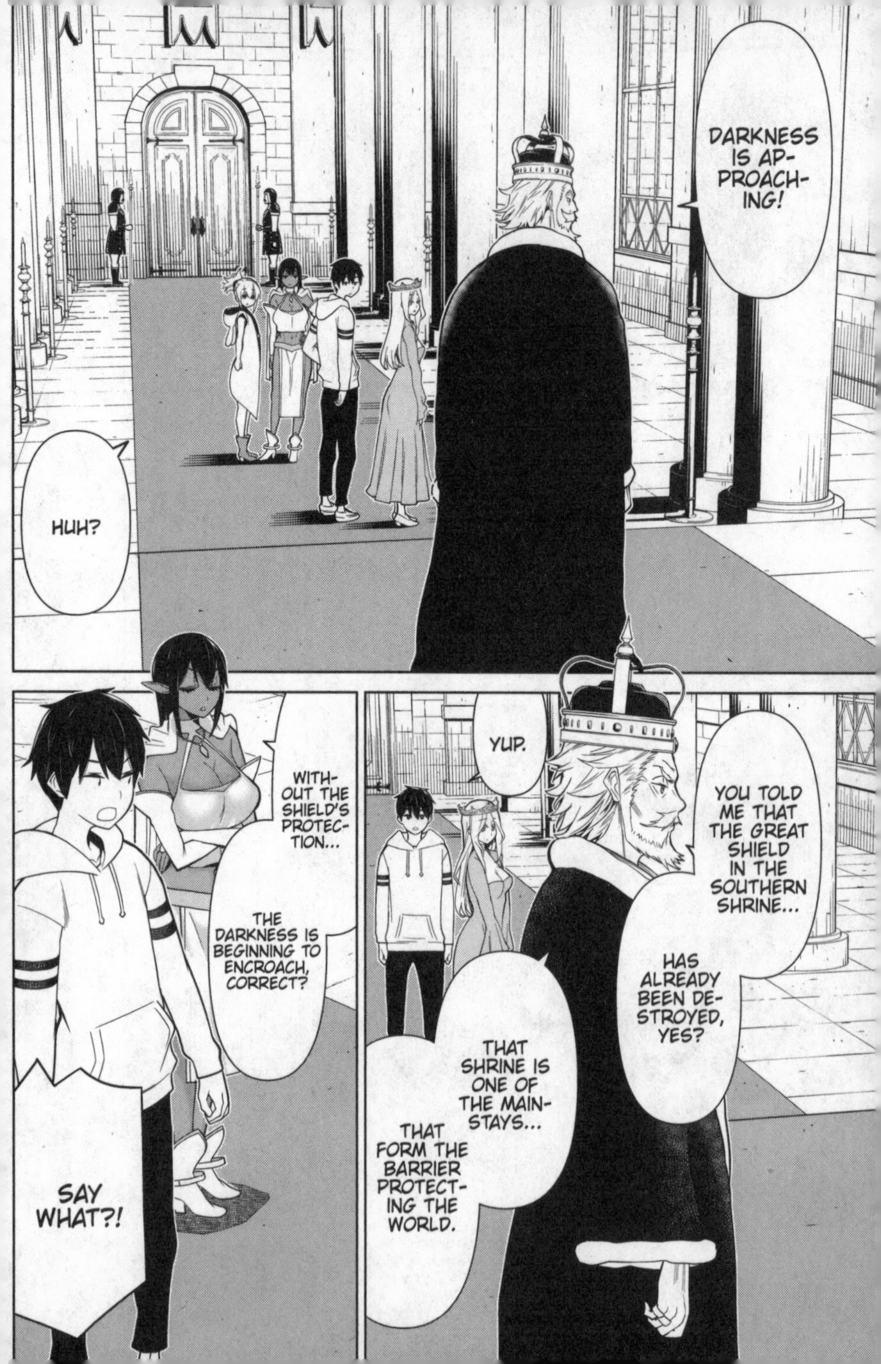
DARKNESS IS APPROACHING!
HUH?
YOU TOLD ME THAT THE GREAT SHIELD IN THE SOUTHERN SHRINE...
HAS ALREADY BEEN DESTROYED, YES?
YUP.
THAT SHRINE IS ONE OF THE MAINSTAYS...
THAT FORM THE BARRIER PROTECTING THE WORLD.
WITHOUT THE SHIELD'S PROTECTION...
THE DARKNESS IS BEGINNING TO ENCROACH, CORRECT?
SAY WHAT?!

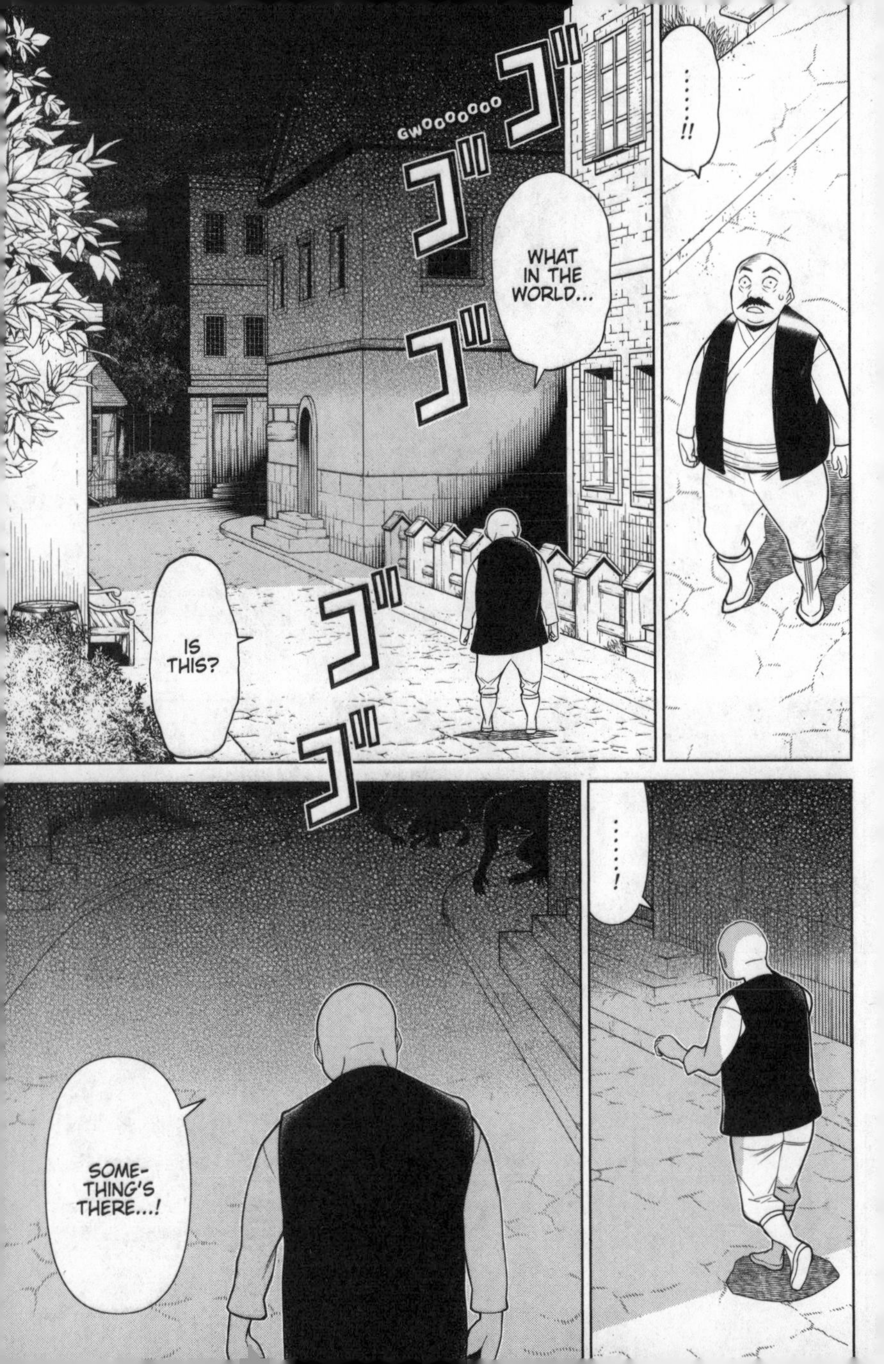
......!!
GWOOOOOOO
ゴゴゴゴゴ
WHAT IN THE WORLD...
IS THIS?
......!
SOME-THING'S THERE...!

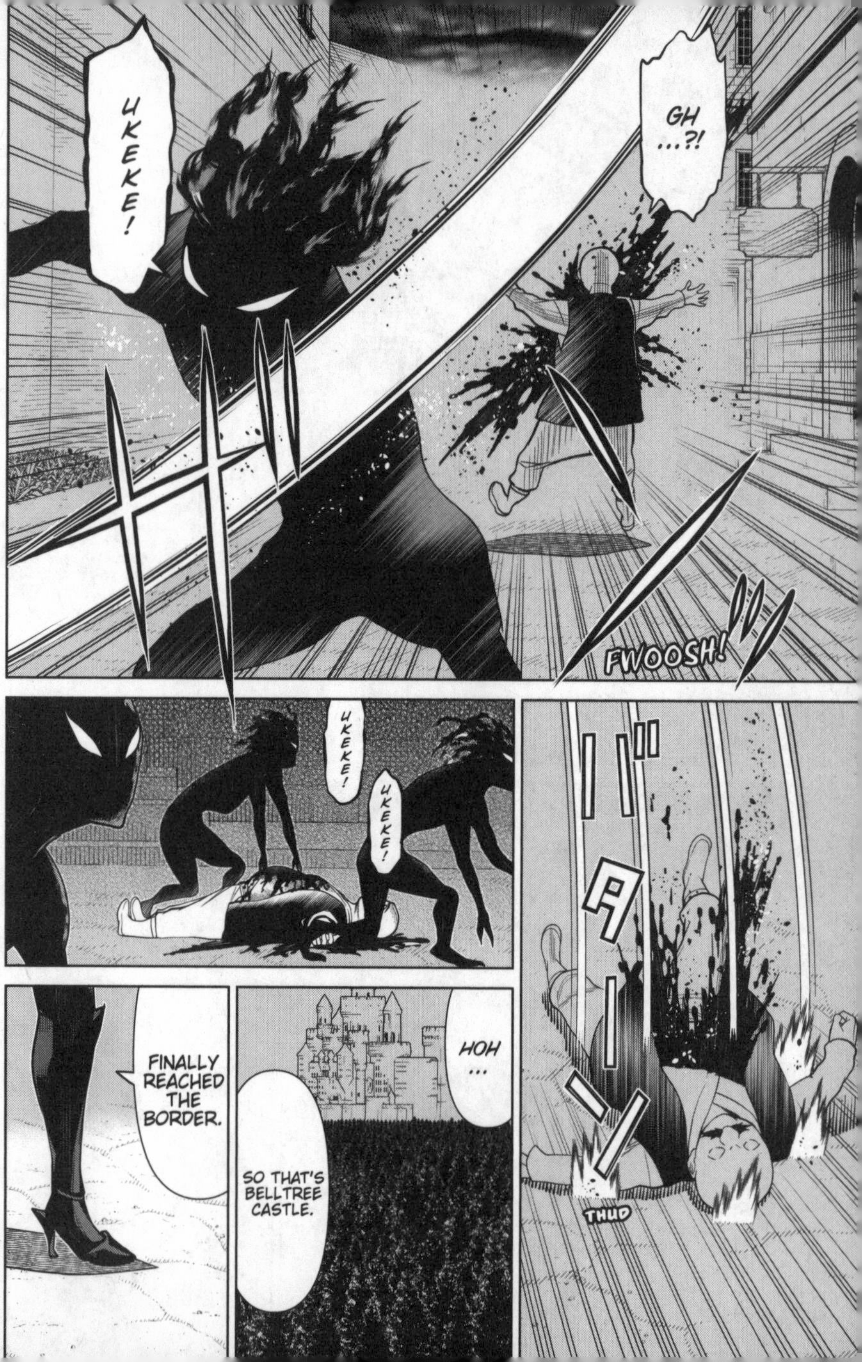
GH ...?!
UKEKE!
FWOOSH!
THUD
UKEKE!
UKEKE!
HOH ...
SO THAT'S BELLTREE CASTLE.
FINALLY REACHED THE BORDER.

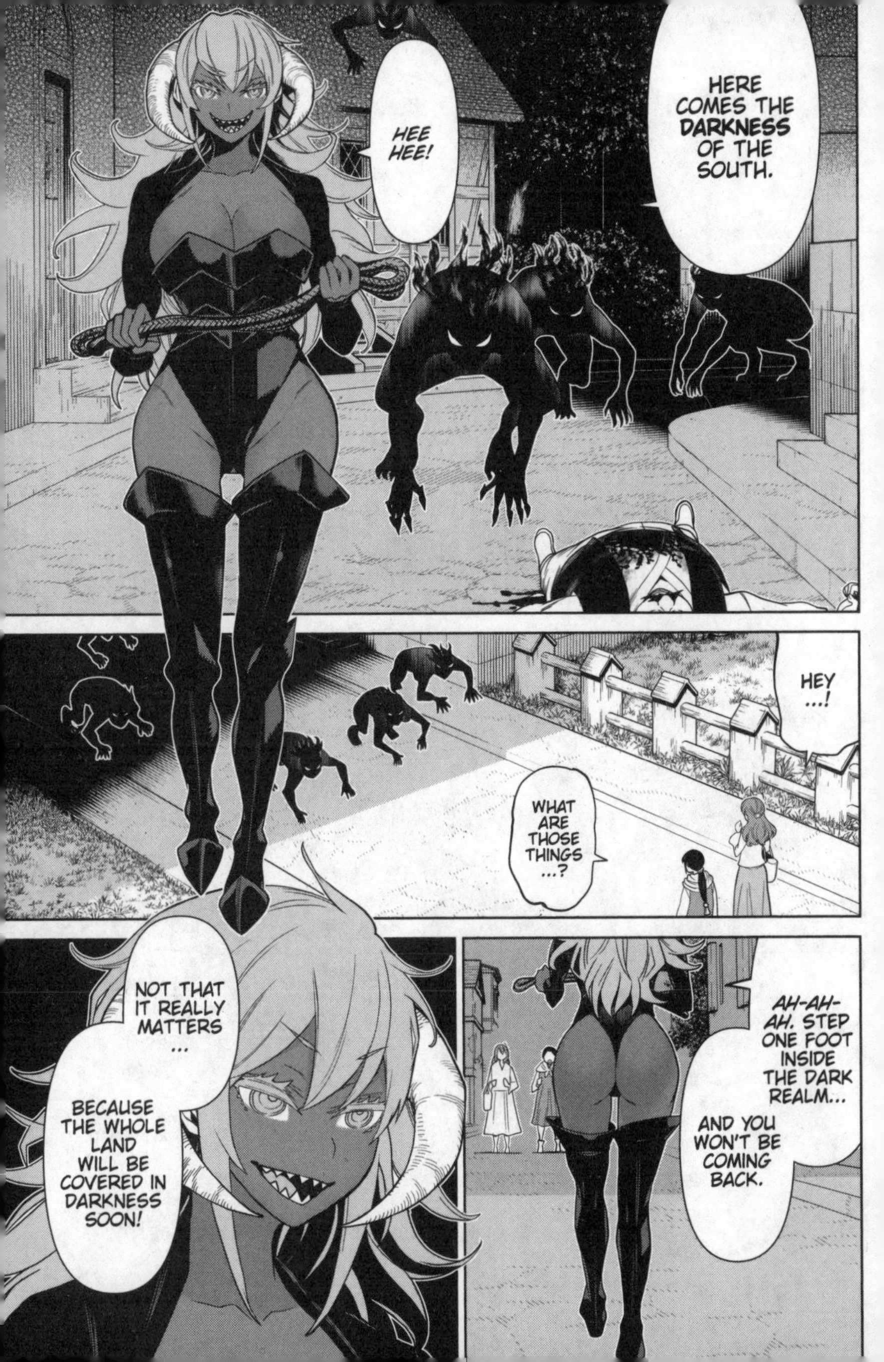
HERE COMES THE DARKNESS OF THE SOUTH.
HEE HEE!
HEY ...!
WHAT ARE THOSE THINGS ...?
AH-AH-AH. STEP ONE FOOT INSIDE THE DARK REALM...
AND YOU WON'T BE COMING BACK.
NOT THAT IT REALLY MATTERS ...
BECAUSE THE WHOLE LAND WILL BE COVERED IN DARKNESS SOON!

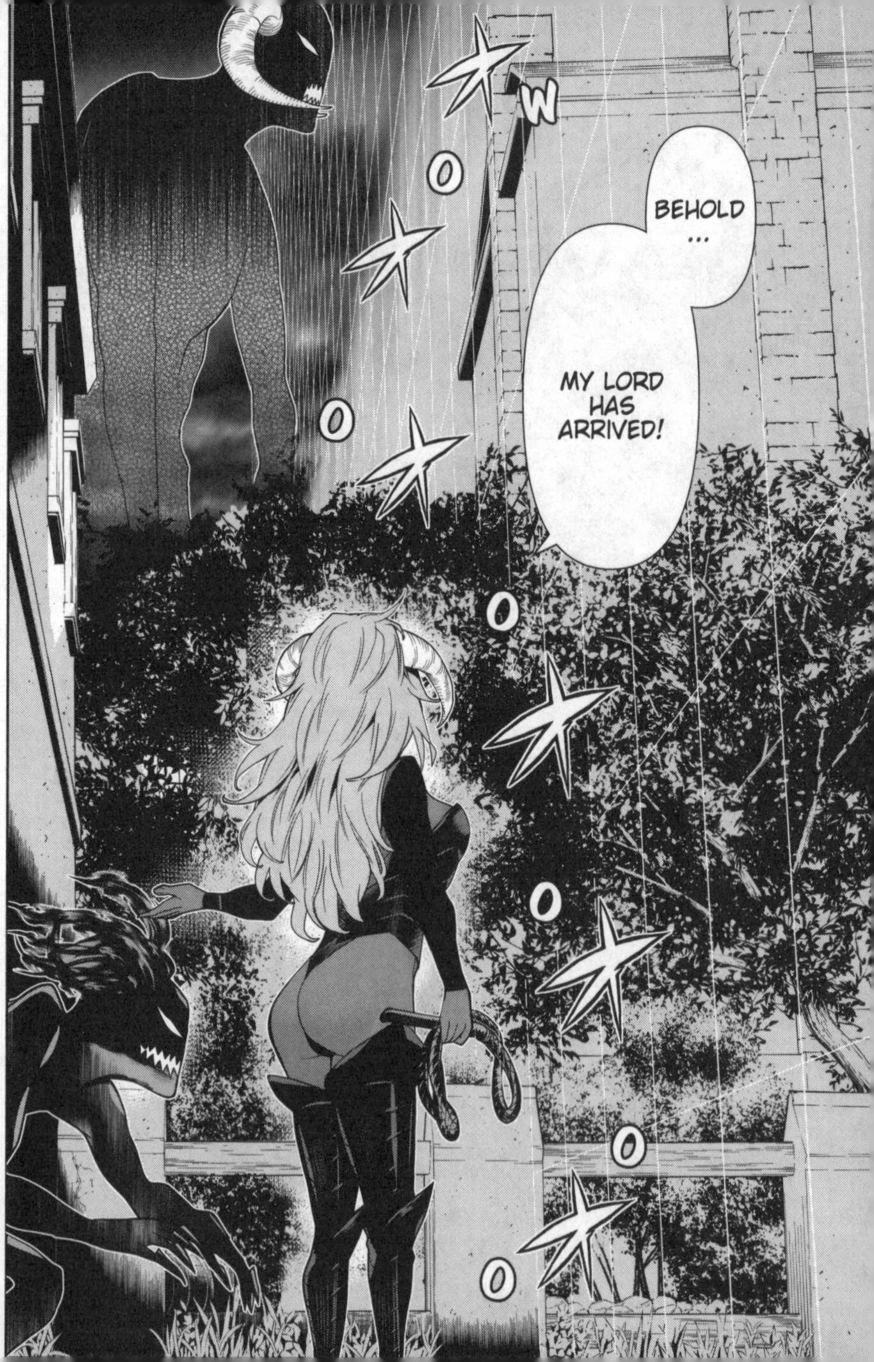
BEHOLD ...
MY LORD HAS ARRIVED!
WOOOOOO

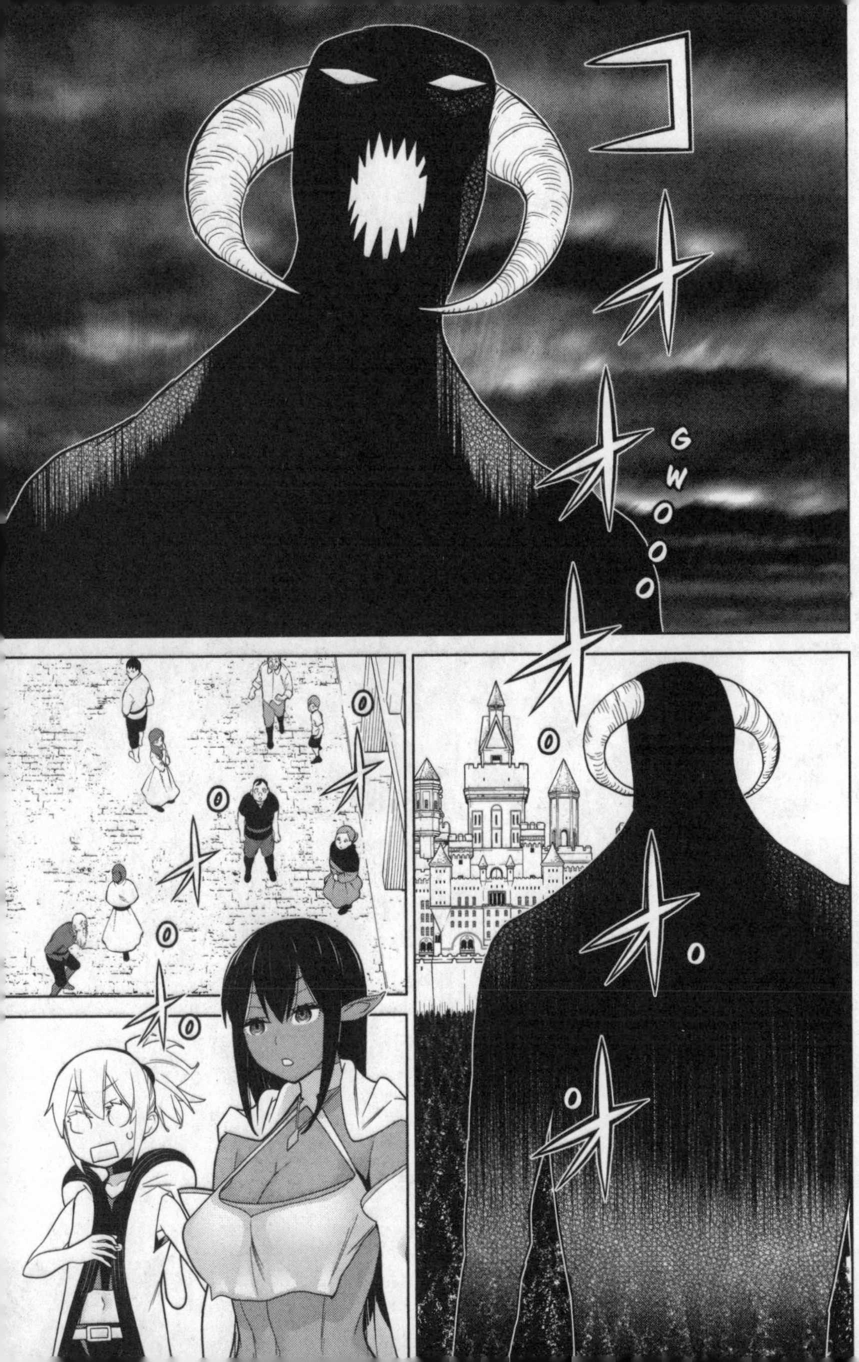
ゴ
GWOOO
O
O
O
O
O
O
O

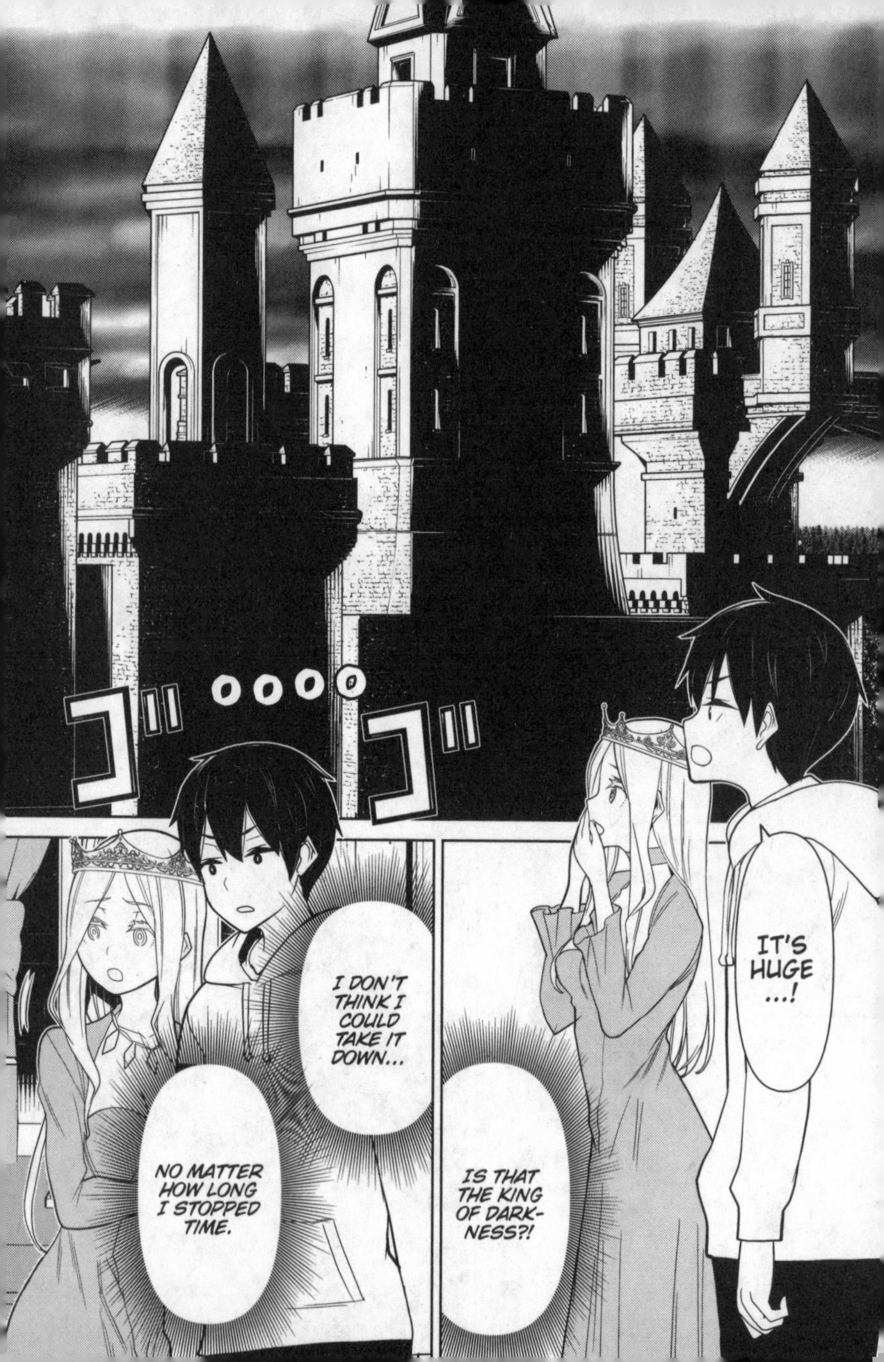
IT'S HUGE ...!
IS THAT THE KING OF DARK-NESS?!
I DON'T THINK I COULD TAKE IT DOWN...
NO MATTER HOW LONG I STOPPED TIME.

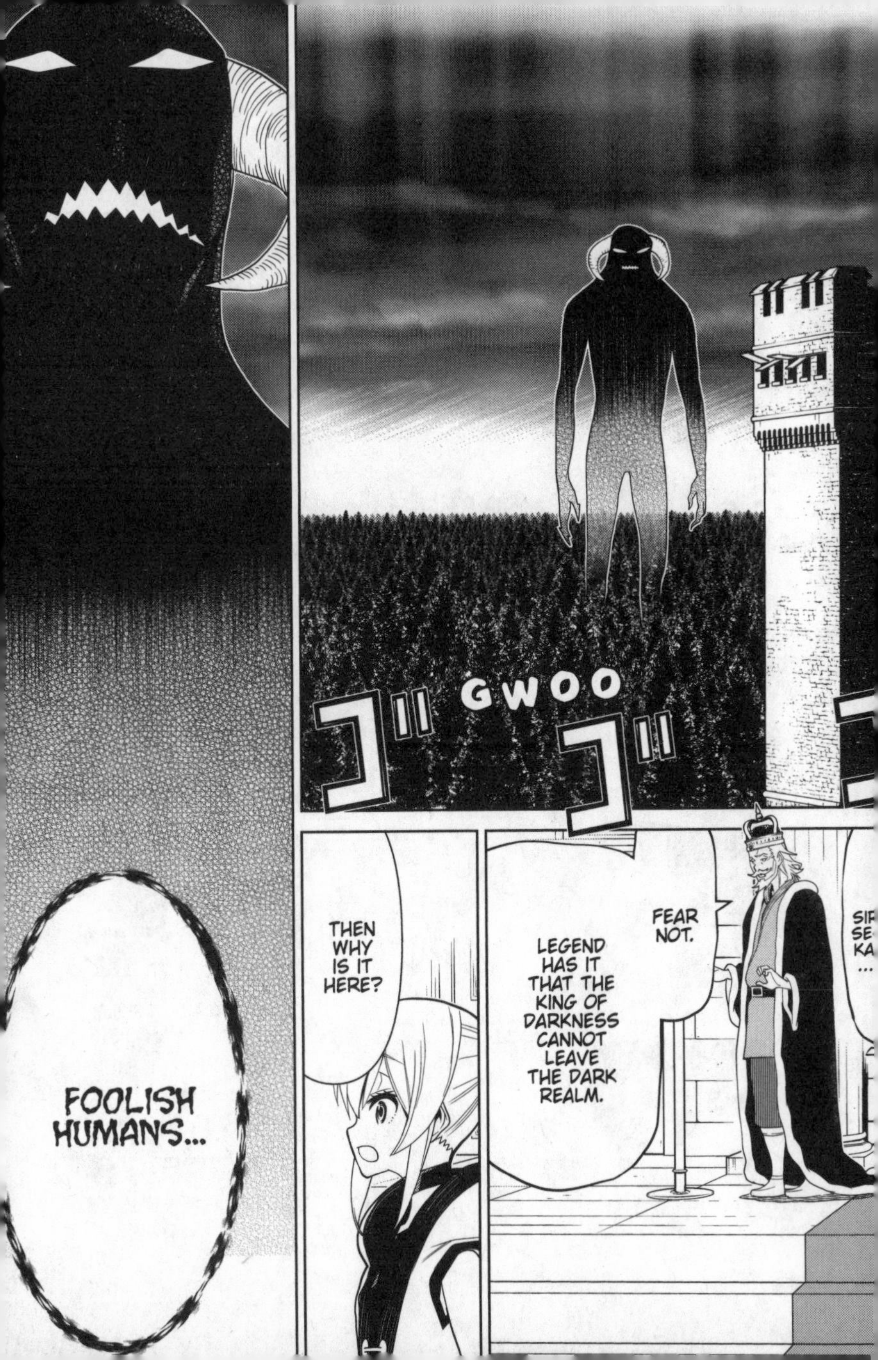
GWOO
FEAR NOT.
LEGEND HAS IT THAT THE KING OF DARKNESS CANNOT LEAVE THE DARK REALM.
THEN WHY IS IT HERE?
FOOLISH HUMANS...

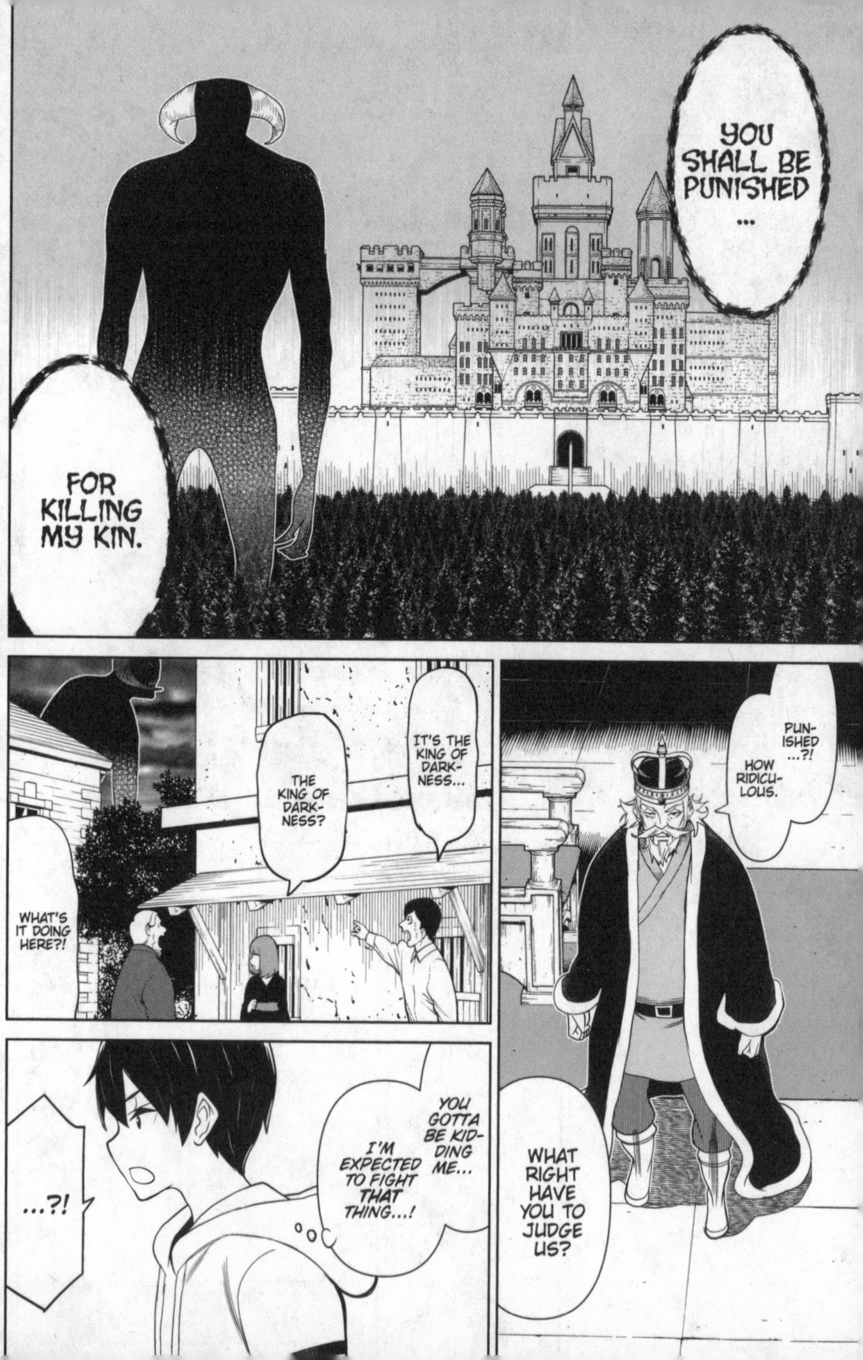

YOU SHALL BE PUNISHED ...
FOR KILLING MY KIN.
PUN-ISHED ...?!
HOW RIDICU-LOUS.
WHAT RIGHT HAVE YOU TO JUDGE US?
IT'S THE KING OF DARK-NESS...
THE KING OF DARK-NESS?
WHAT'S IT DOING HERE?!
YOU GOTTA BE KID-DING ME...
I'M EXPECTED TO FIGHT THAT THING...!
...?!

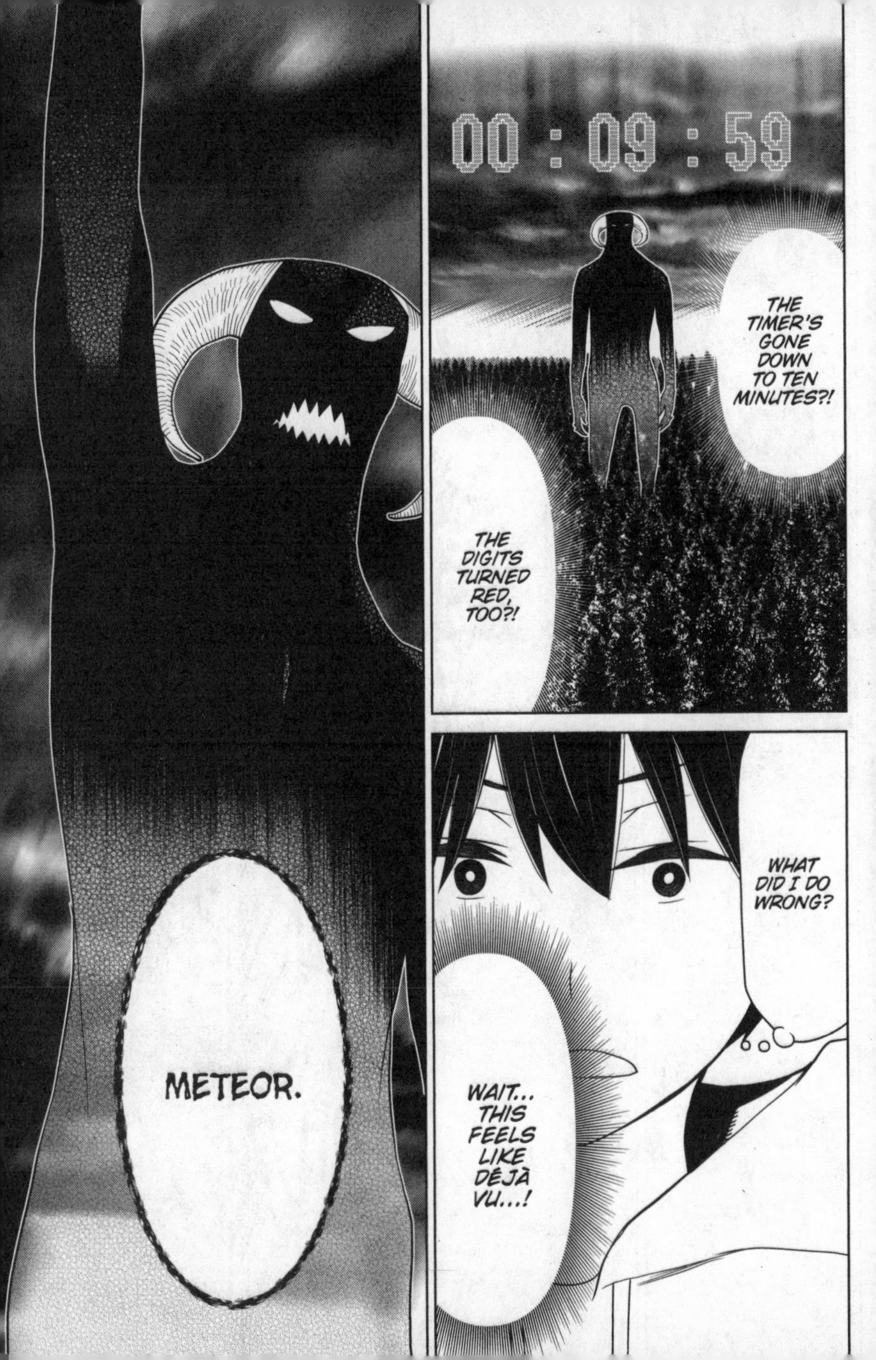
00 : 09 : 59
THE TIMER'S GONE DOWN TO TEN MINUTES?!
THE DIGITS TURNED RED, TOO?!
WHAT DID I DO WRONG?
WAIT... THIS FEELS LIKE DÉJÀ VU...!
METEOR.

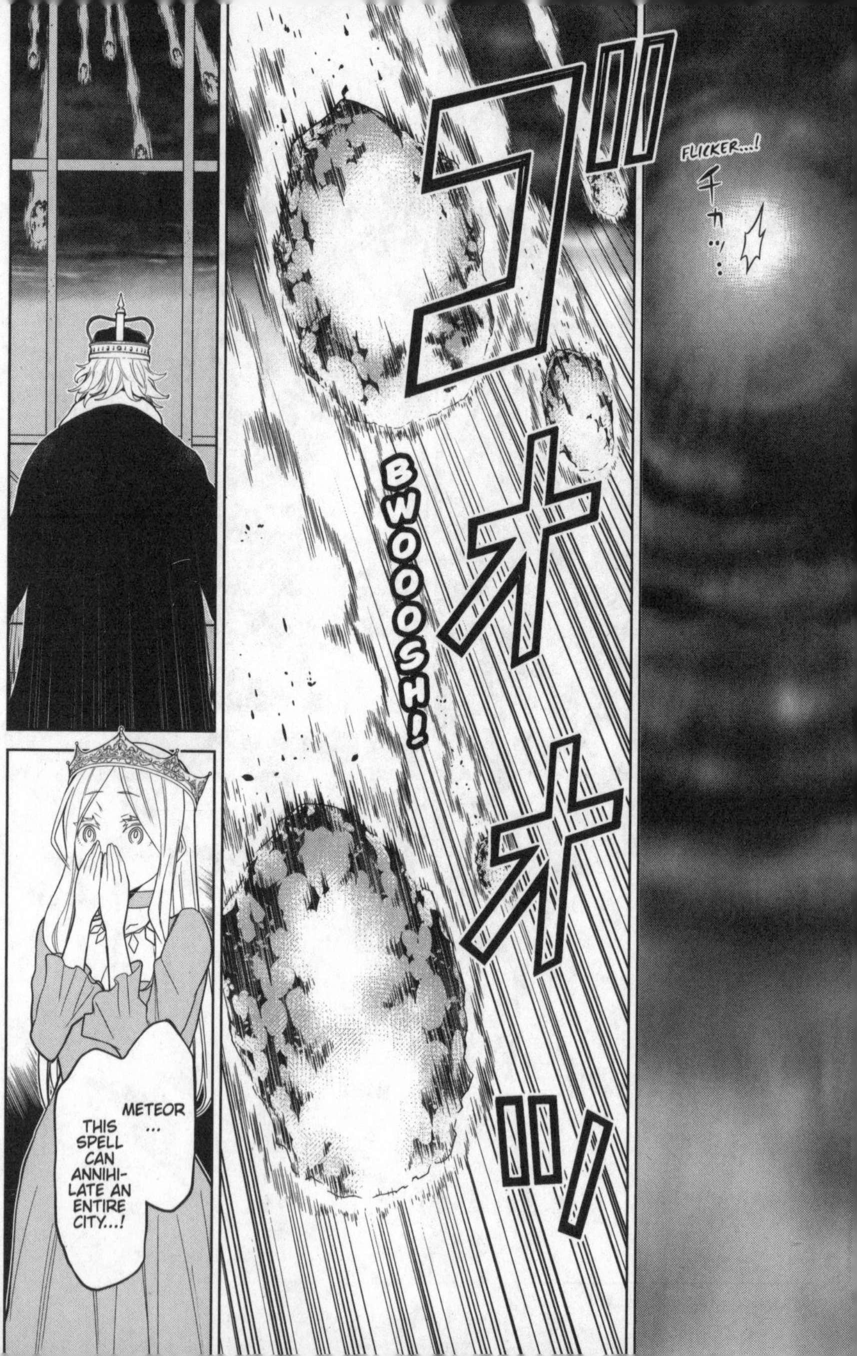
FLICKER...!
チカッ…
ゴオオオ
BWOOOOSH!
METEOR... THIS SPELL CAN ANNIHILATE AN ENTIRE CITY...!

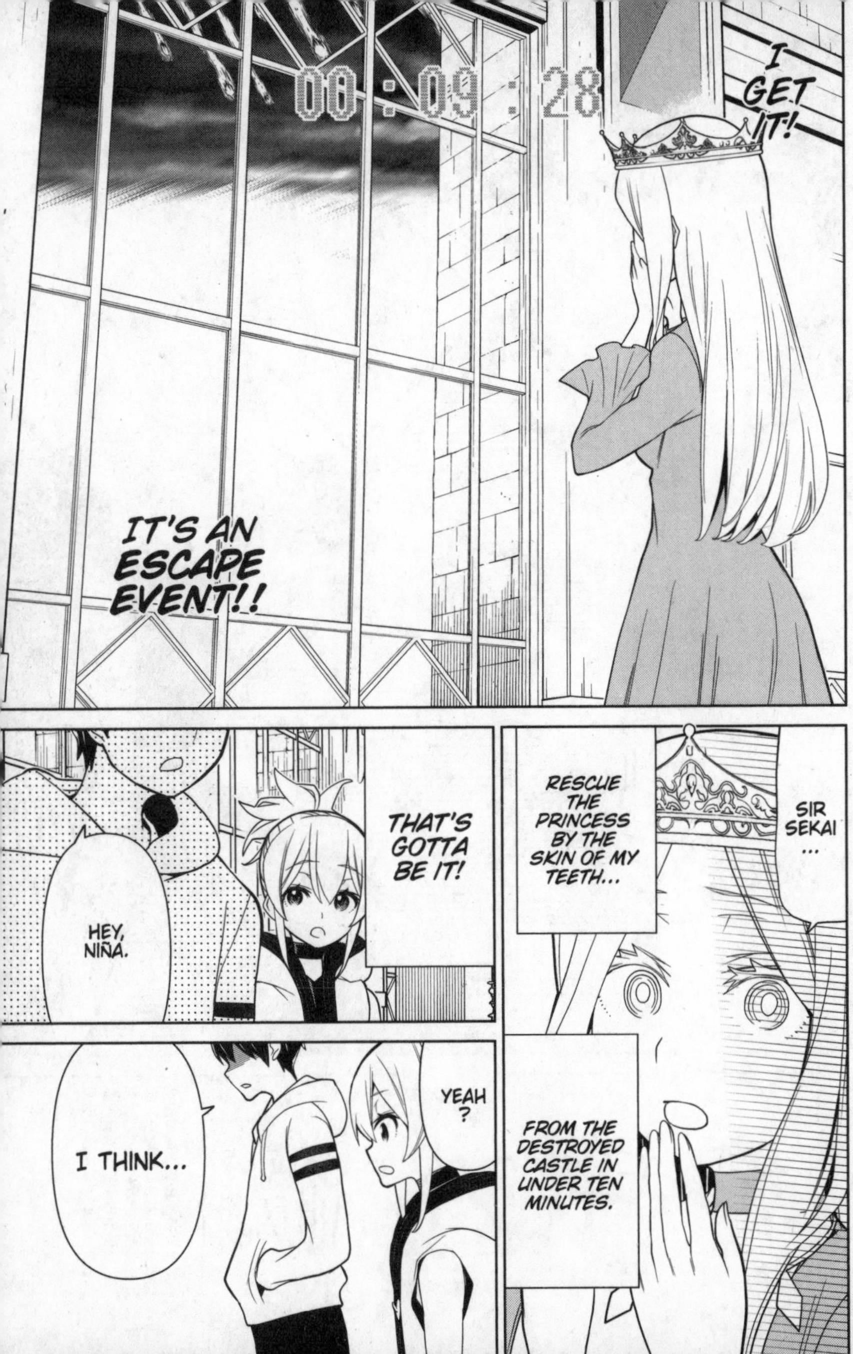
I GET IT!
00:09:28
IT'S AN ESCAPE EVENT!!
SIR SEKAI...
RESCUE THE PRINCESS BY THE SKIN OF MY TEETH...
FROM THE DESTROYED CASTLE IN UNDER TEN MINUTES.
THAT'S GOTTA BE IT!
HEY, NIÑA.
YEAH?
I THINK...

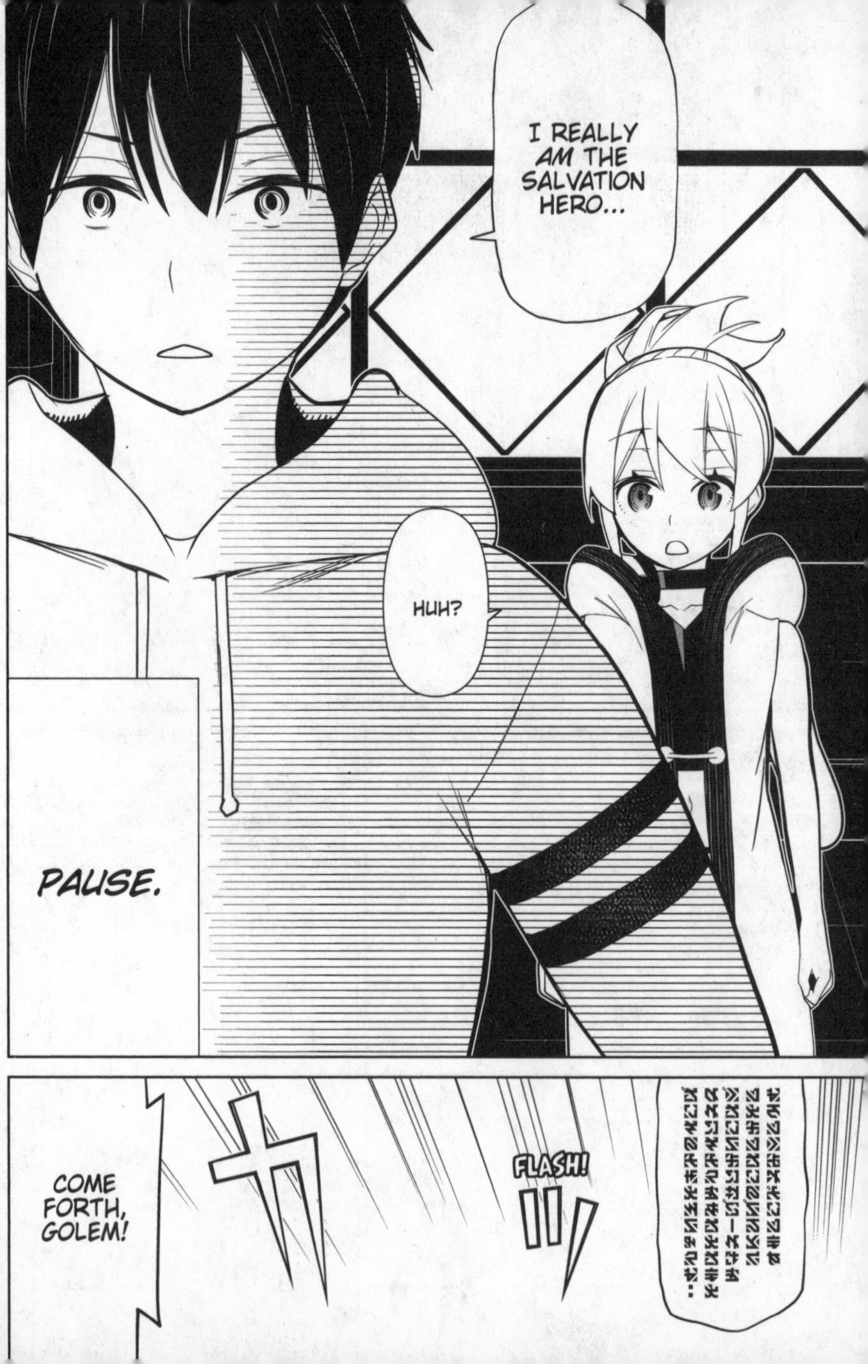
I REALLY AM THE SALVATION HERO...
HUH?
PAUSE.
FLASH!
COME FORTH, GOLEM!

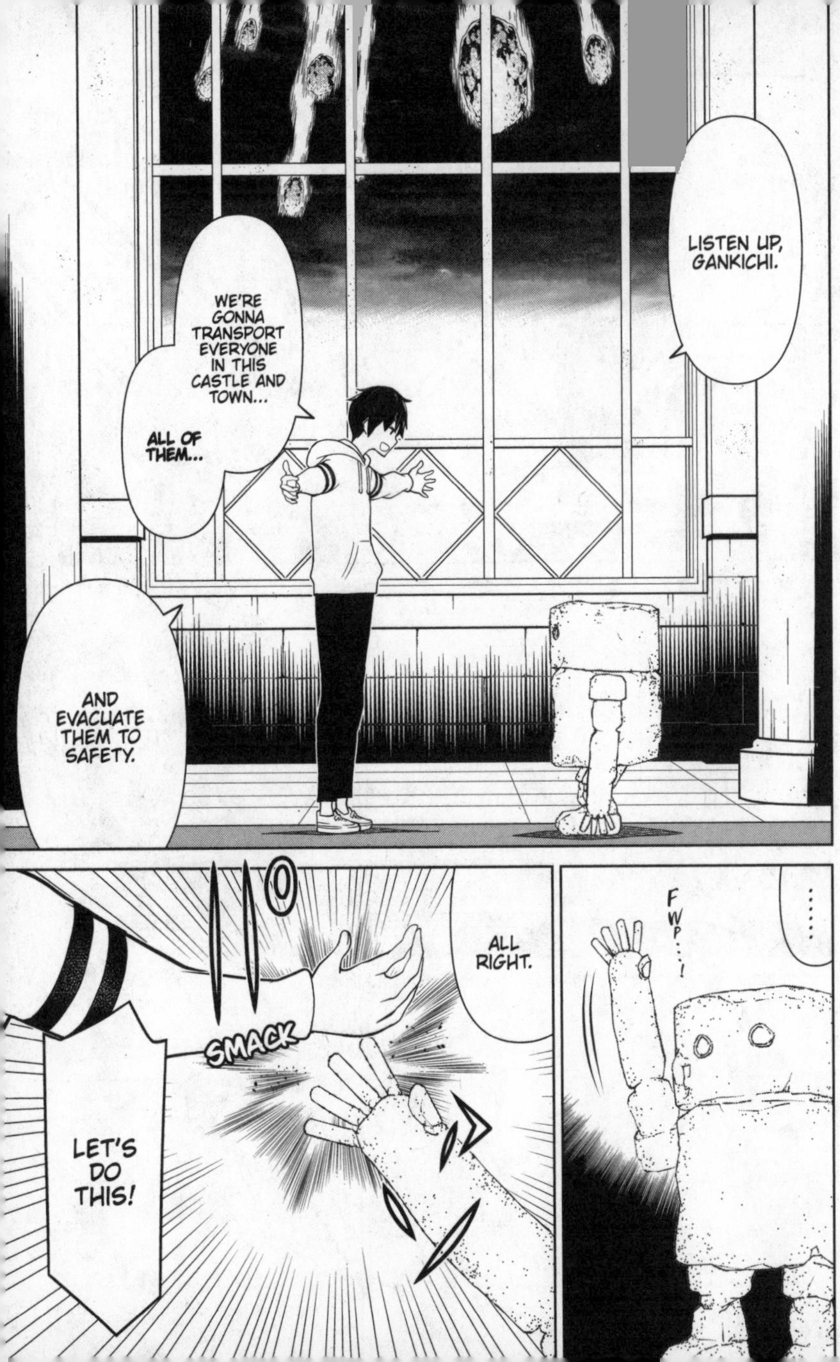
LISTEN UP, GANKICHI.
WE'RE GONNA TRANSPORT EVERYONE IN THIS CASTLE AND TOWN...
ALL OF THEM...
AND EVACUATE THEM TO SAFETY.
......
FWP...!
ALL RIGHT.
SMACK
LET'S DO THIS!

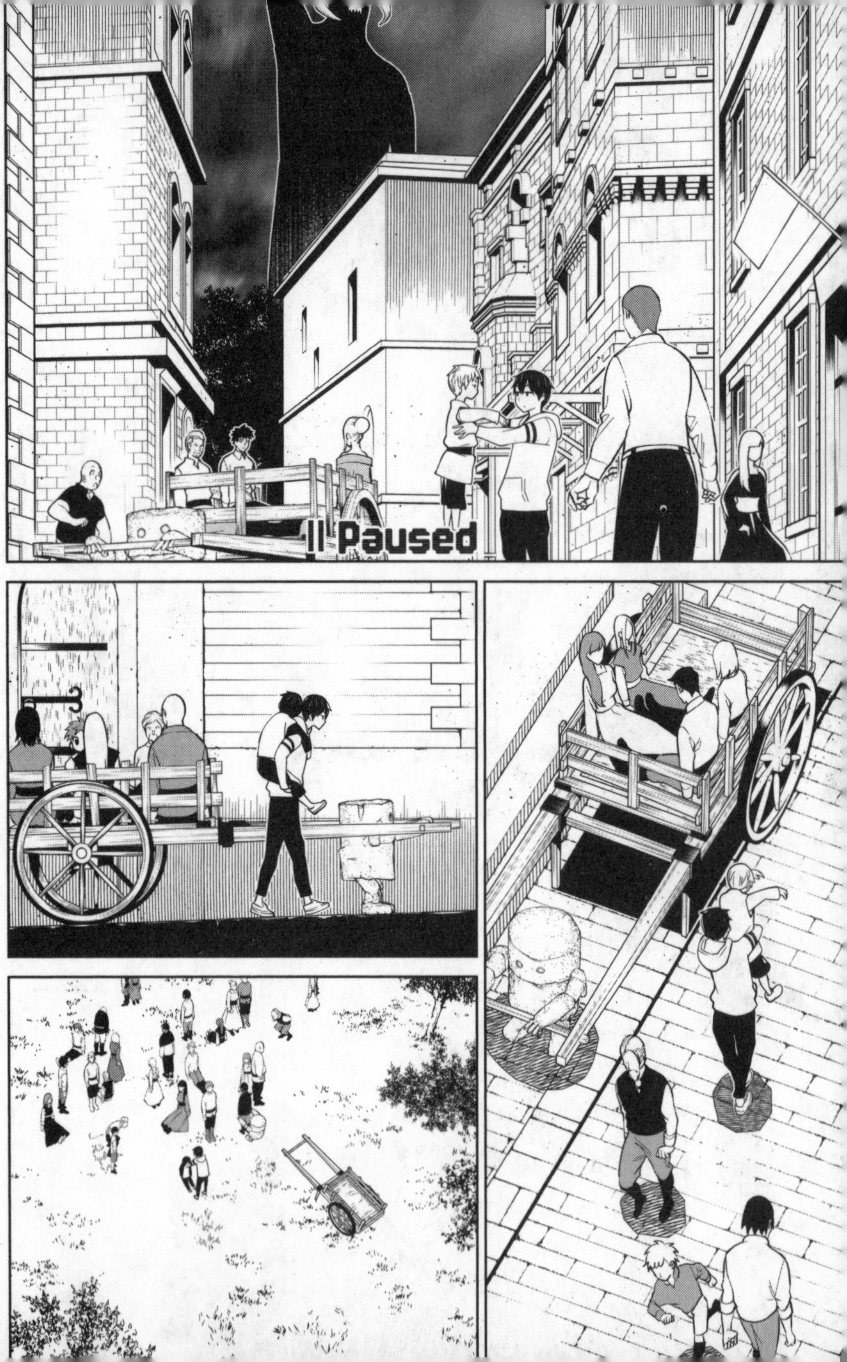
|| Paused

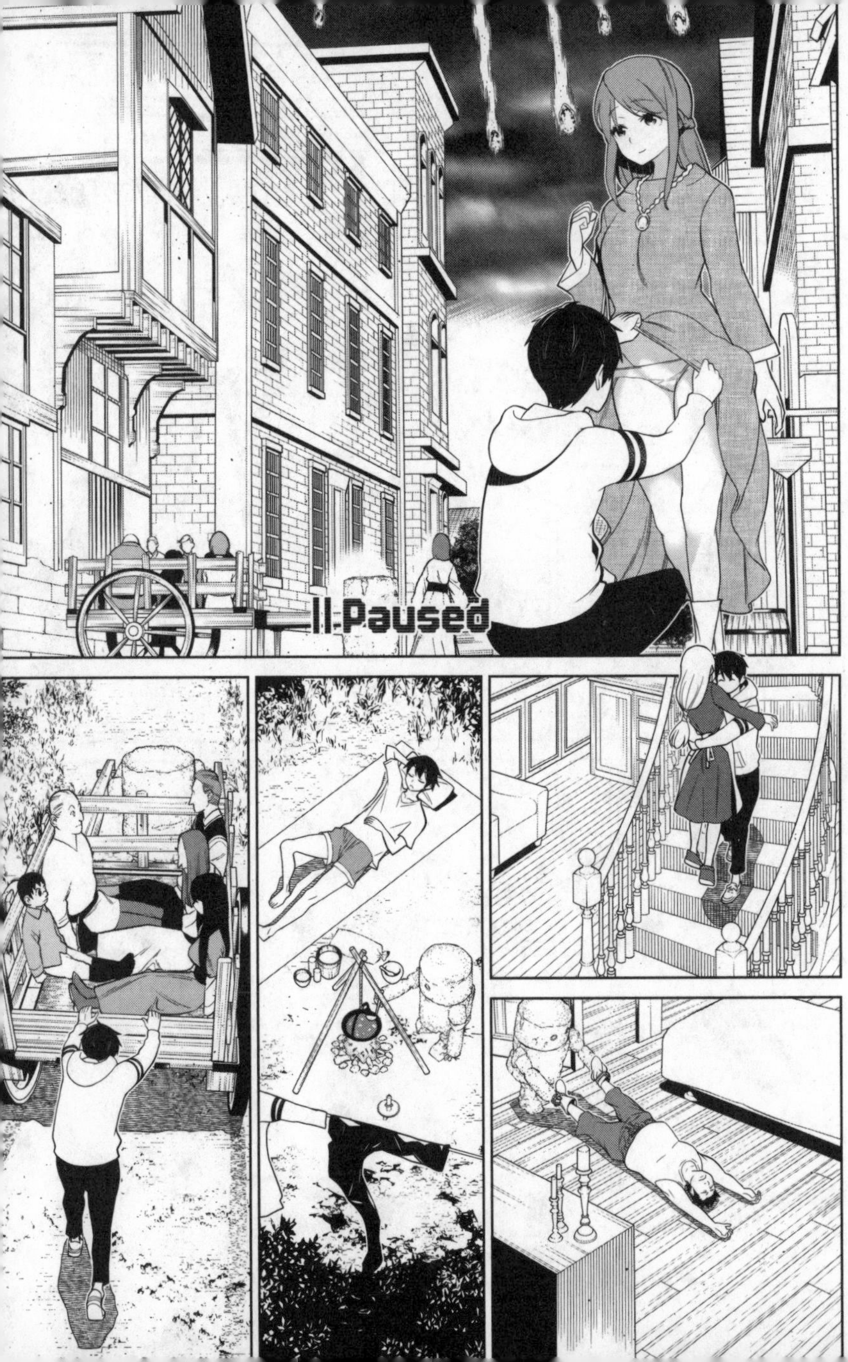
II Paused

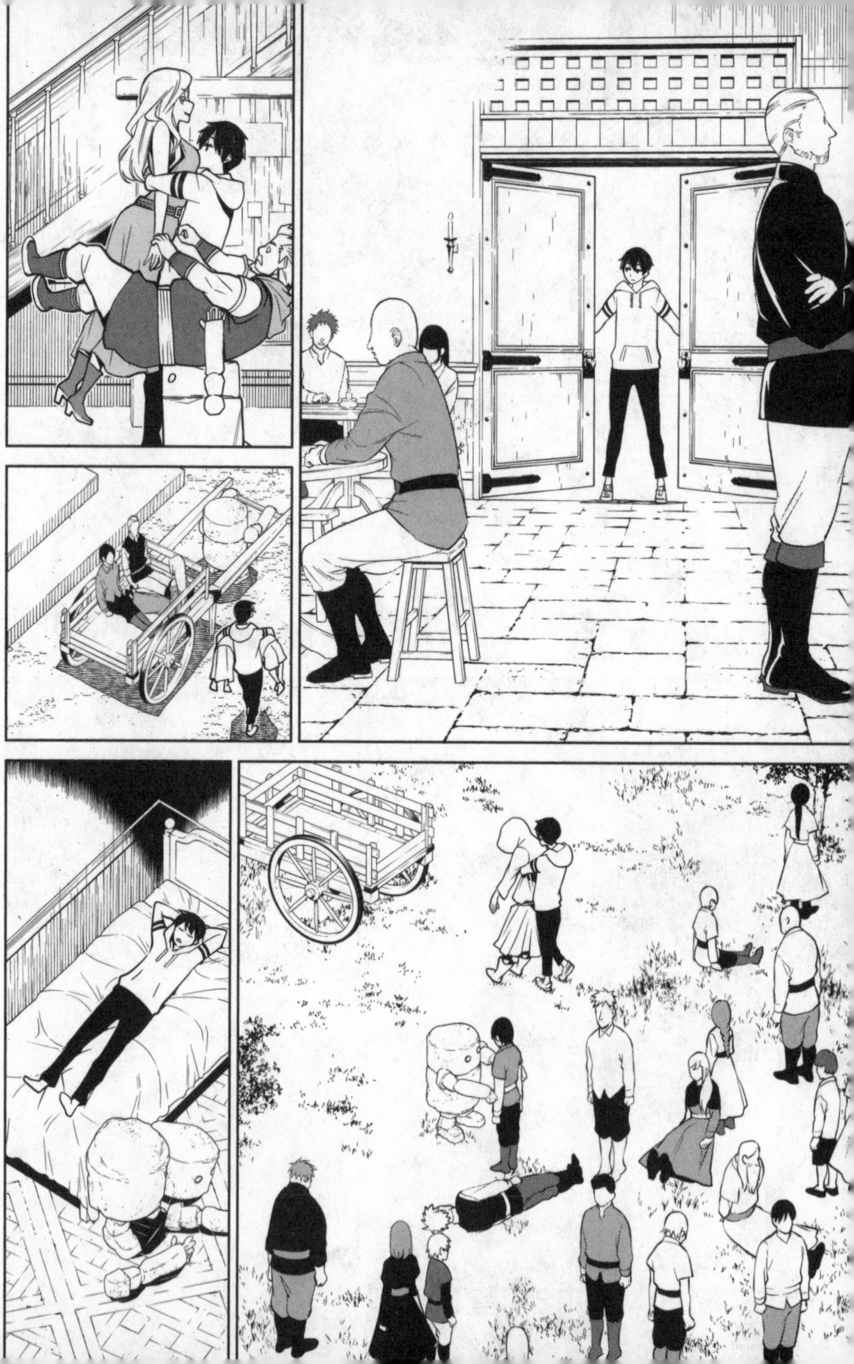

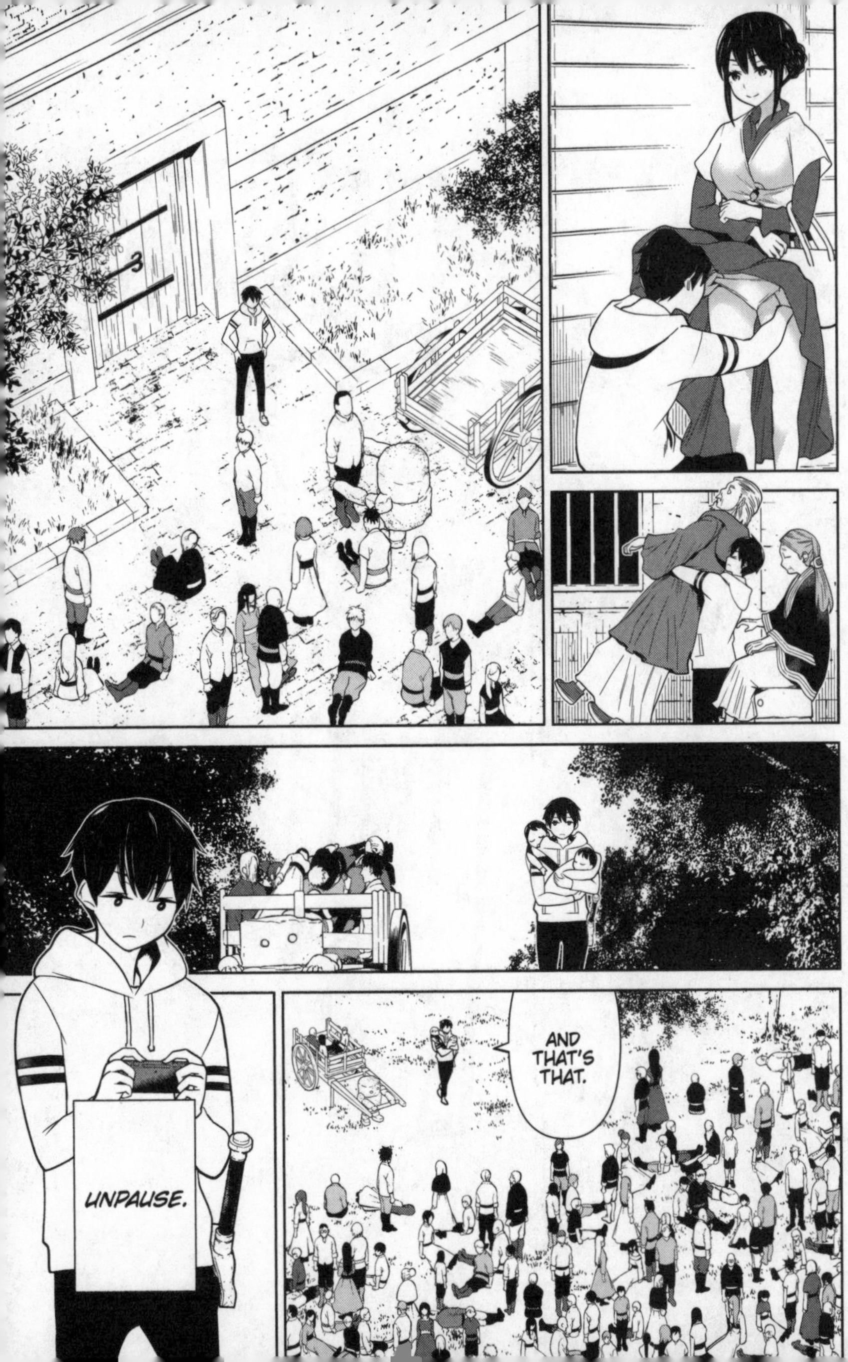
AND THAT'S THAT.
UNPAUSE.

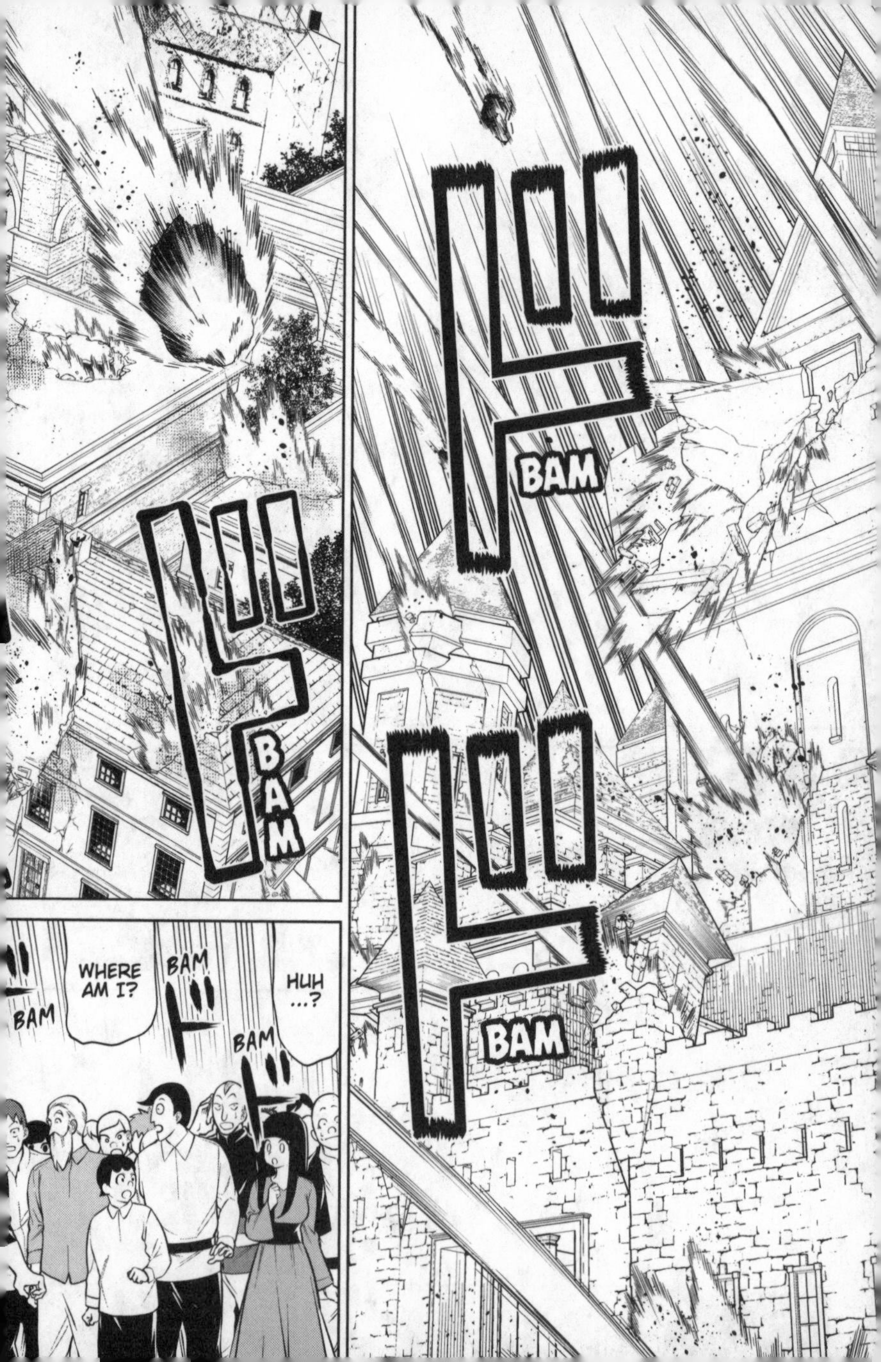
BAM
BAM
BAM
HUH ...?
BAM
BAM
WHERE AM I?
BAM

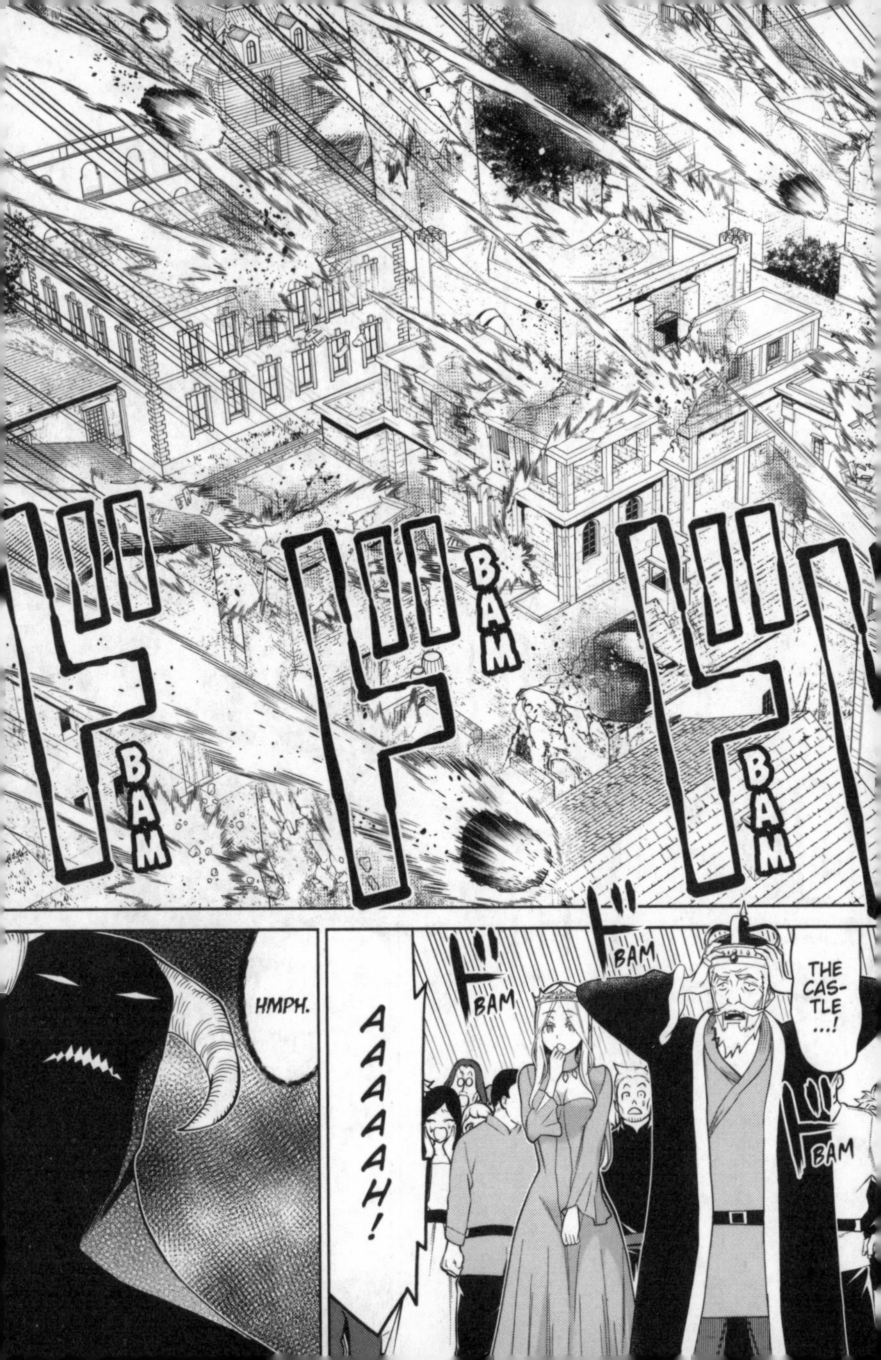

ドドド
BAM
BAM
BAM
THE CASTLE...!
BAM
BAM
BAM
AAAAAAH!
HMPH.

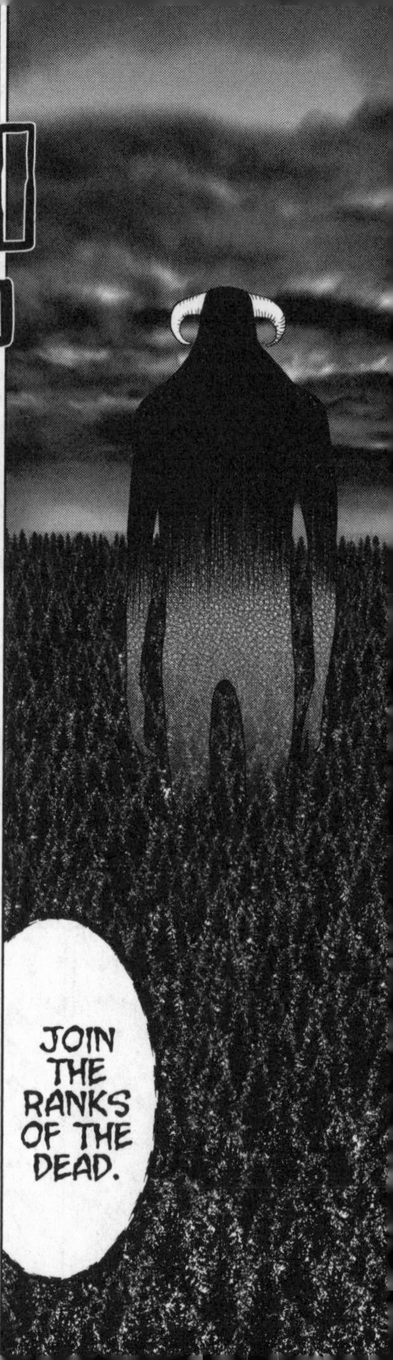
JOIN THE RANKS OF THE DEAD.
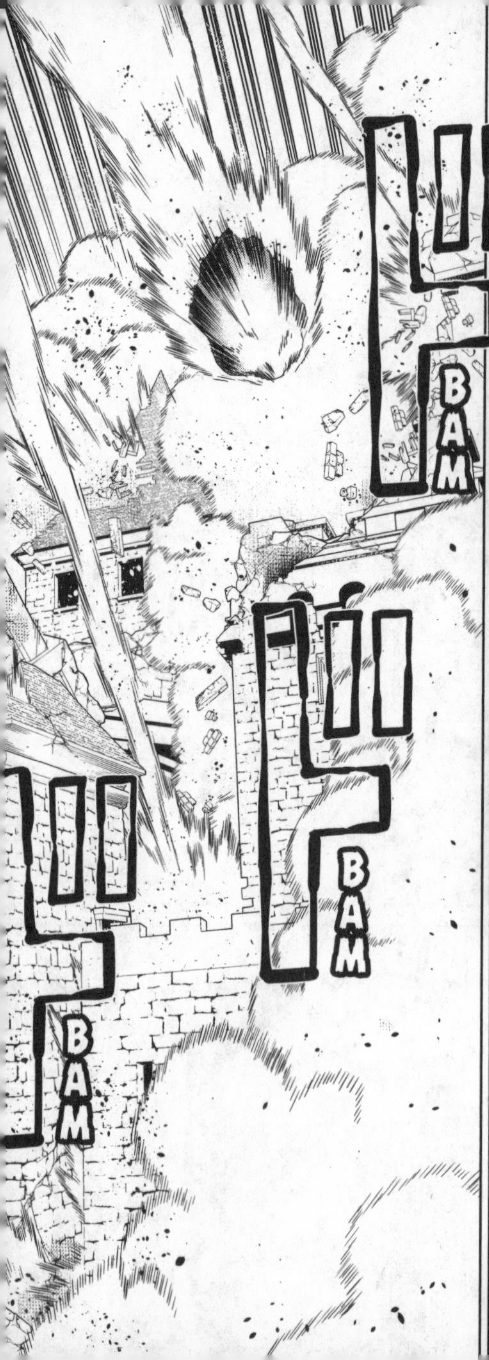
BAM
BAM
BAM

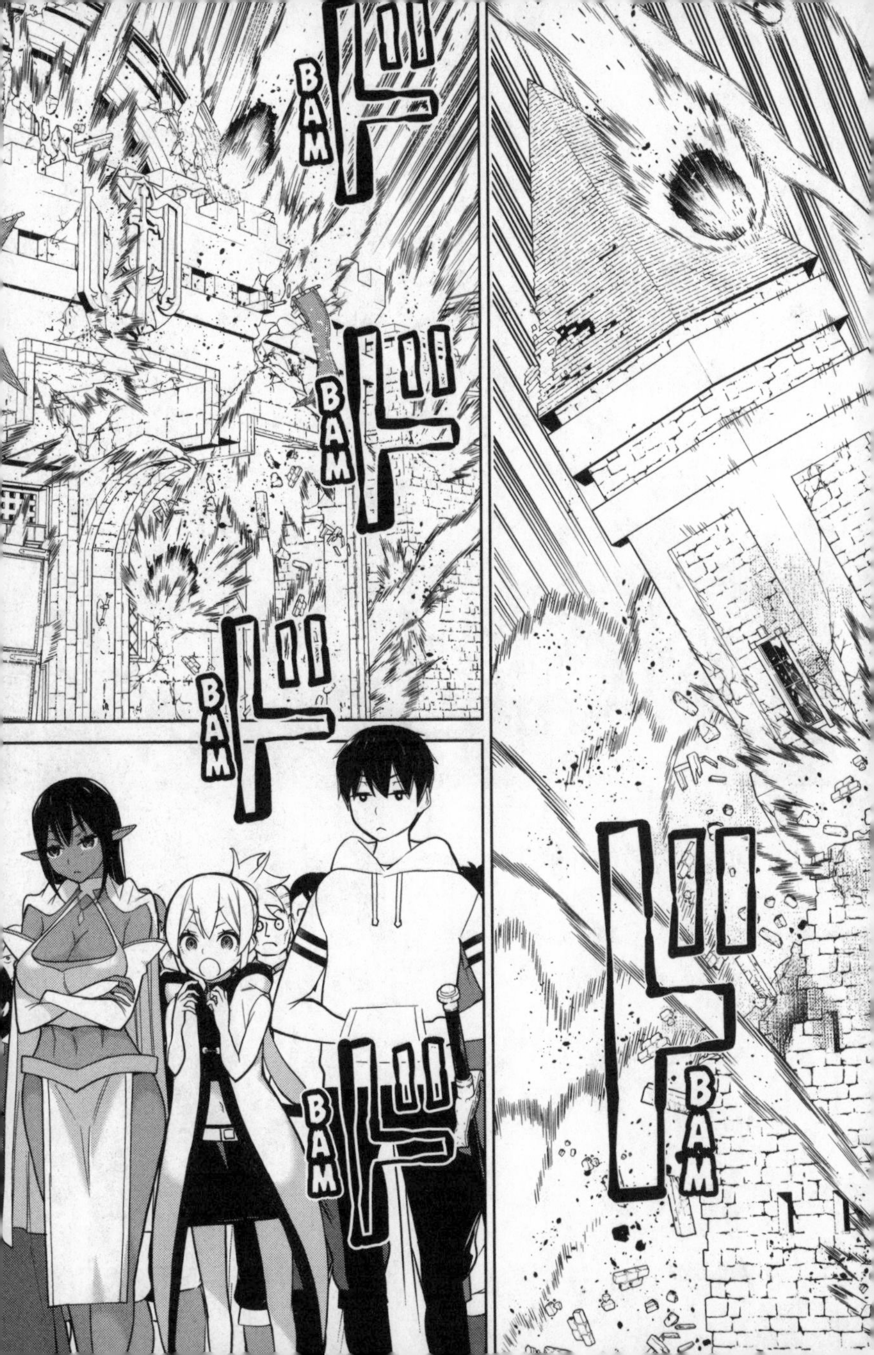
ド
BAM
ド
BAM
ド
BAM
ド
BAM
ド
BAM

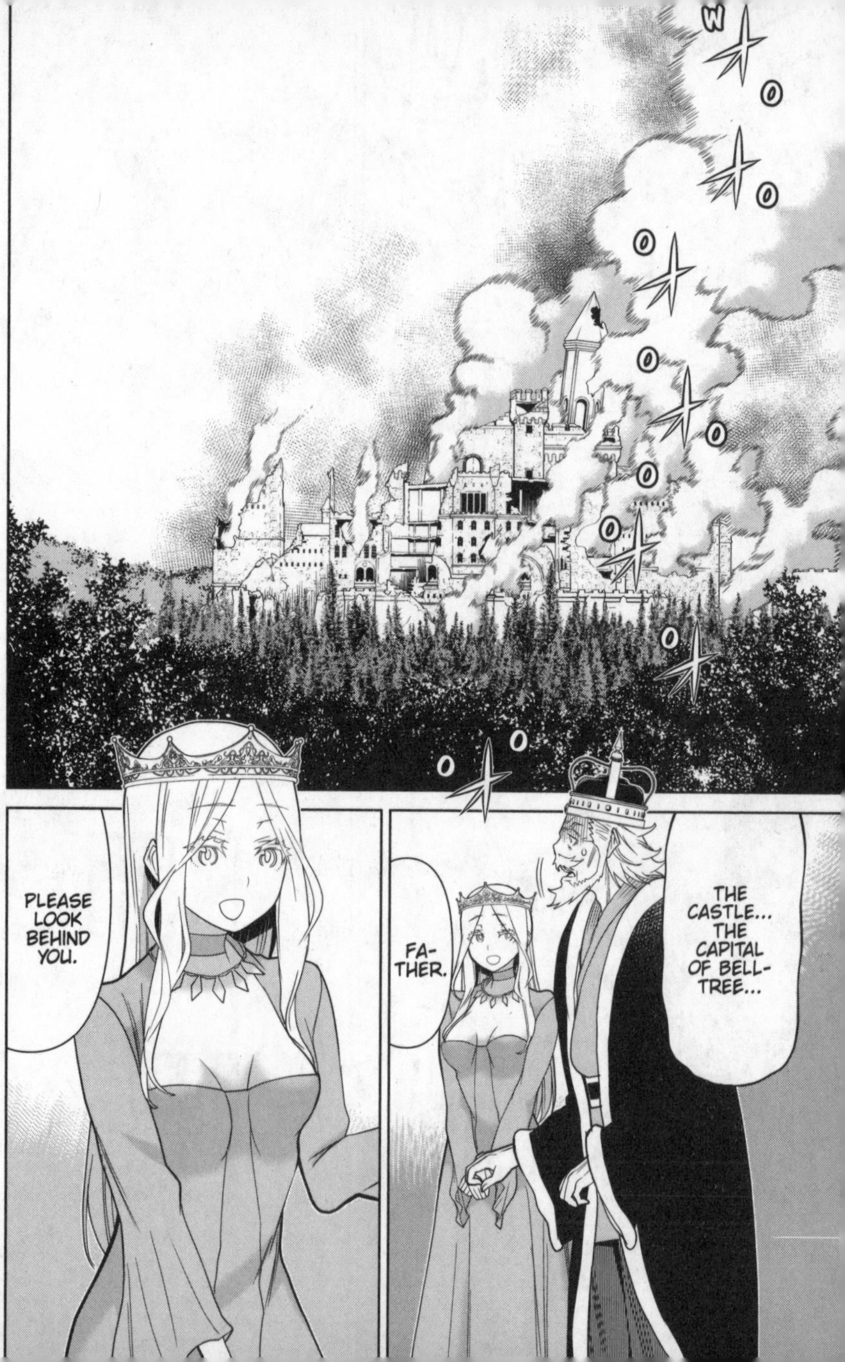
WOOOOOOOOOO
THE CASTLE... THE CAPITAL OF BELL-TREE...
FA-THER.
PLEASE LOOK BEHIND YOU.

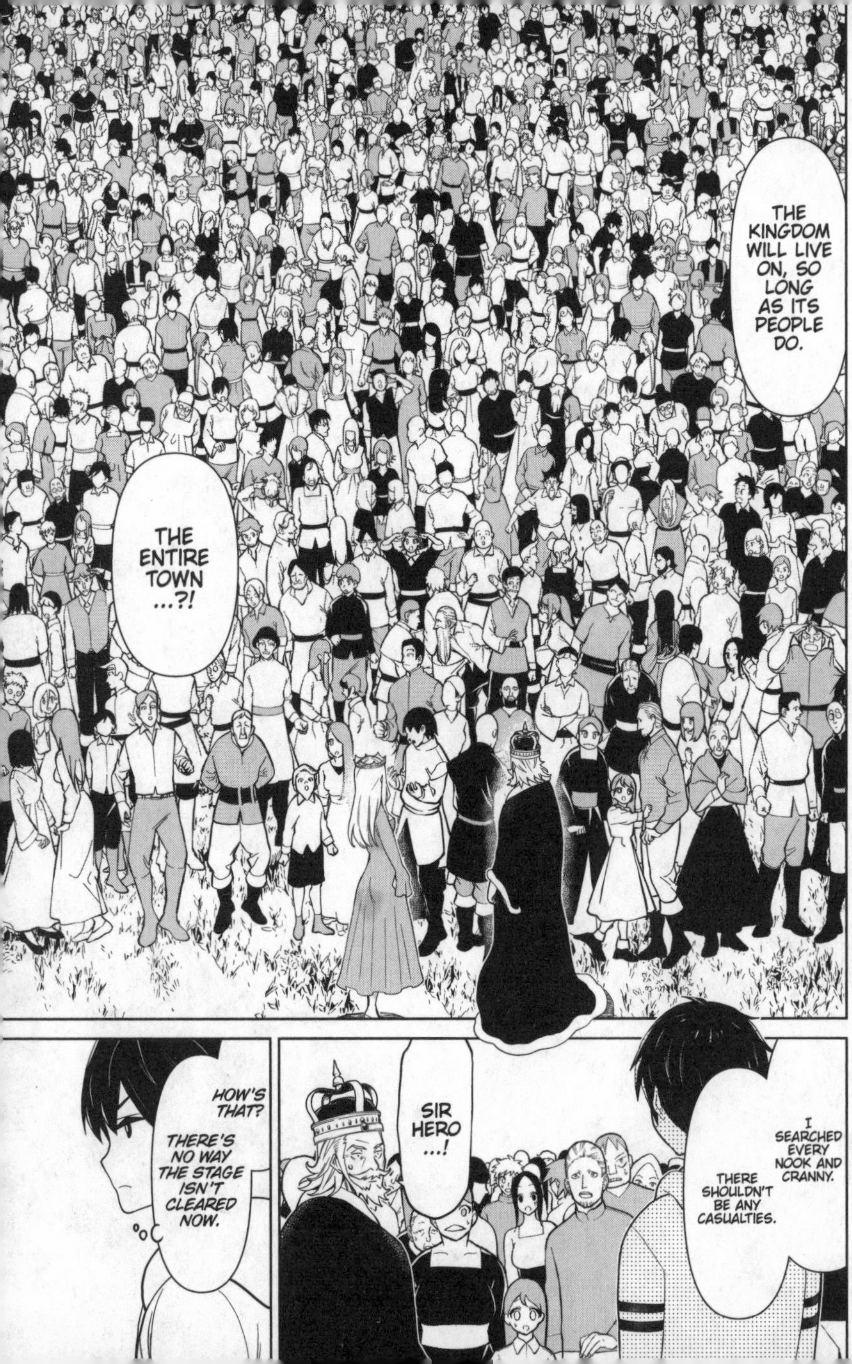
THE KINGDOM WILL LIVE ON, SO LONG AS ITS PEOPLE DO.
THE ENTIRE TOWN ...?!
I SEARCHED EVERY NOOK AND CRANNY.
THERE SHOULDN'T BE ANY CASUALTIES.
SIR HERO ...!
HOW'S THAT?
THERE'S NO WAY THE STAGE ISN'T CLEARED NOW.

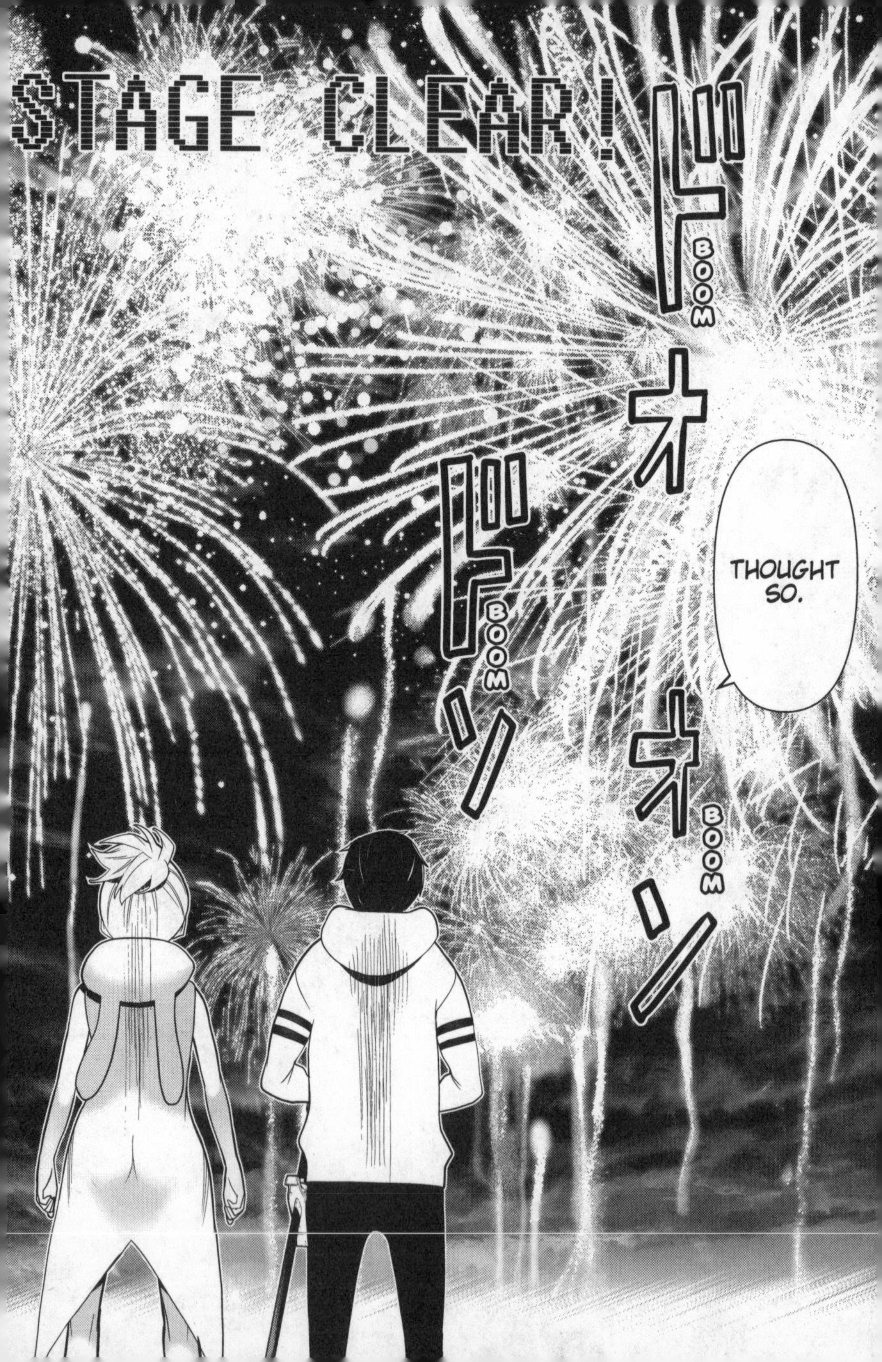
STAGE CLEAR!
BOOM
BOOM
THOUGHT SO.
BOOM

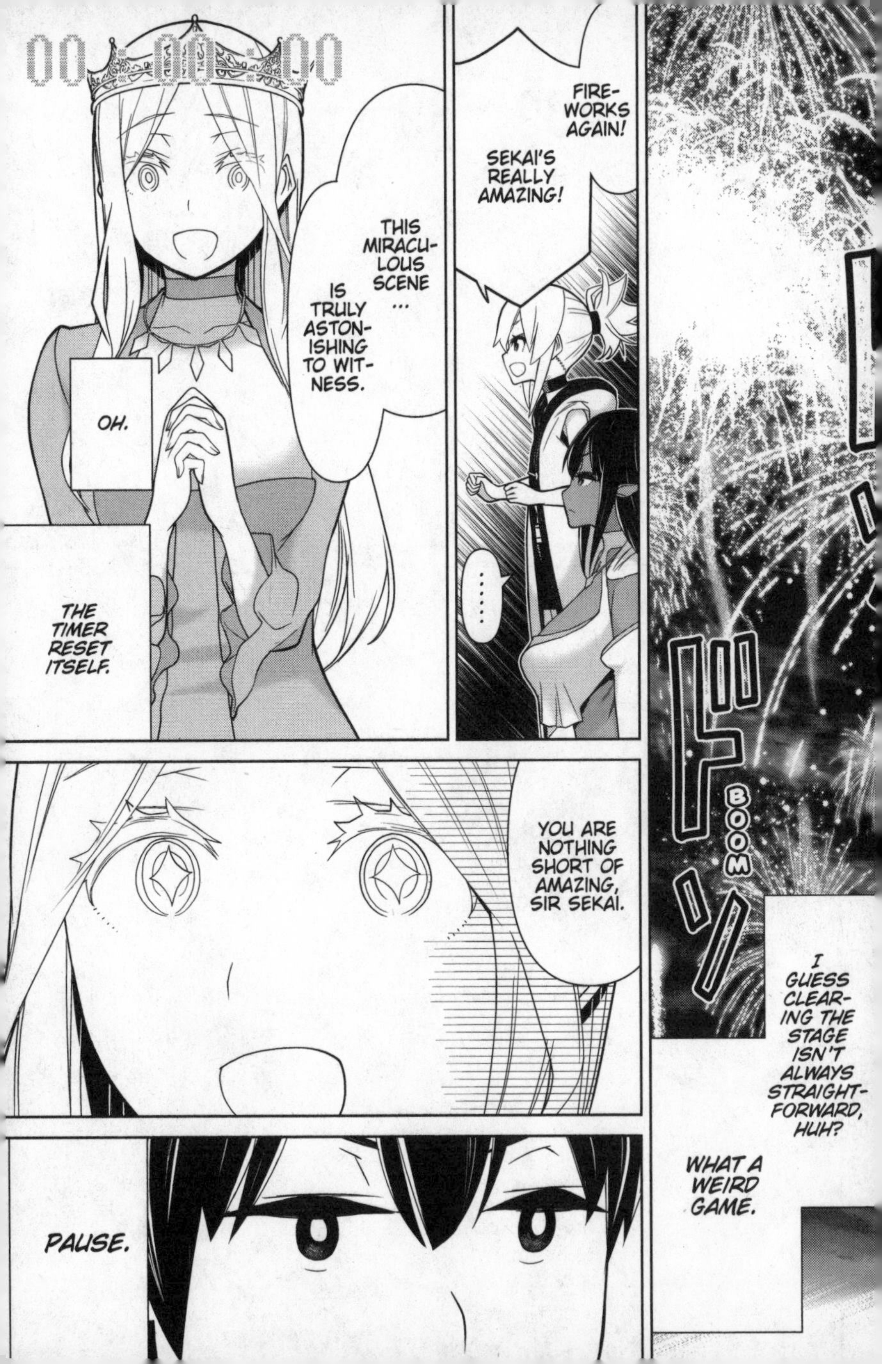
BOOM
I GUESS CLEARING THE STAGE ISN'T ALWAYS STRAIGHTFORWARD, HUH?
WHAT A WEIRD GAME.
FIRE-WORKS AGAIN!
SEKAI'S REALLY AMAZING!
......
00:00:00
THIS MIRACULOUS SCENE ... IS TRULY ASTONISHING TO WITNESS.
OH.
THE TIMER RESET ITSELF.
YOU ARE NOTHING SHORT OF AMAZING, SIR SEKAI.
PAUSE.

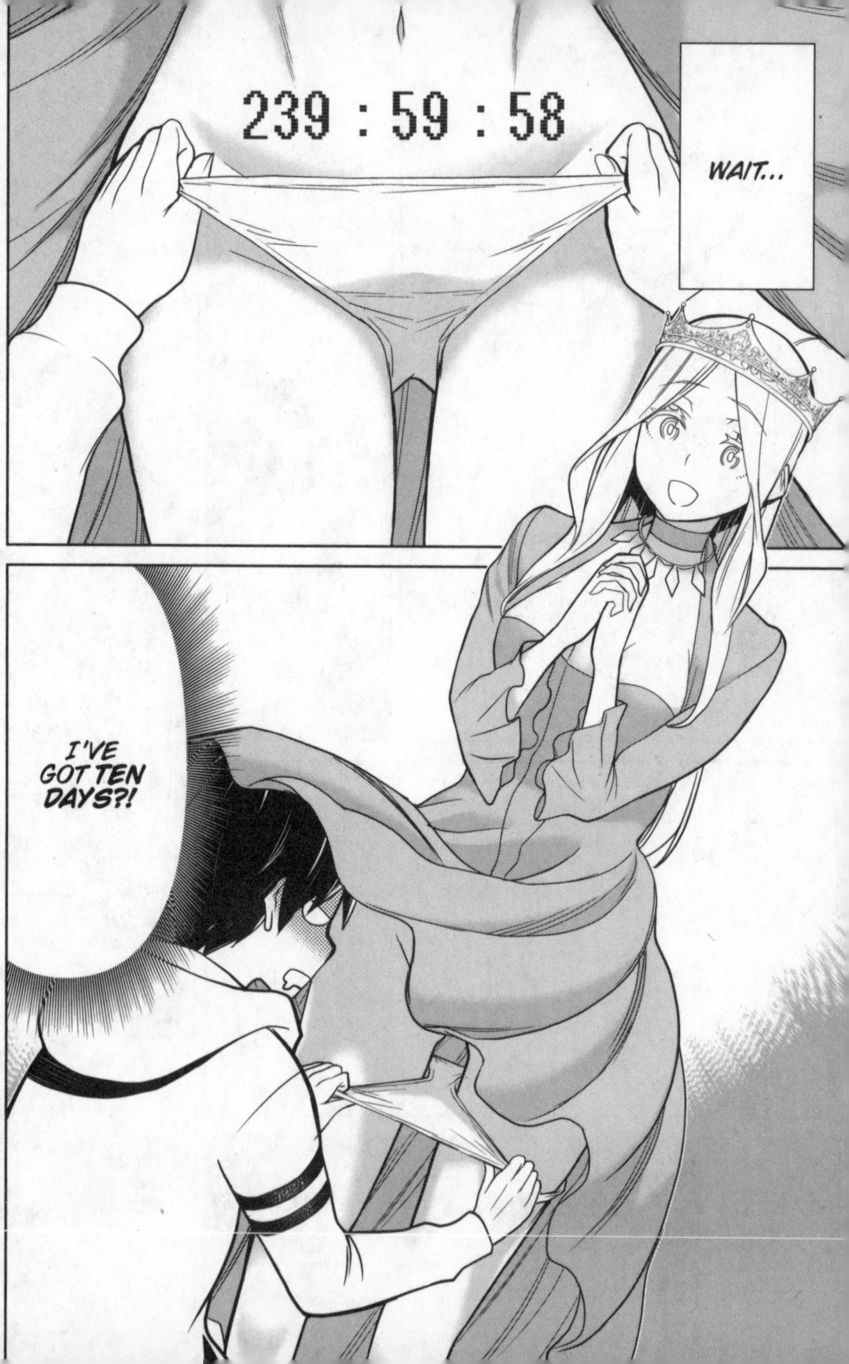
239 : 59 : 58
WAIT...
I'VE GOT TEN DAYS?!

Chapter 9 - End

2 3 4 5 6 7 8

START
▶ PAUSE

▶START
PAUSE

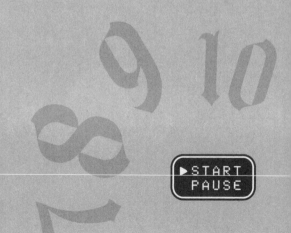

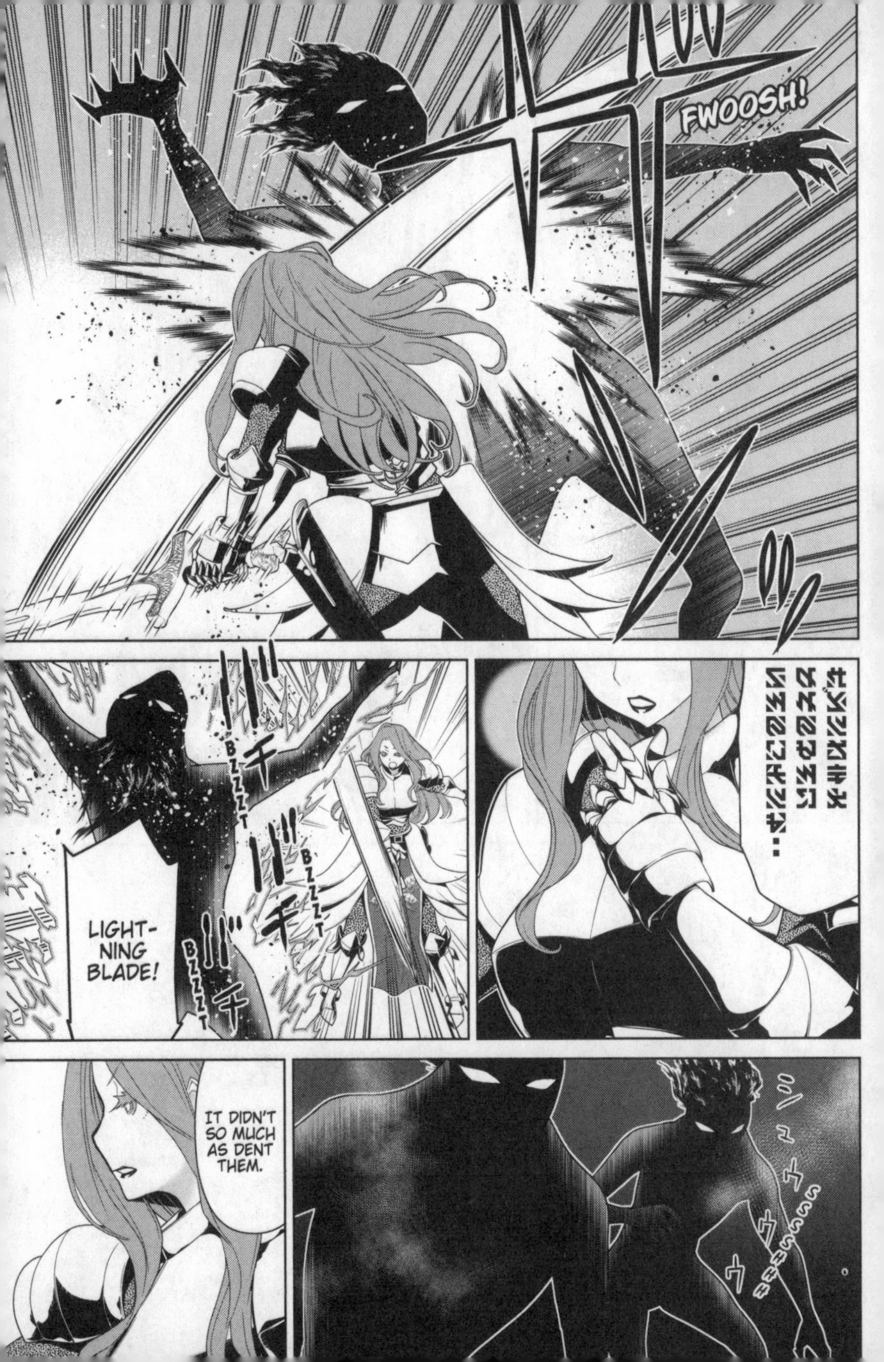
FWOOSH!
BZZZT
BZZZT
BZZZT
LIGHTNING BLADE!
IT DIDN'T SO MUCH AS DENT THEM.

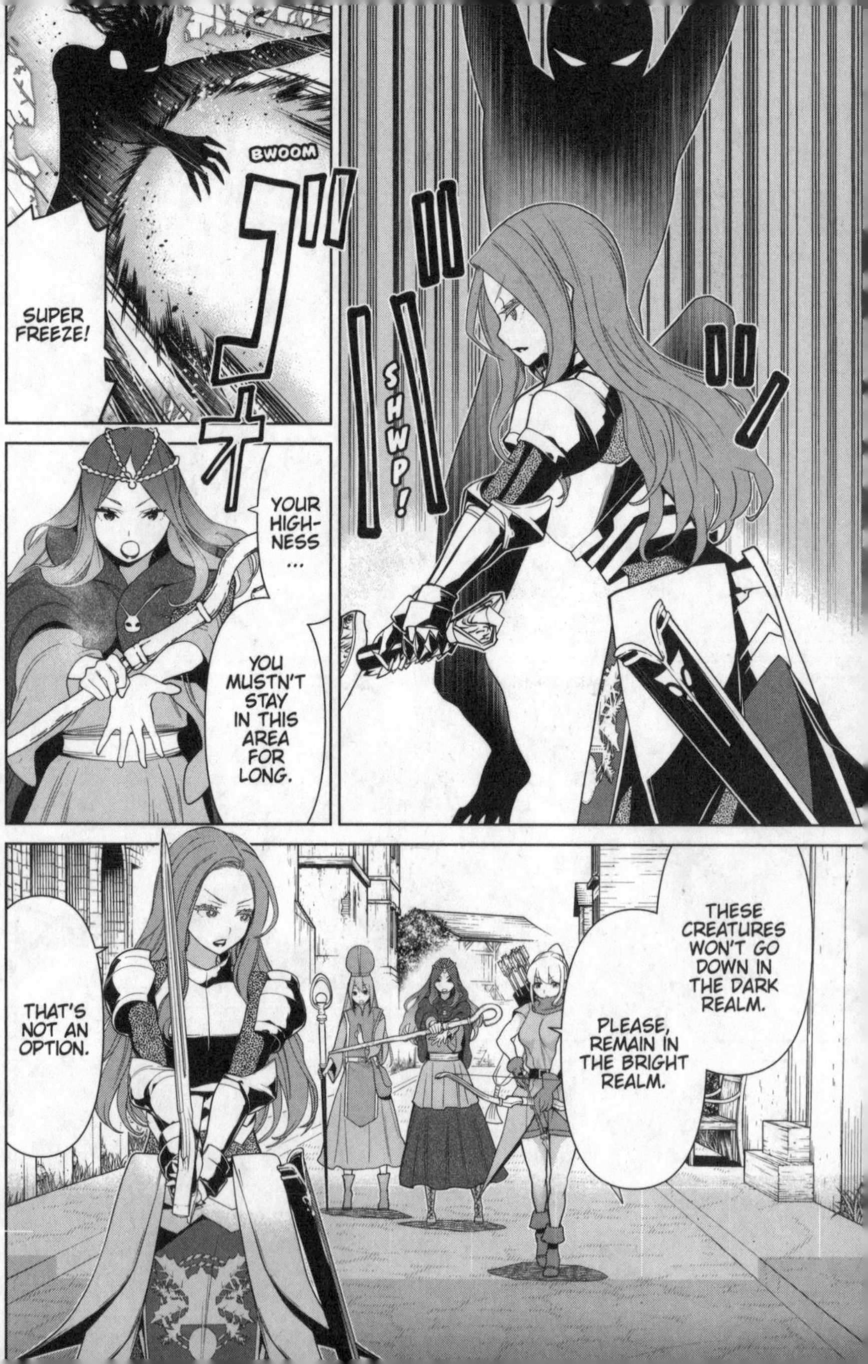
SHWP!
BWOOM
SUPER FREEZE!
YOUR HIGHNESS...
YOU MUSTN'T STAY IN THIS AREA FOR LONG.
THESE CREATURES WON'T GO DOWN IN THE DARK REALM.
PLEASE, REMAIN IN THE BRIGHT REALM.
THAT'S NOT AN OPTION.

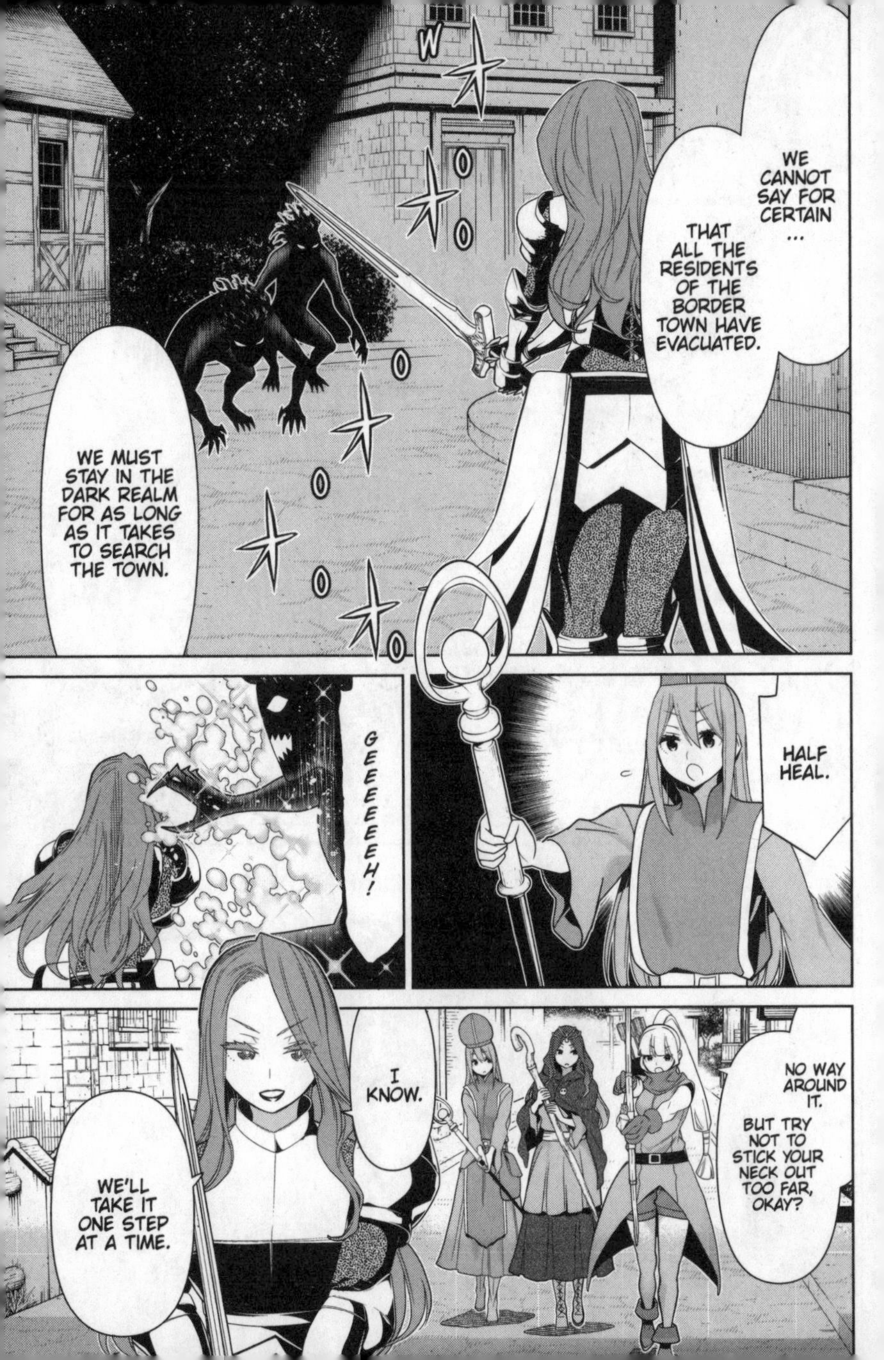
W
WE CANNOT SAY FOR CERTAIN ...
THAT ALL THE RESIDENTS OF THE BORDER TOWN HAVE EVACUATED.
WE MUST STAY IN THE DARK REALM FOR AS LONG AS IT TAKES TO SEARCH THE TOWN.
HALF HEAL.
GEEEEEEEH!
NO WAY AROUND IT.
BUT TRY NOT TO STICK YOUR NECK OUT TOO FAR, OKAY?
I KNOW.
WE'LL TAKE IT ONE STEP AT A TIME.

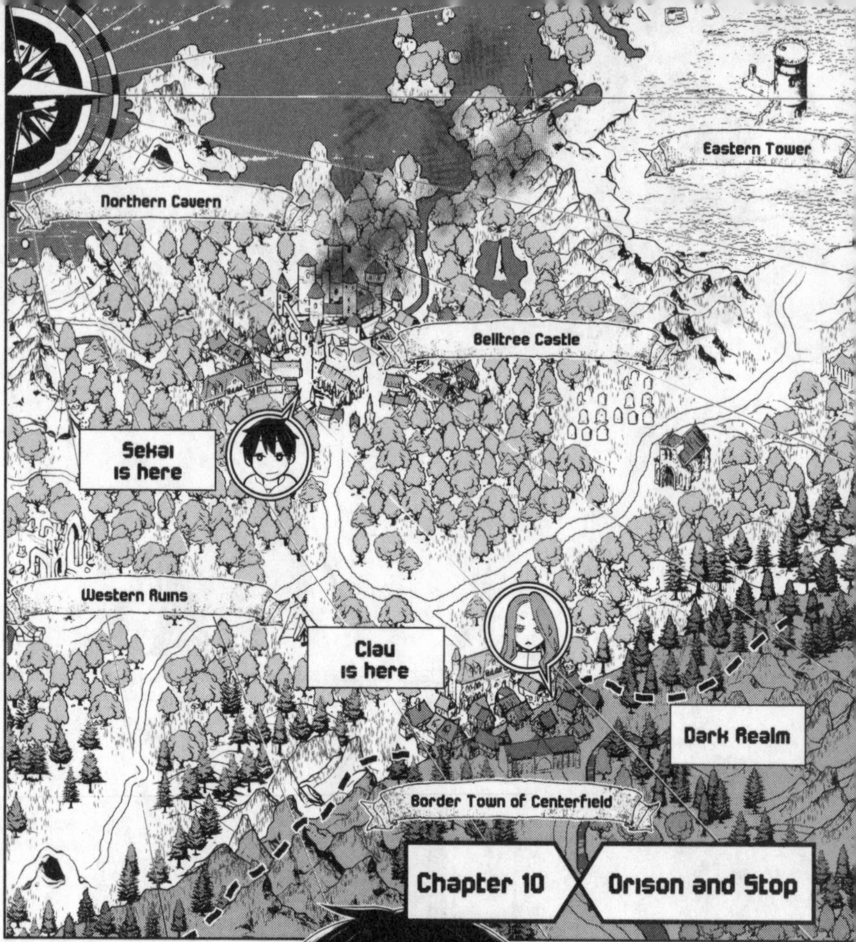
Eastern Tower
Northern Cavern
Belltree Castle
Sekai is here
Western Ruins
Clau is here
Dark Realm
Border Town of Centerfield
Chapter 10
Orison and Stop
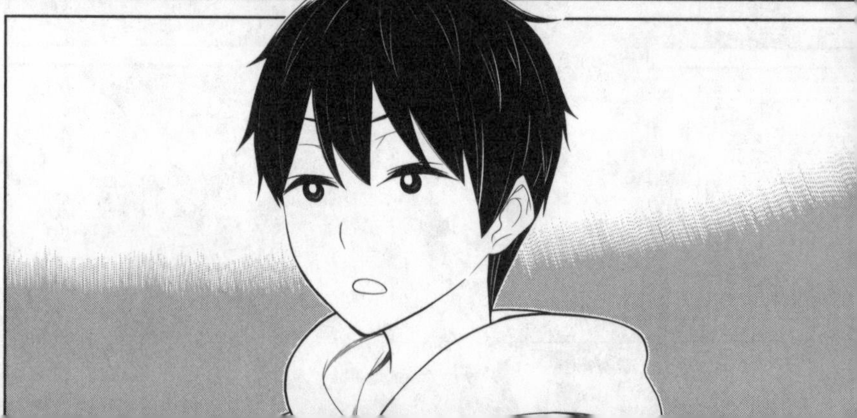

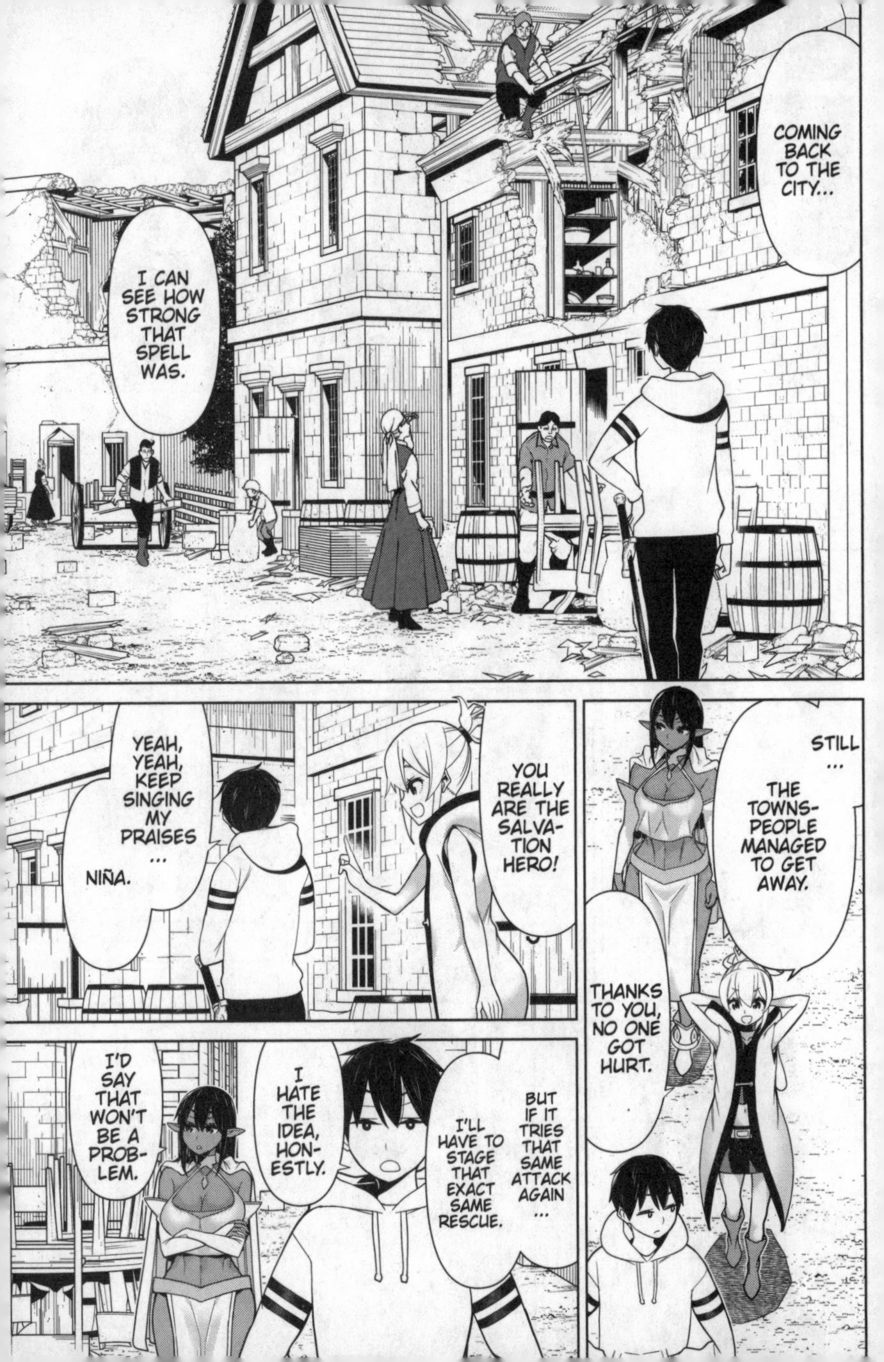
COMING BACK TO THE CITY...
I CAN SEE HOW STRONG THAT SPELL WAS.
STILL ... THE TOWNS-PEOPLE MANAGED TO GET AWAY.
THANKS TO YOU, NO ONE GOT HURT.
YOU REALLY ARE THE SALVA-TION HERO!
YEAH, YEAH, KEEP SINGING MY PRAISES ... NIÑA.
BUT IF IT TRIES THAT SAME ATTACK AGAIN ...
I'LL HAVE TO STAGE THAT EXACT SAME RESCUE.
I HATE THE IDEA, HON-ESTLY.
I'D SAY THAT WON'T BE A PROB-LEM.

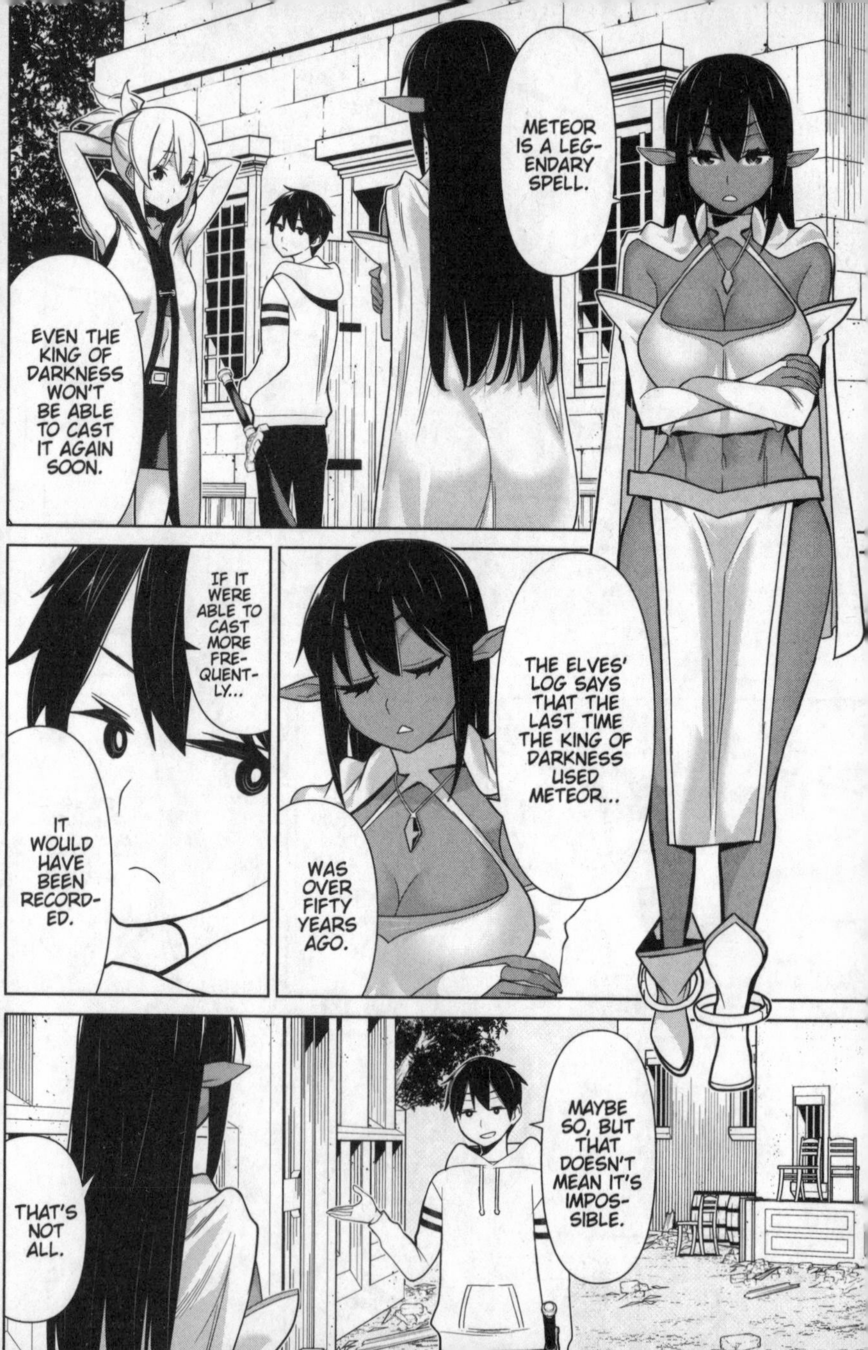
METEOR IS A LEG-ENDARY SPELL.
EVEN THE KING OF DARKNESS WON'T BE ABLE TO CAST IT AGAIN SOON.
THE ELVES' LOG SAYS THAT THE LAST TIME THE KING OF DARKNESS USED METEOR...
WAS OVER FIFTY YEARS AGO.
IF IT WERE ABLE TO CAST MORE FRE-QUENT-LY...
IT WOULD HAVE BEEN RECORD-ED.
MAYBE SO, BUT THAT DOESN'T MEAN IT'S IMPOS-SIBLE.
THAT'S NOT ALL.

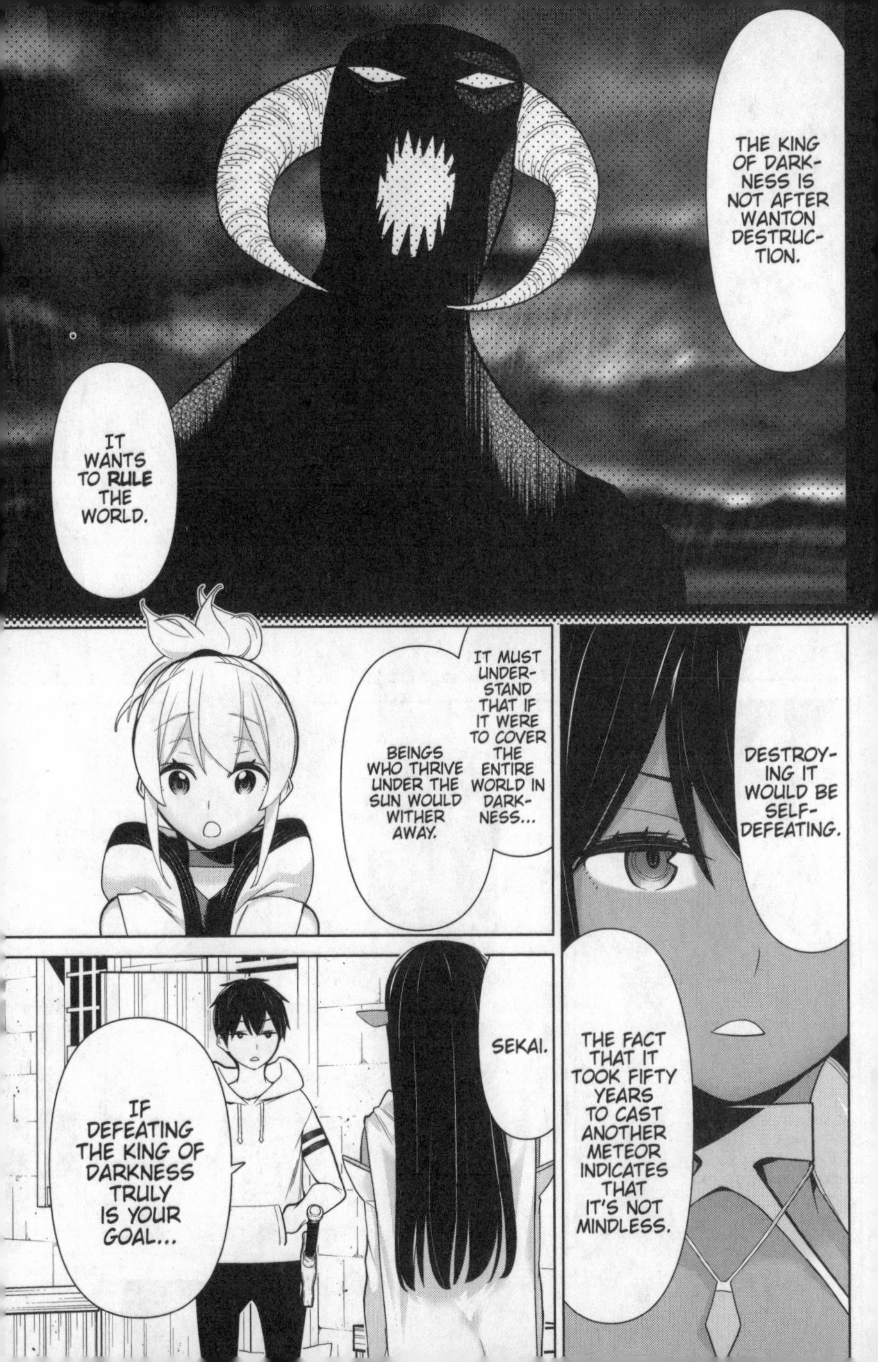
THE KING OF DARKNESS IS NOT AFTER WANTON DESTRUCTION.
IT WANTS TO RULE THE WORLD.
DESTROYING IT WOULD BE SELF-DEFEATING.
THE FACT THAT IT TOOK FIFTY YEARS TO CAST ANOTHER METEOR INDICATES THAT IT'S NOT MINDLESS.
IT MUST UNDERSTAND THAT IF IT WERE TO COVER THE ENTIRE WORLD IN DARKNESS...
BEINGS WHO THRIVE UNDER THE SUN WOULD WITHER AWAY.
SEKAI.
IF DEFEATING THE KING OF DARKNESS TRULY IS YOUR GOAL...

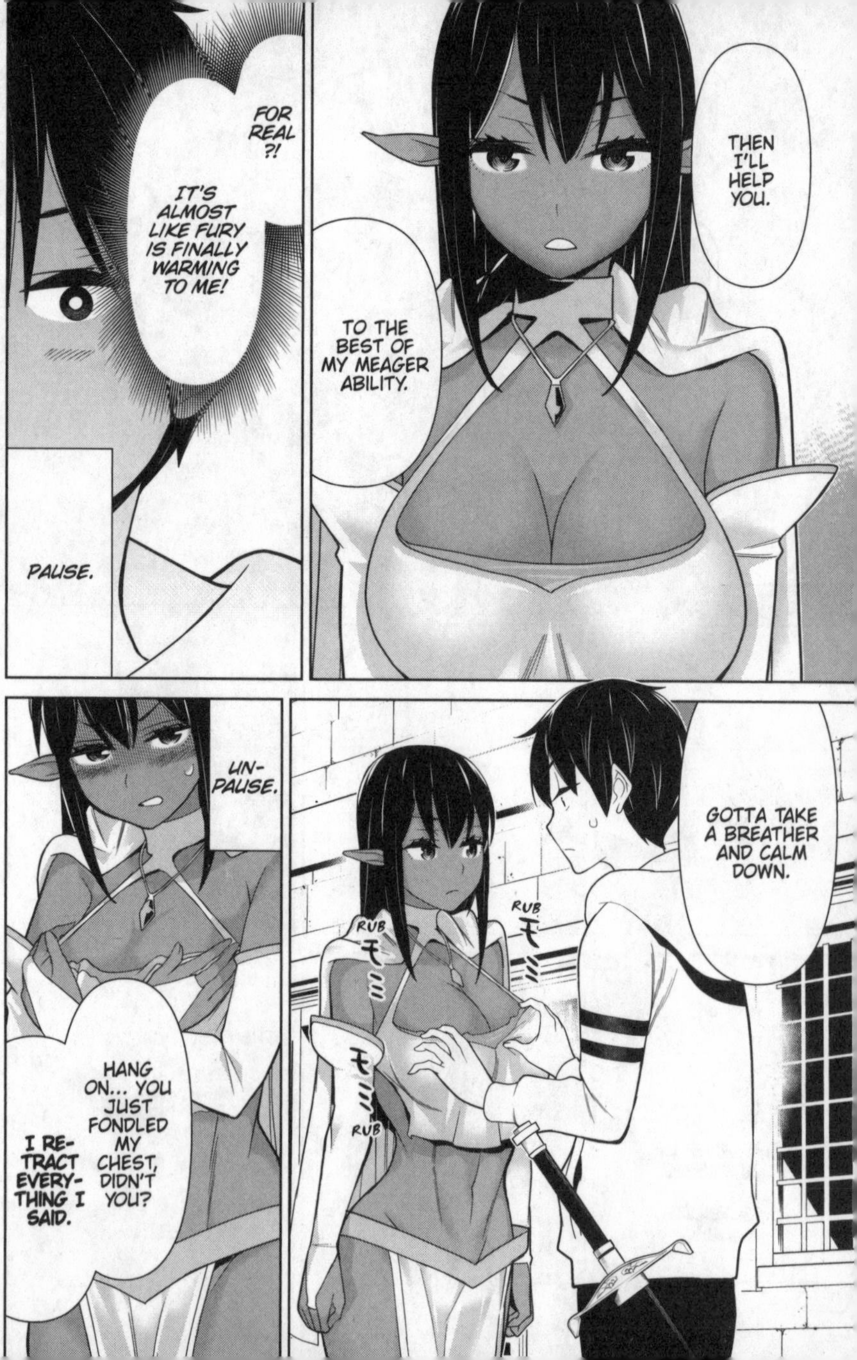
THEN I'LL HELP YOU.
TO THE BEST OF MY MEAGER ABILITY.
FOR REAL?!
IT'S ALMOST LIKE FURY IS FINALLY WARMING TO ME!
PAUSE.
GOTTA TAKE A BREATHER AND CALM DOWN.
RUB モミ
RUB モミ
モミ RUB
UN-PAUSE.
HANG ON... YOU JUST FONDLED MY CHEST, DIDN'T YOU?
I RETRACT EVERYTHING I SAID.

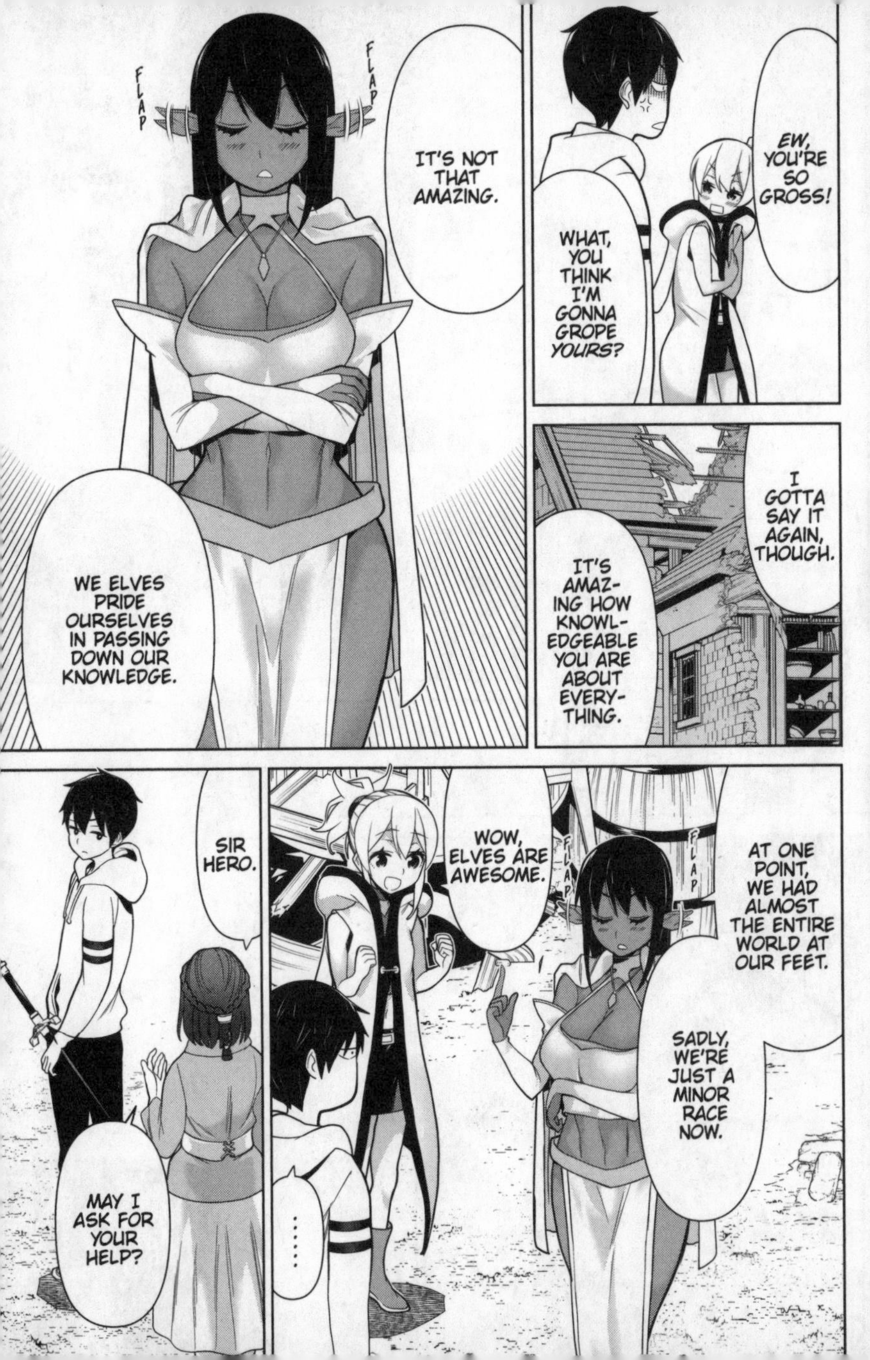
EW, YOU'RE SO GROSS!
WHAT, YOU THINK I'M GONNA GROPE YOURS?
I GOTTA SAY IT AGAIN, THOUGH.
IT'S AMAZING HOW KNOWLEDGEABLE YOU ARE ABOUT EVERYTHING.
FLAP
FLAP
IT'S NOT THAT AMAZING.
WE ELVES PRIDE OURSELVES IN PASSING DOWN OUR KNOWLEDGE.
AT ONE POINT, WE HAD ALMOST THE ENTIRE WORLD AT OUR FEET.
FLAP
FLAP
WOW, ELVES ARE AWESOME.
SADLY, WE'RE JUST A MINOR RACE NOW.
......
SIR HERO.
MAY I ASK FOR YOUR HELP?

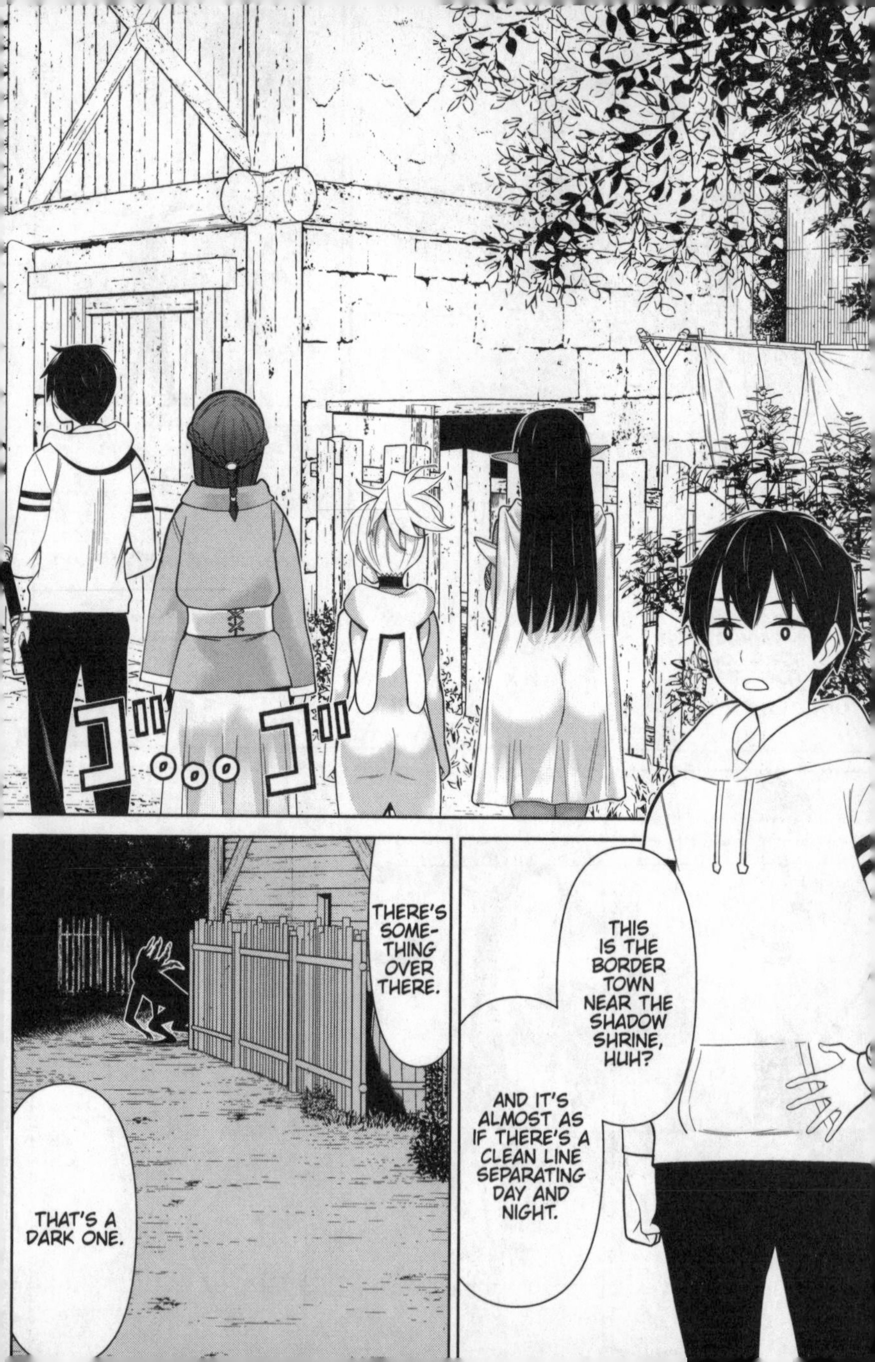
THIS IS THE BORDER TOWN NEAR THE SHADOW SHRINE, HUH?
AND IT'S ALMOST AS IF THERE'S A CLEAN LINE SEPARATING DAY AND NIGHT.
THERE'S SOME-THING OVER THERE.
THAT'S A DARK ONE.

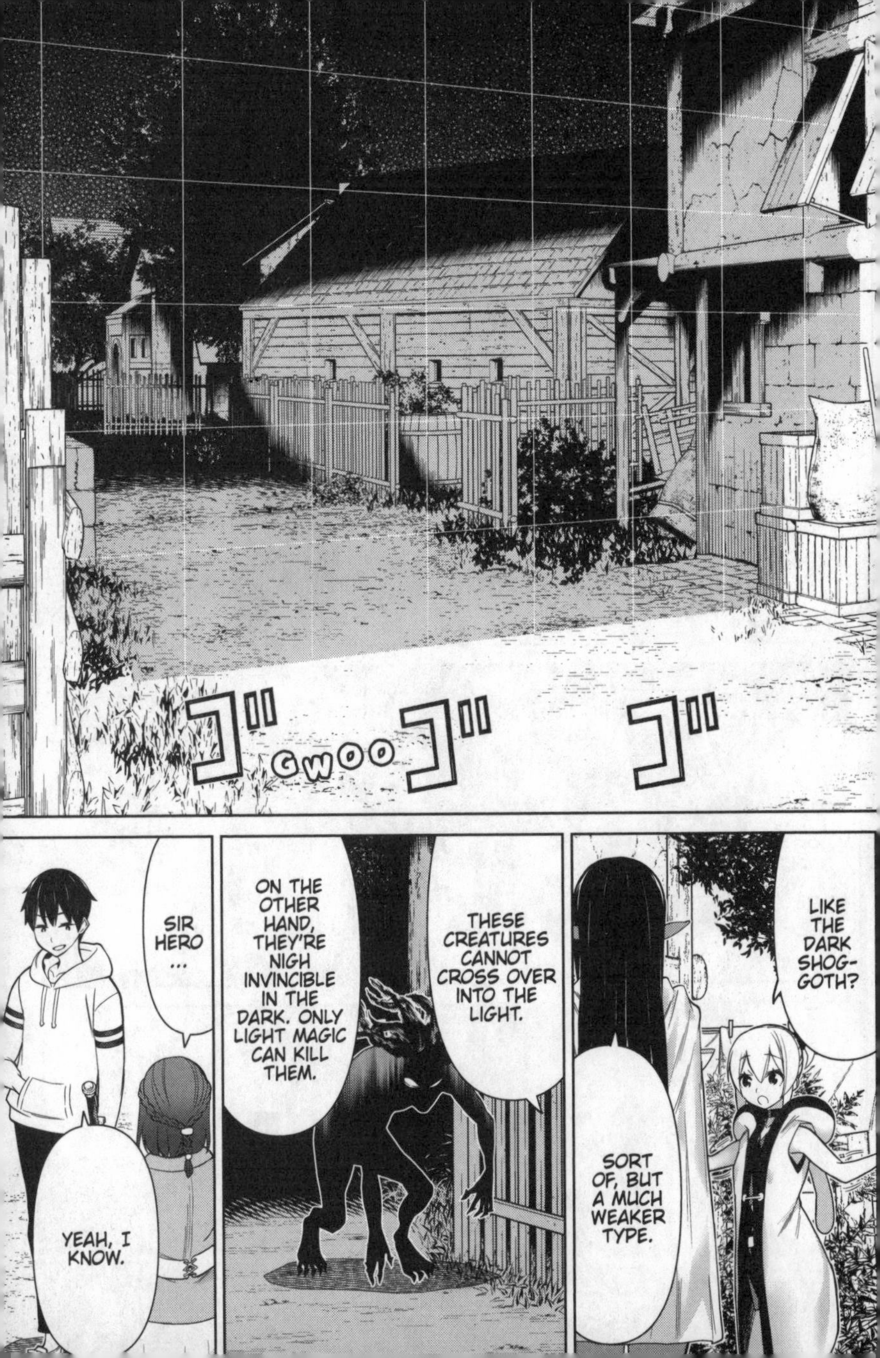
GWOO
LIKE THE DARK SHOG-GOTH?
SORT OF, BUT A MUCH WEAKER TYPE.
THESE CREATURES CANNOT CROSS OVER INTO THE LIGHT.
ON THE OTHER HAND, THEY'RE NIGH INVINCIBLE IN THE DARK. ONLY LIGHT MAGIC CAN KILL THEM.
SIR HERO ...
YEAH, I KNOW.

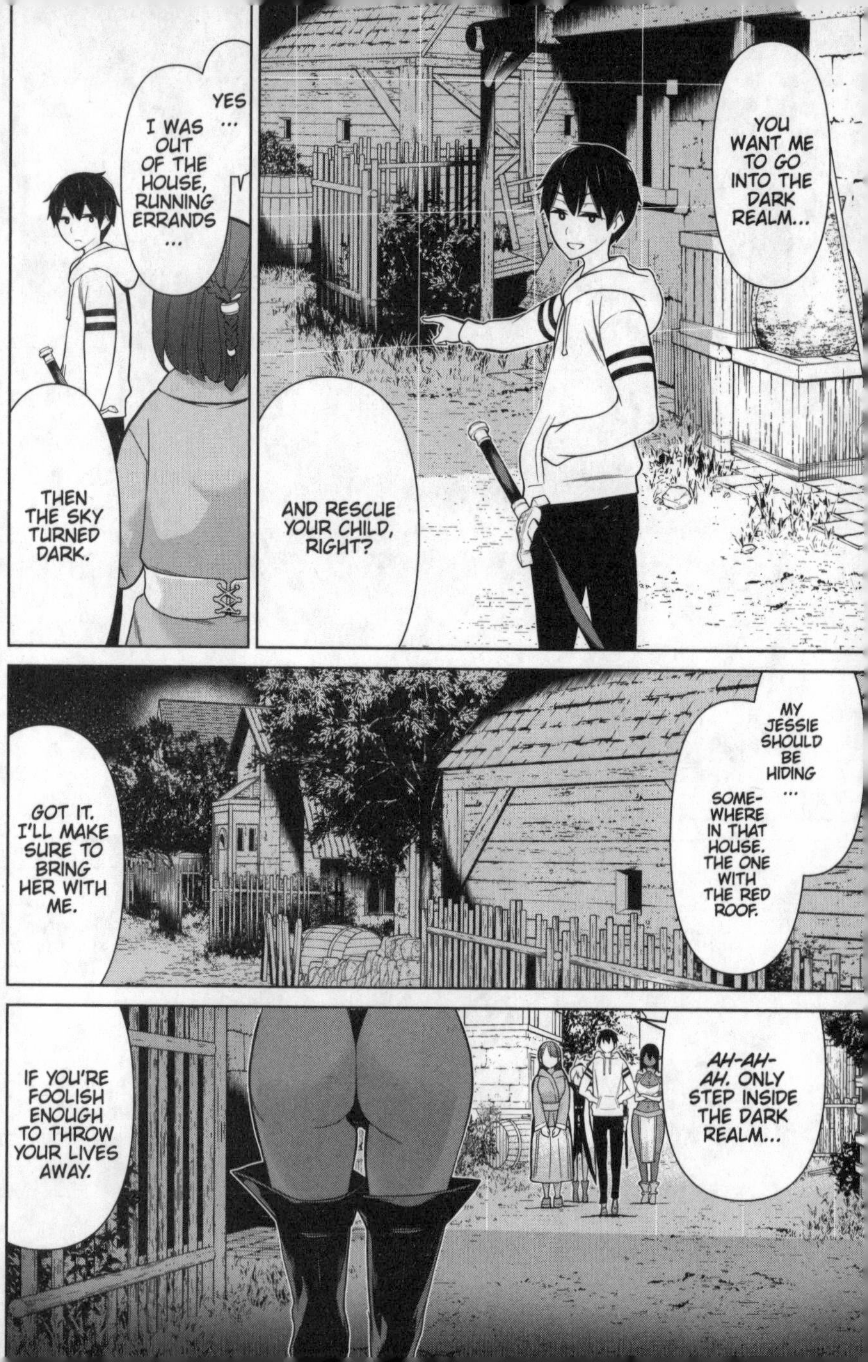
YOU WANT ME TO GO INTO THE DARK REALM...
AND RESCUE YOUR CHILD, RIGHT?
YES... I WAS OUT OF THE HOUSE, RUNNING ERRANDS...
THEN THE SKY TURNED DARK.
MY JESSIE SHOULD BE HIDING...
SOME-WHERE IN THAT HOUSE. THE ONE WITH THE RED ROOF.
GOT IT. I'LL MAKE SURE TO BRING HER WITH ME.
AH-AH-AH. ONLY STEP INSIDE THE DARK REALM...
IF YOU'RE FOOLISH ENOUGH TO THROW YOUR LIVES AWAY.

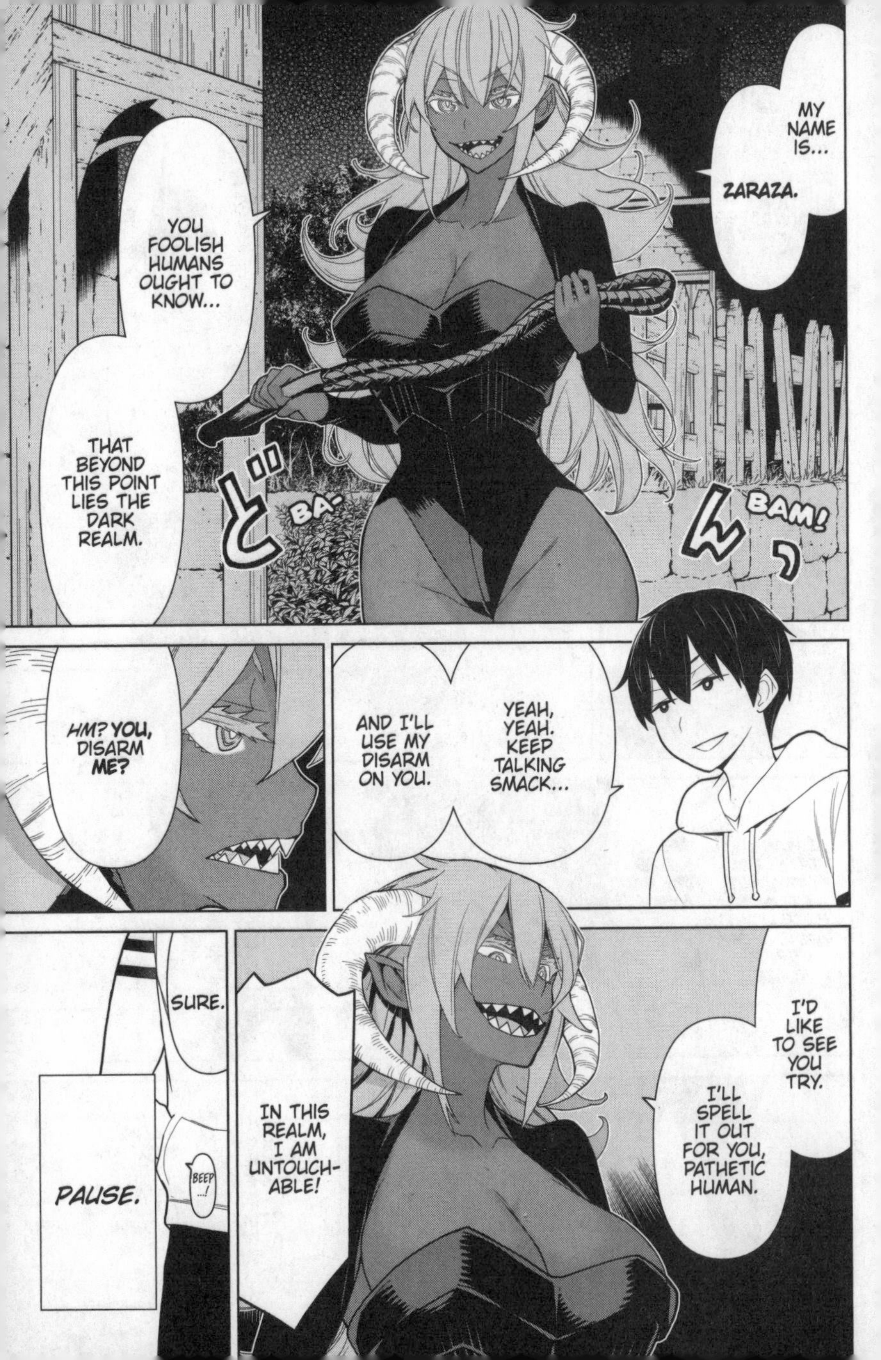
MY NAME IS...
ZARAZA.
YOU FOOLISH HUMANS OUGHT TO KNOW...
THAT BEYOND THIS POINT LIES THE DARK REALM.
BA-
BAM!
YEAH, YEAH. KEEP TALKING SMACK...
AND I'LL USE MY DISARM ON YOU.
HM? YOU, DISARM ME?
I'D LIKE TO SEE YOU TRY.
I'LL SPELL IT OUT FOR YOU, PATHETIC HUMAN.
IN THIS REALM, I AM UNTOUCHABLE!
SURE.
BEEP ...!
PAUSE.

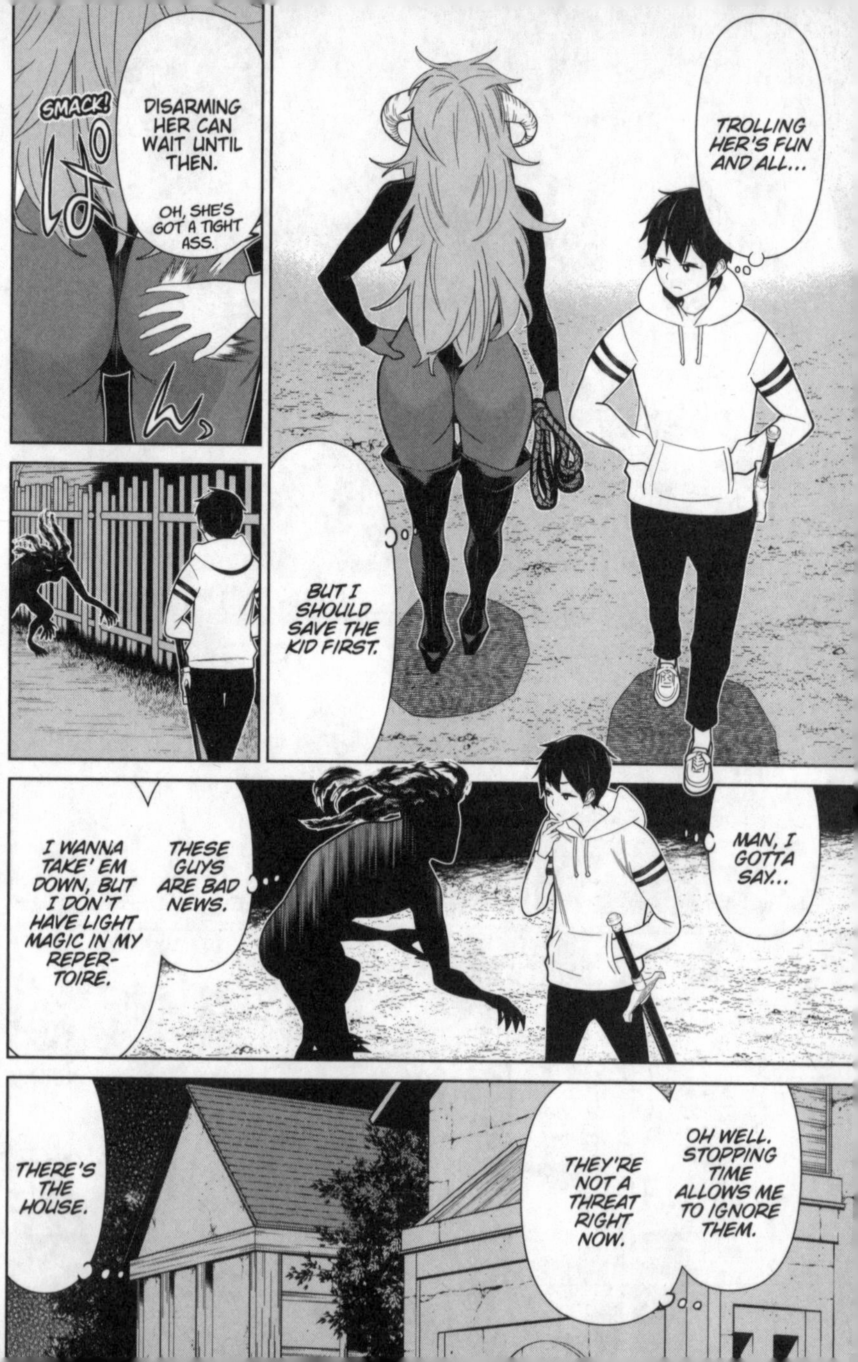

TROLLING HER'S FUN AND ALL...
BUT I SHOULD SAVE THE KID FIRST.
DISARMING HER CAN WAIT UNTIL THEN.
OH, SHE'S GOT A TIGHT ASS.
SMACK!
MAN, I GOTTA SAY...
THESE GUYS ARE BAD NEWS.
I WANNA TAKE' EM DOWN, BUT I DON'T HAVE LIGHT MAGIC IN MY REPERTOIRE.
OH WELL. STOPPING TIME ALLOWS ME TO IGNORE THEM.
THEY'RE NOT A THREAT RIGHT NOW.
THERE'S THE HOUSE.

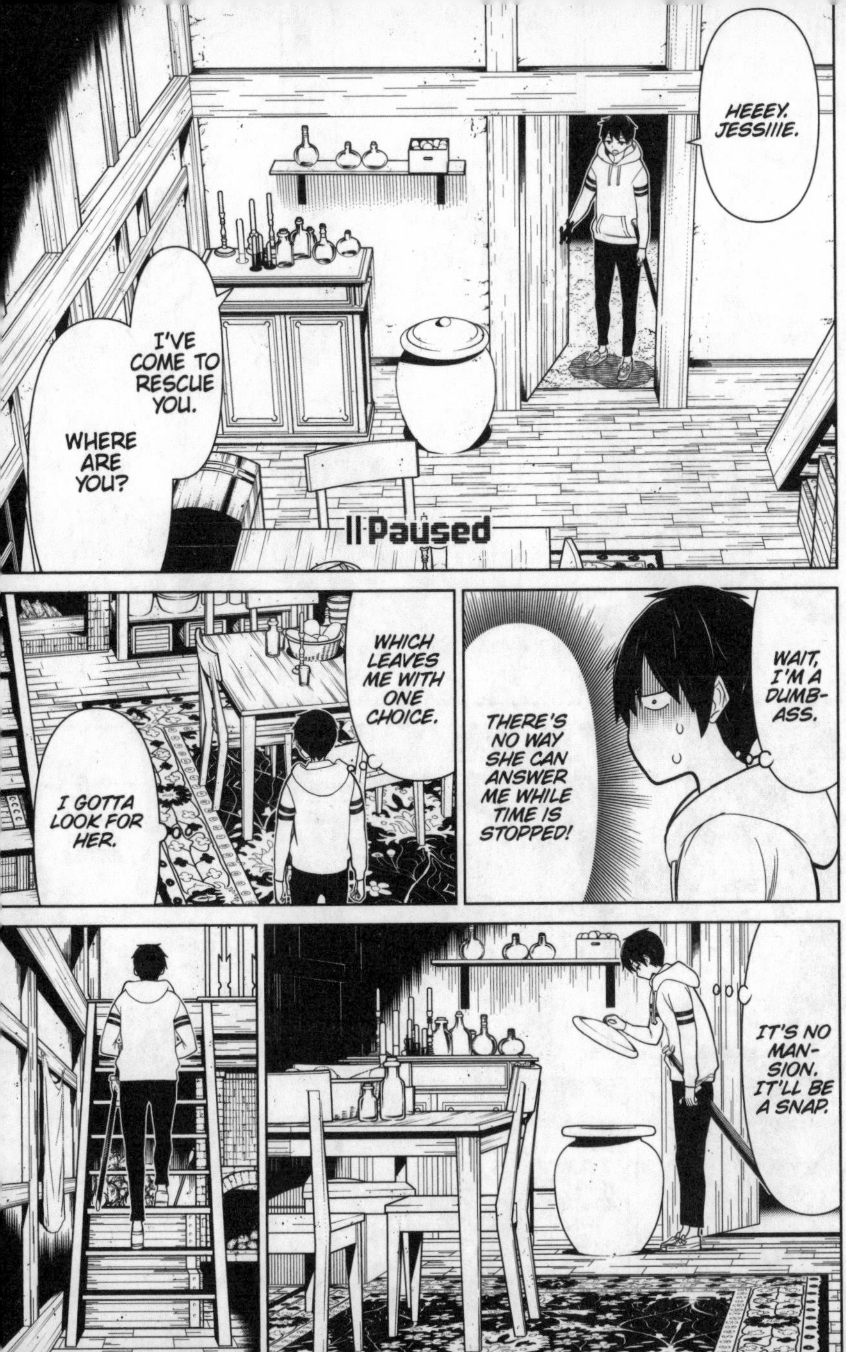
HEEEY. JESSIIIE.
I'VE COME TO RESCUE YOU.
WHERE ARE YOU?
Paused
WAIT, I'M A DUMB-ASS.
THERE'S NO WAY SHE CAN ANSWER ME WHILE TIME IS STOPPED!
WHICH LEAVES ME WITH ONE CHOICE.
I GOTTA LOOK FOR HER.
IT'S NO MAN-SION. IT'LL BE A SNAP.

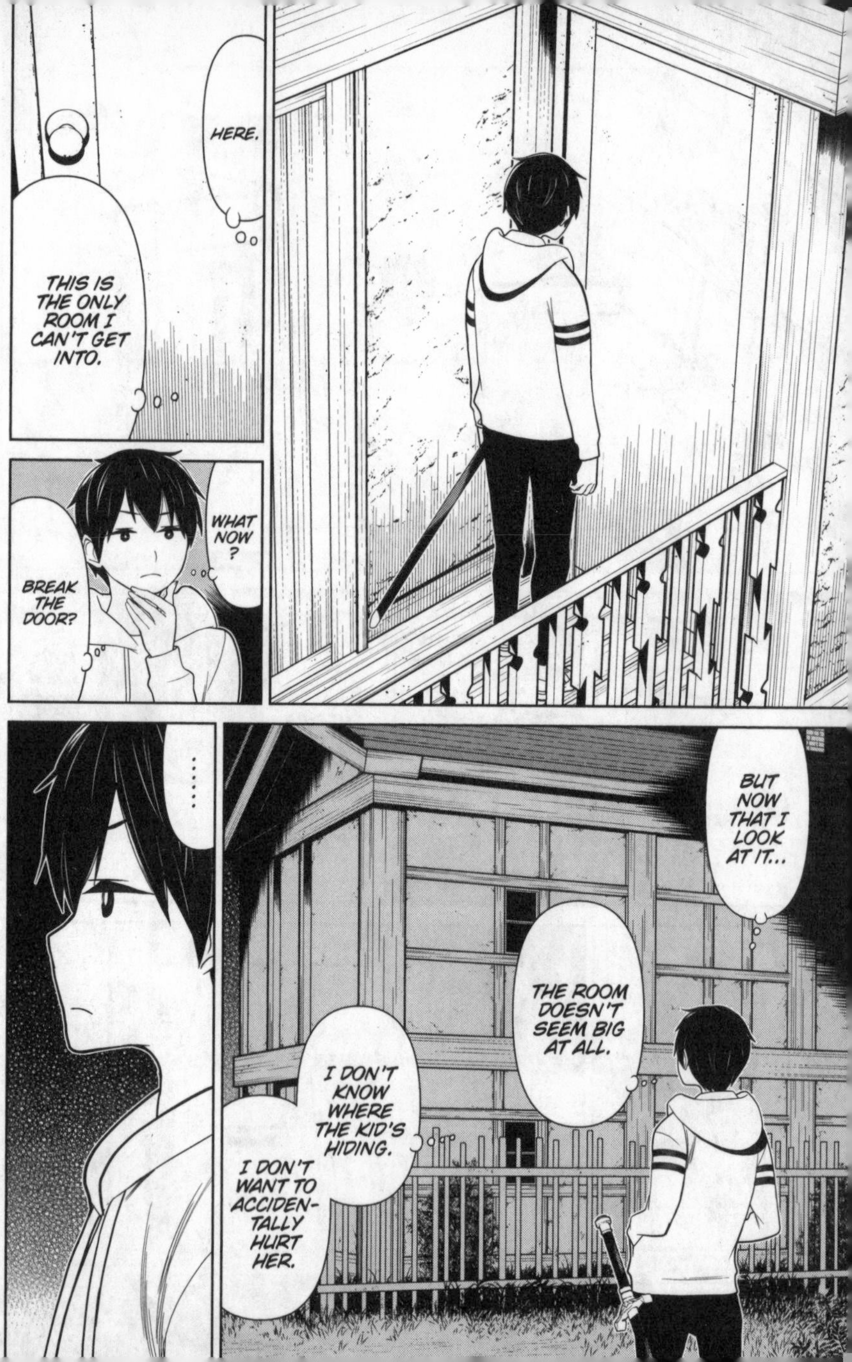
HERE.
THIS IS THE ONLY ROOM I CAN'T GET INTO.
WHAT NOW?
BREAK THE DOOR?
BUT NOW THAT I LOOK AT IT...
THE ROOM DOESN'T SEEM BIG AT ALL.
I DON'T KNOW WHERE THE KID'S HIDING.
I DON'T WANT TO ACCIDEN-TALLY HURT HER.
......

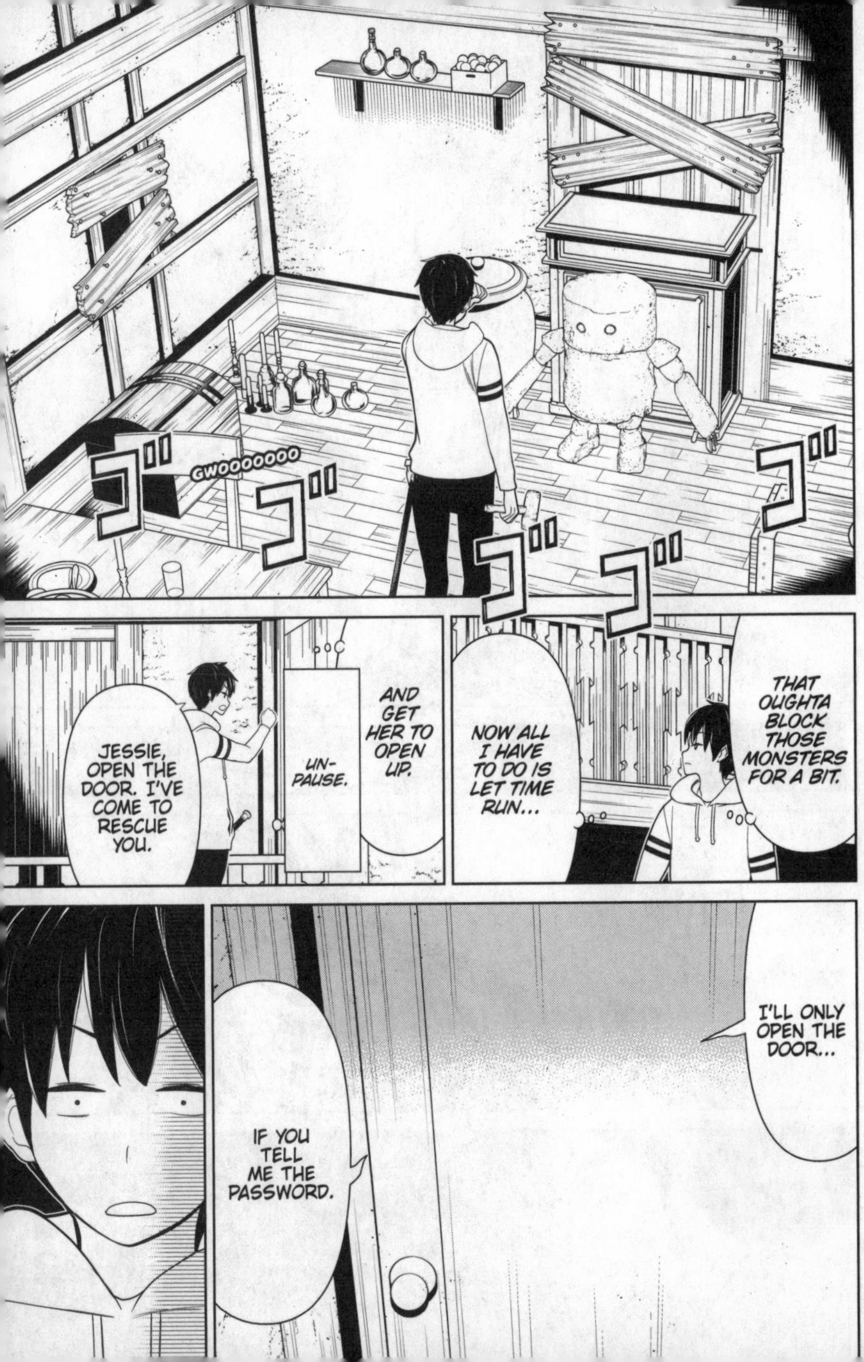
GWOOOOOOO
THAT OUGHTA BLOCK THOSE MONSTERS FOR A BIT.
NOW ALL I HAVE TO DO IS LET TIME RUN...
AND GET HER TO OPEN UP.
UN-PAUSE.
JESSIE, OPEN THE DOOR. I'VE COME TO RESCUE YOU.
I'LL ONLY OPEN THE DOOR...
IF YOU TELL ME THE PASSWORD.

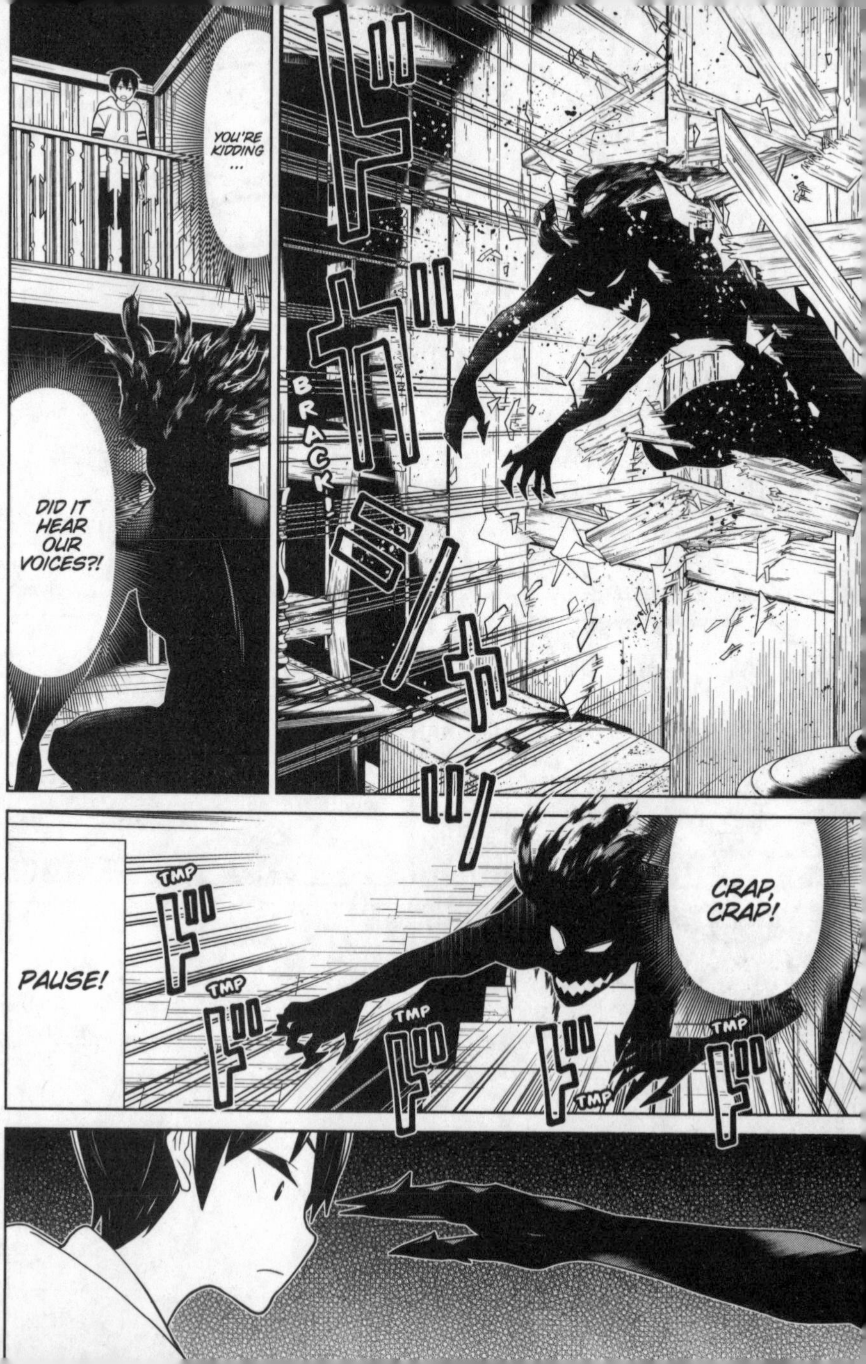
BRACK!
YOU'RE KIDDING ...
DID IT HEAR OUR VOICES?!
CRAP, CRAP!
TMP
TMP
TMP
TMP
TMP
PAUSE!

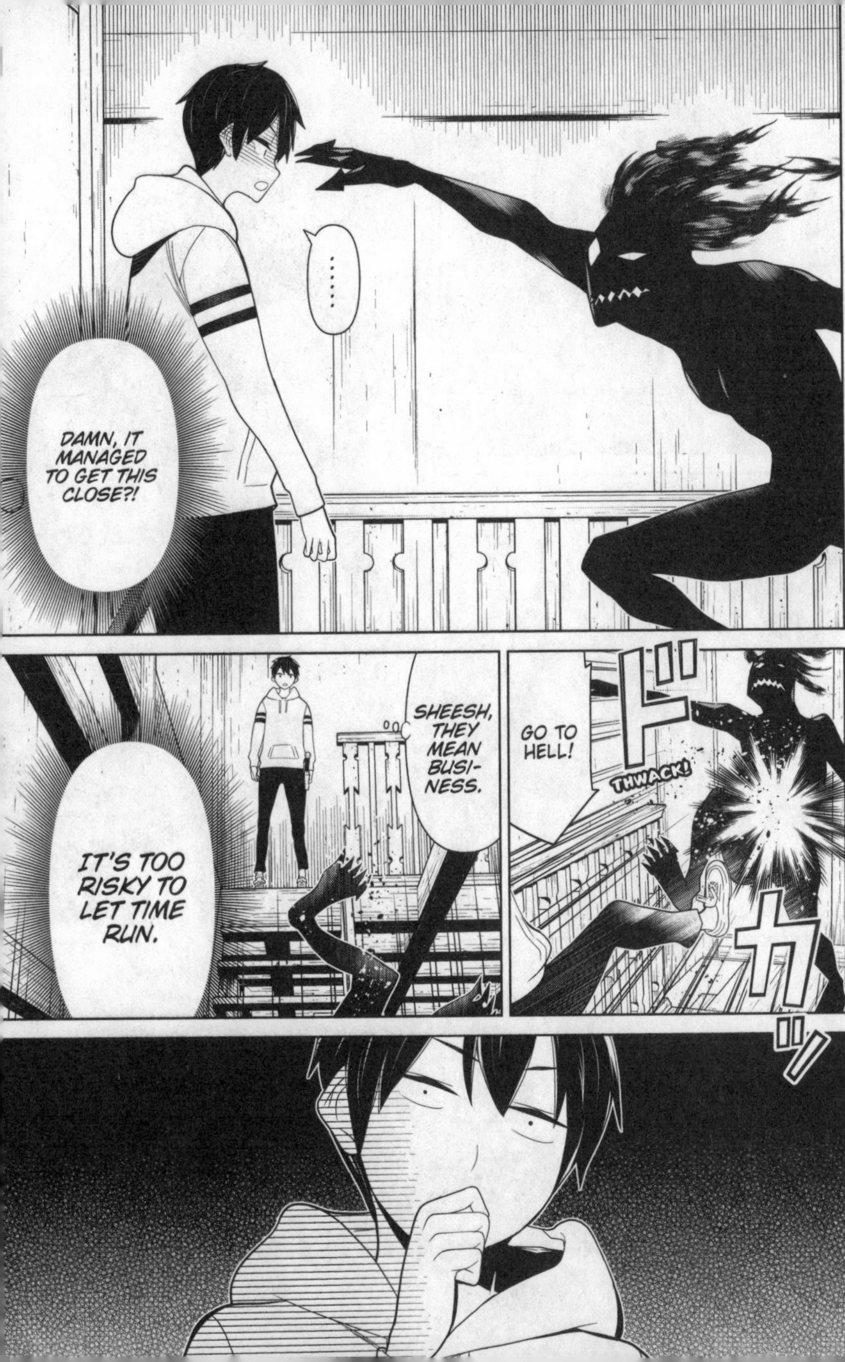

......
DAMN, IT MANAGED TO GET THIS CLOSE?!
ドッ
GO TO HELL!
THWACK!
カッ
SHEESH, THEY MEAN BUSINESS.
IT'S TOO RISKY TO LET TIME RUN.

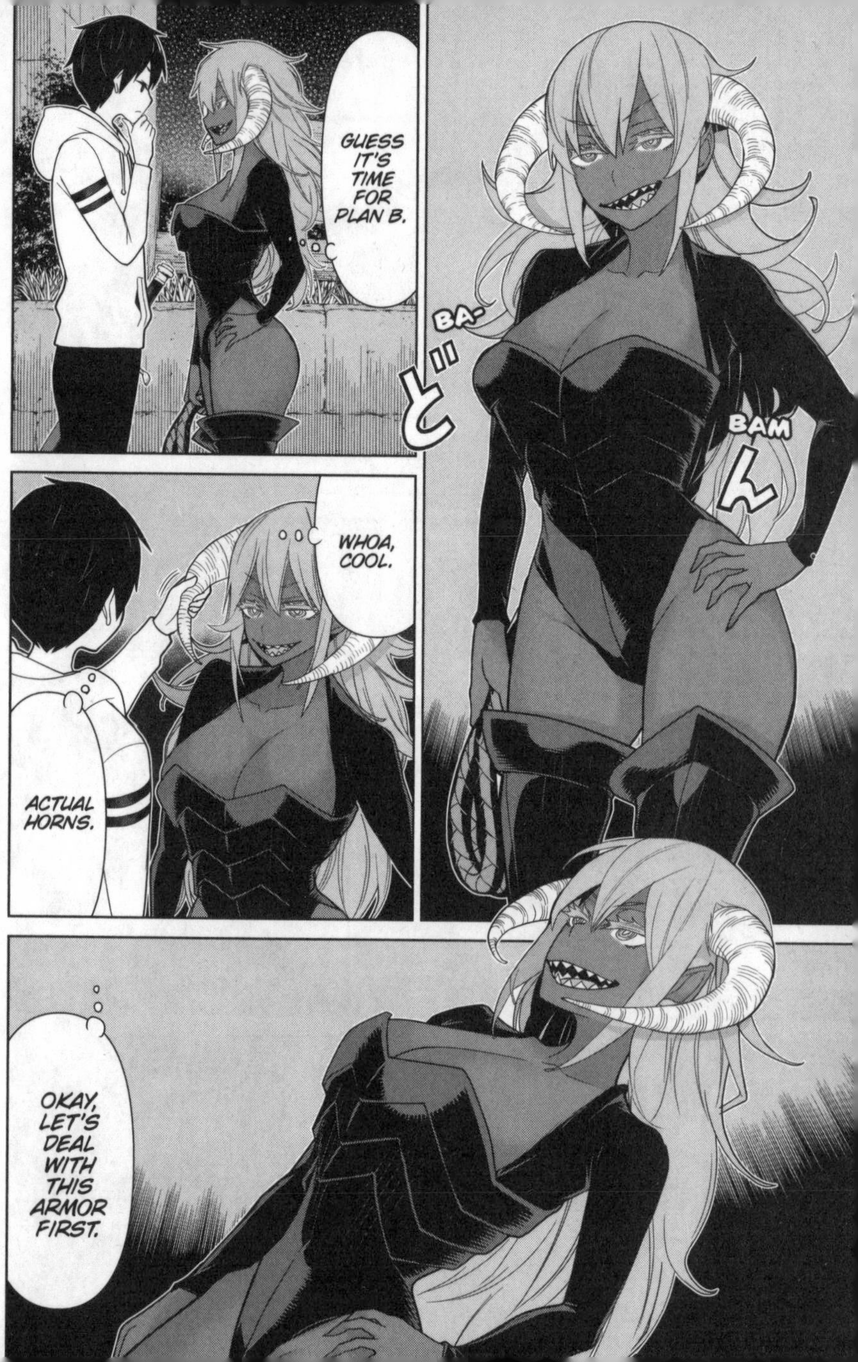
BA-
ど
BAM
ん
GUESS IT'S TIME FOR PLAN B.
WHOA, COOL.
ACTUAL HORNS.
OKAY, LET'S DEAL WITH THIS ARMOR FIRST.

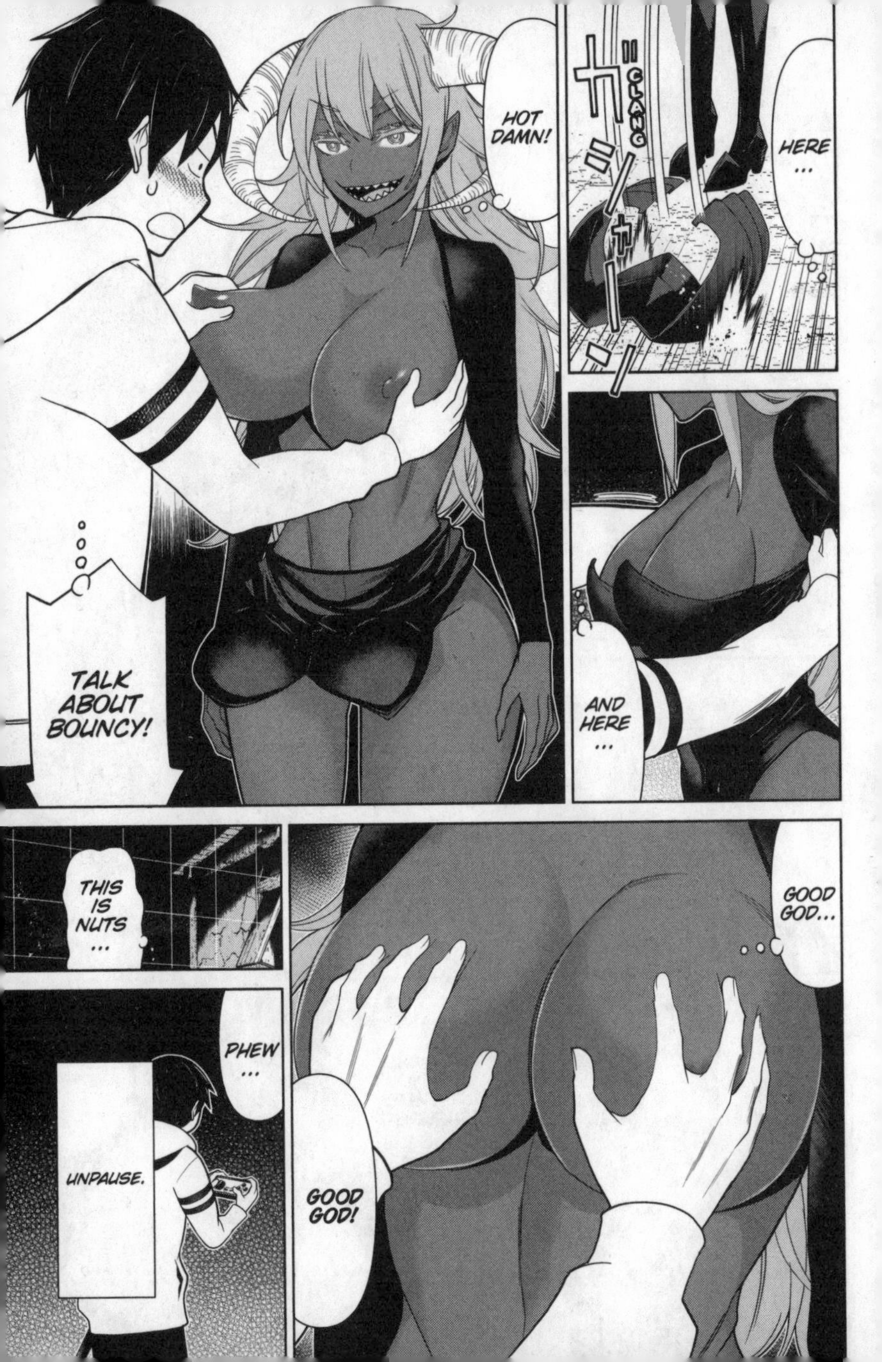
HERE ...
CLANG
AND HERE ...
HOT DAMN!
TALK ABOUT BOUNCY!
GOOD GOD...
GOOD GOD!
THIS IS NUTS ...
PHEW ...
UNPAUSE.

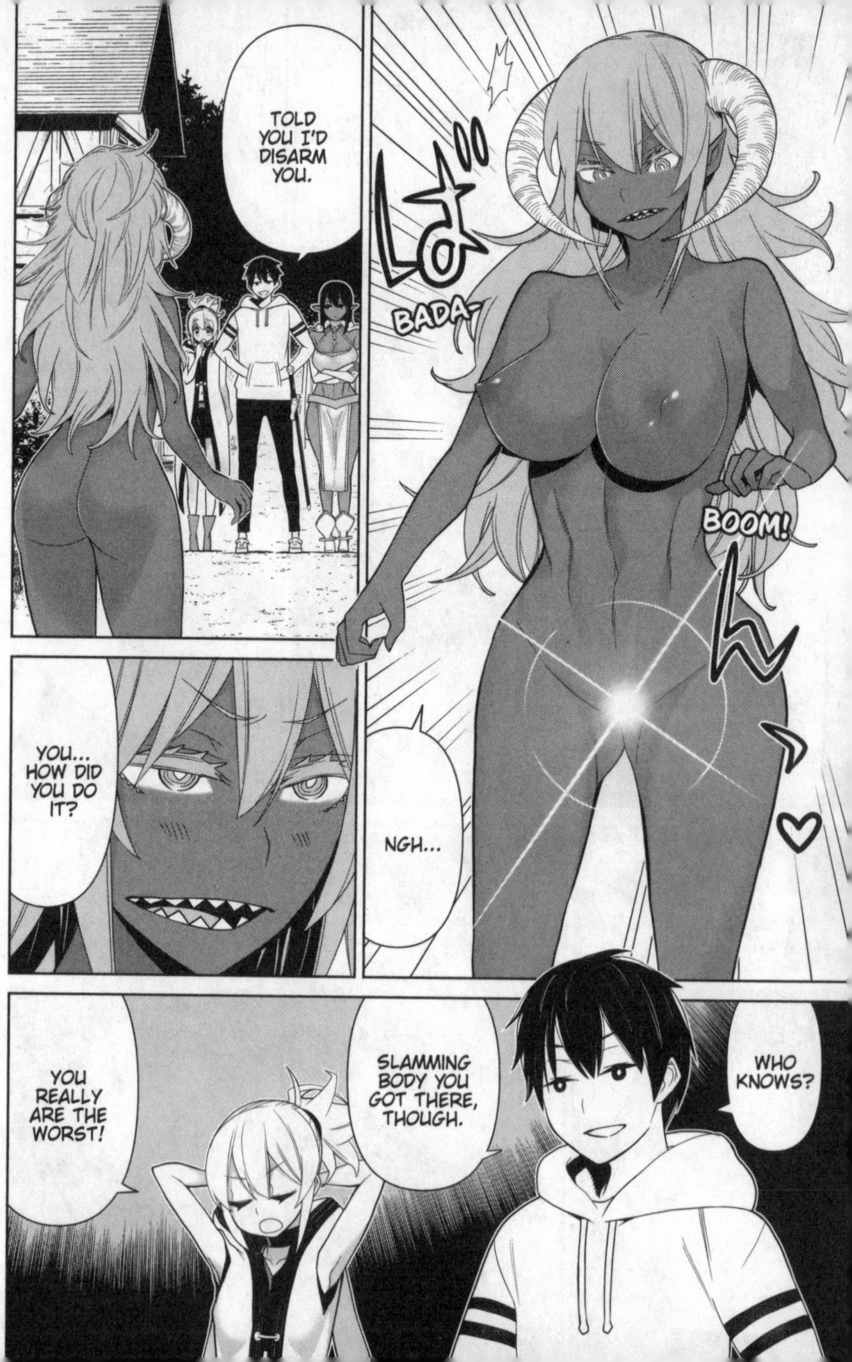
BADA-
BOOM!
NGH...
TOLD YOU I'D DISARM YOU.
YOU... HOW DID YOU DO IT?
WHO KNOWS?
SLAMMING BODY YOU GOT THERE, THOUGH.
YOU REALLY ARE THE WORST!

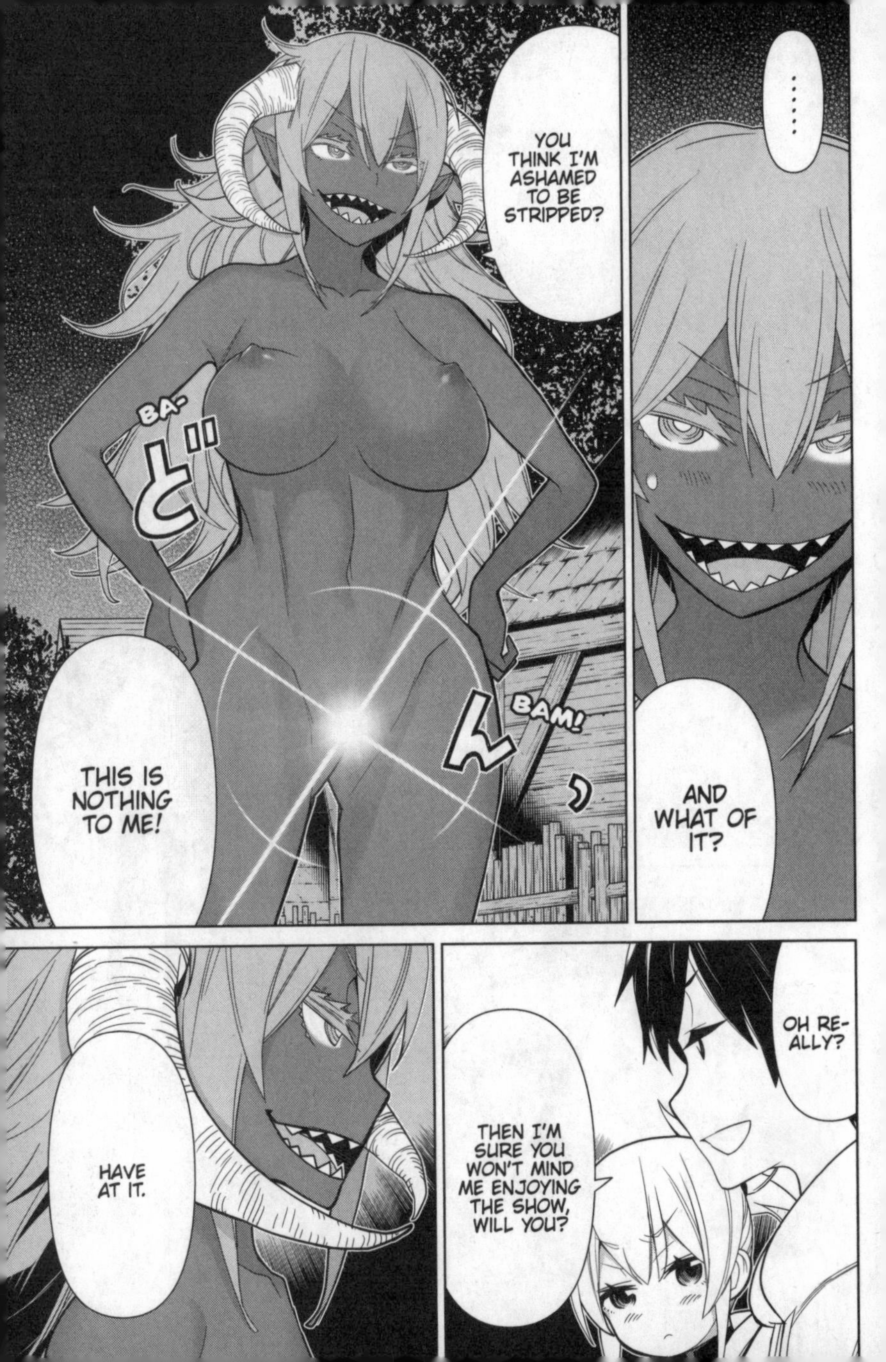
......
AND WHAT OF IT?
YOU THINK I'M ASHAMED TO BE STRIPPED?
BA-
BAM!
THIS IS NOTHING TO ME!
OH RE-ALLY?
THEN I'M SURE YOU WON'T MIND ME ENJOYING THE SHOW, WILL YOU?
HAVE AT IT.

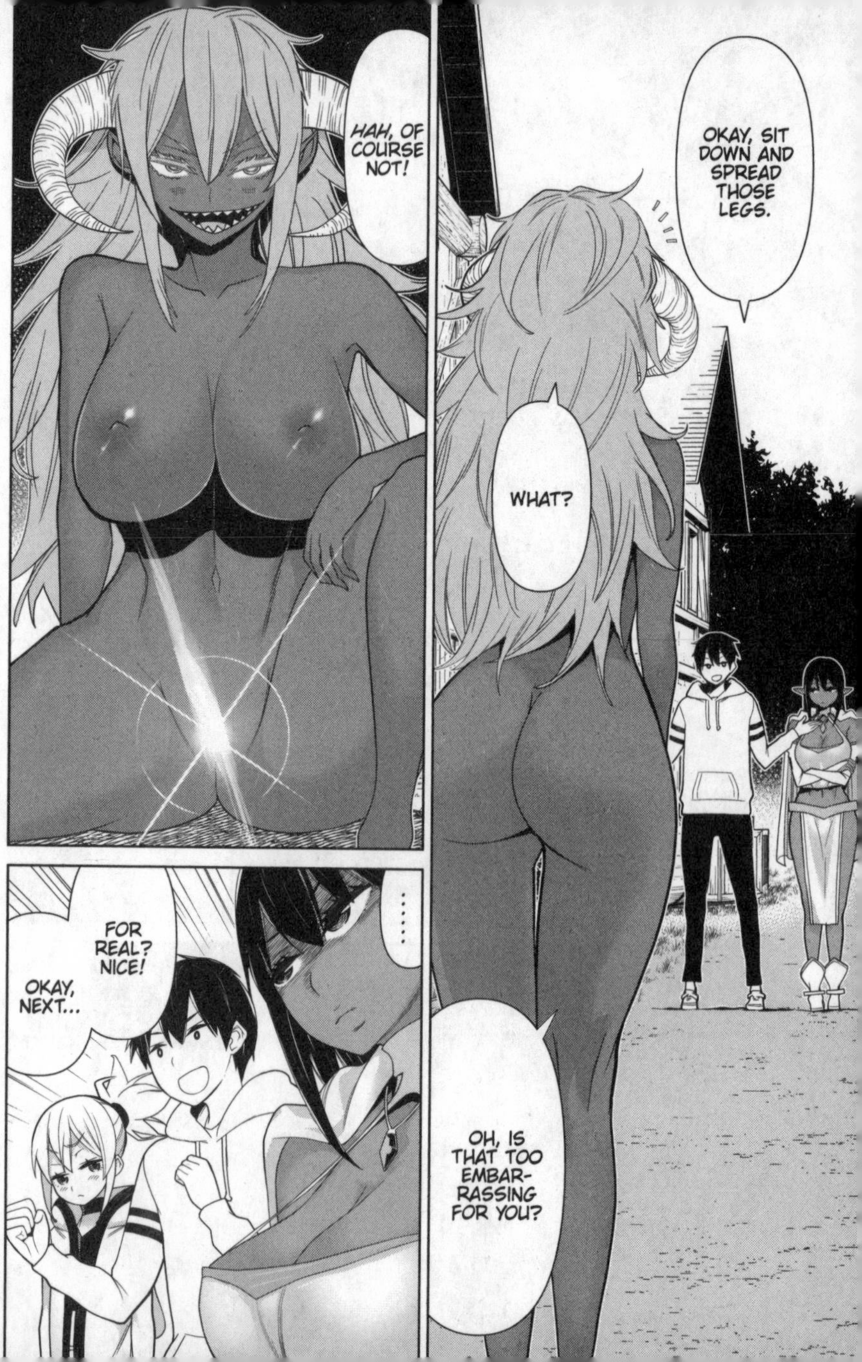
OKAY, SIT DOWN AND SPREAD THOSE LEGS.
WHAT?
OH, IS THAT TOO EMBAR-RASSING FOR YOU?
HAH, OF COURSE NOT!
......
FOR REAL? NICE!
OKAY, NEXT...

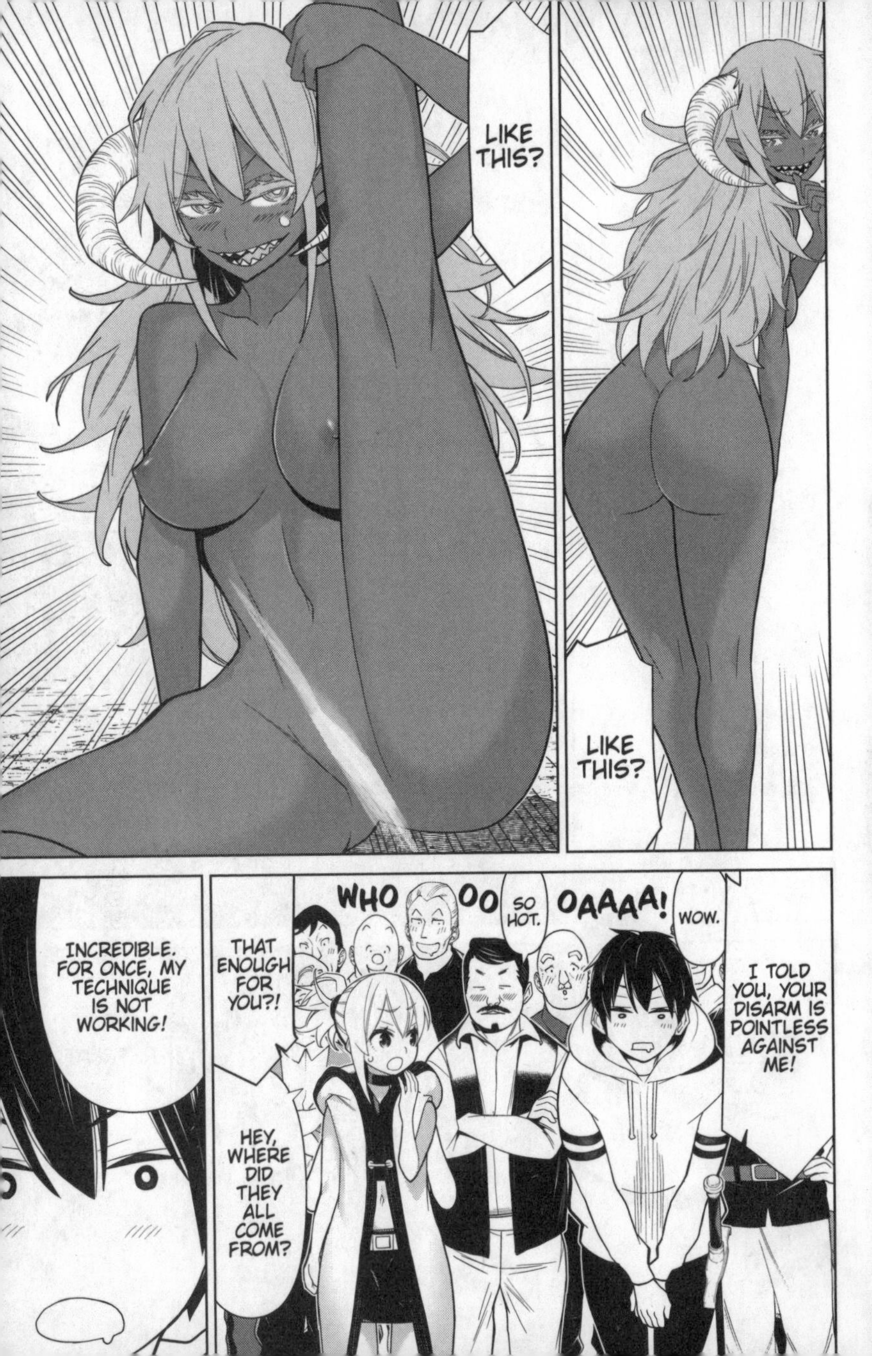
LIKE THIS?
LIKE THIS?
WOW.
I TOLD YOU, YOUR DISARM IS POINTLESS AGAINST ME!
WHOOOOAAAA!
SO HOT.
THAT ENOUGH FOR YOU?!
HEY, WHERE DID THEY ALL COME FROM?
INCREDIBLE. FOR ONCE, MY TECHNIQUE IS NOT WORKING!

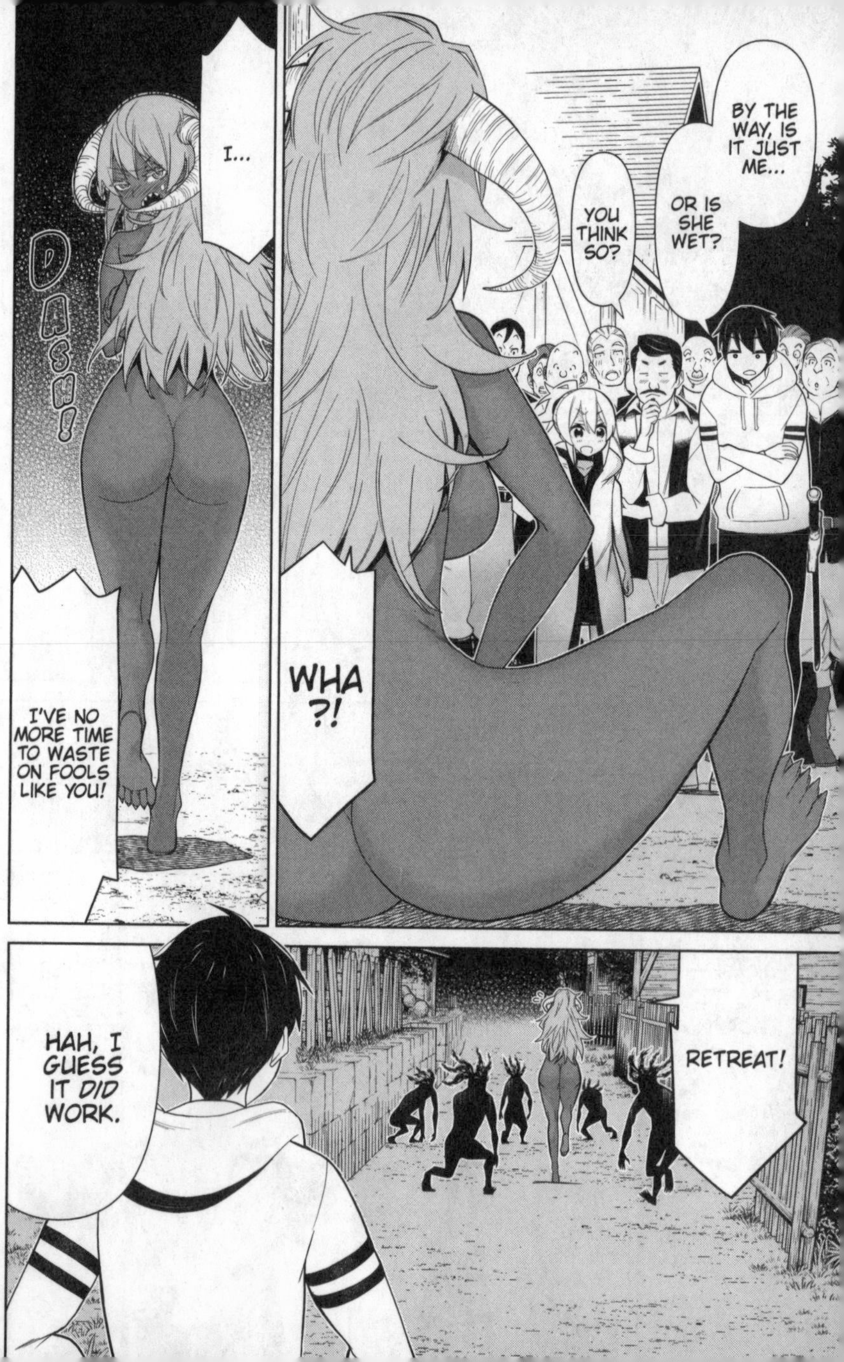
BY THE WAY, IS IT JUST ME...
OR IS SHE WET?
YOU THINK SO?
WHA?!
I...
DASH!
I'VE NO MORE TIME TO WASTE ON FOOLS LIKE YOU!
RETREAT!
HAH, I GUESS IT *DID* WORK.

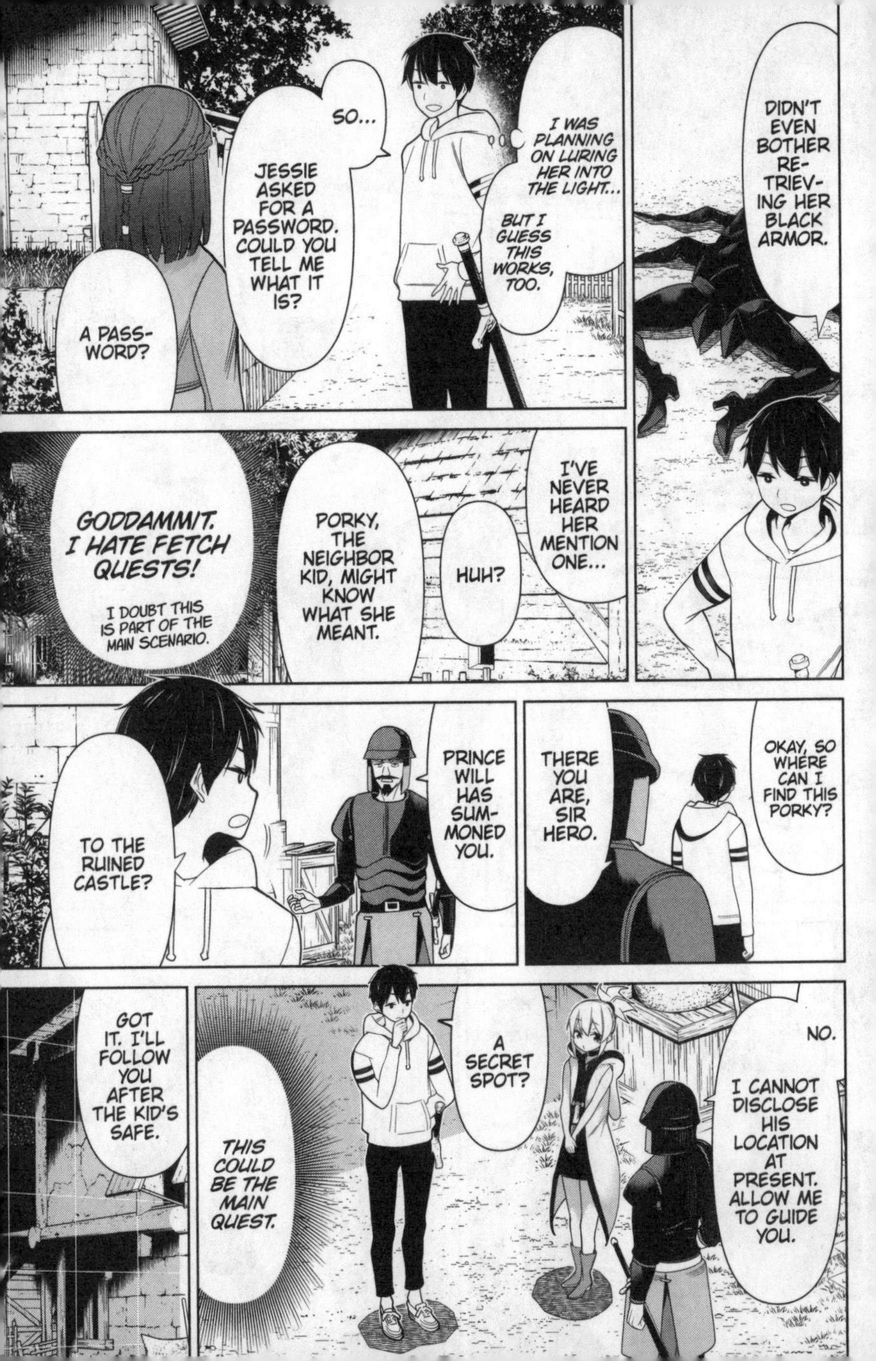
DIDN'T EVEN BOTHER RETRIEVING HER BLACK ARMOR.
I WAS PLANNING ON LURING HER INTO THE LIGHT...
BUT I GUESS THIS WORKS, TOO.
SO...
JESSIE ASKED FOR A PASSWORD. COULD YOU TELL ME WHAT IT IS?
A PASSWORD?
I'VE NEVER HEARD HER MENTION ONE...
HUH?
PORKY, THE NEIGHBOR KID, MIGHT KNOW WHAT SHE MEANT.
GODDAMMIT. I HATE FETCH QUESTS!
I DOUBT THIS IS PART OF THE MAIN SCENARIO.
OKAY, SO WHERE CAN I FIND THIS PORKY?
THERE YOU ARE, SIR HERO.
PRINCE WILL HAS SUMMONED YOU.
TO THE RUINED CASTLE?
NO.
I CANNOT DISCLOSE HIS LOCATION AT PRESENT. ALLOW ME TO GUIDE YOU.
A SECRET SPOT?
THIS COULD BE THE MAIN QUEST.
GOT IT. I'LL FOLLOW YOU AFTER THE KID'S SAFE.

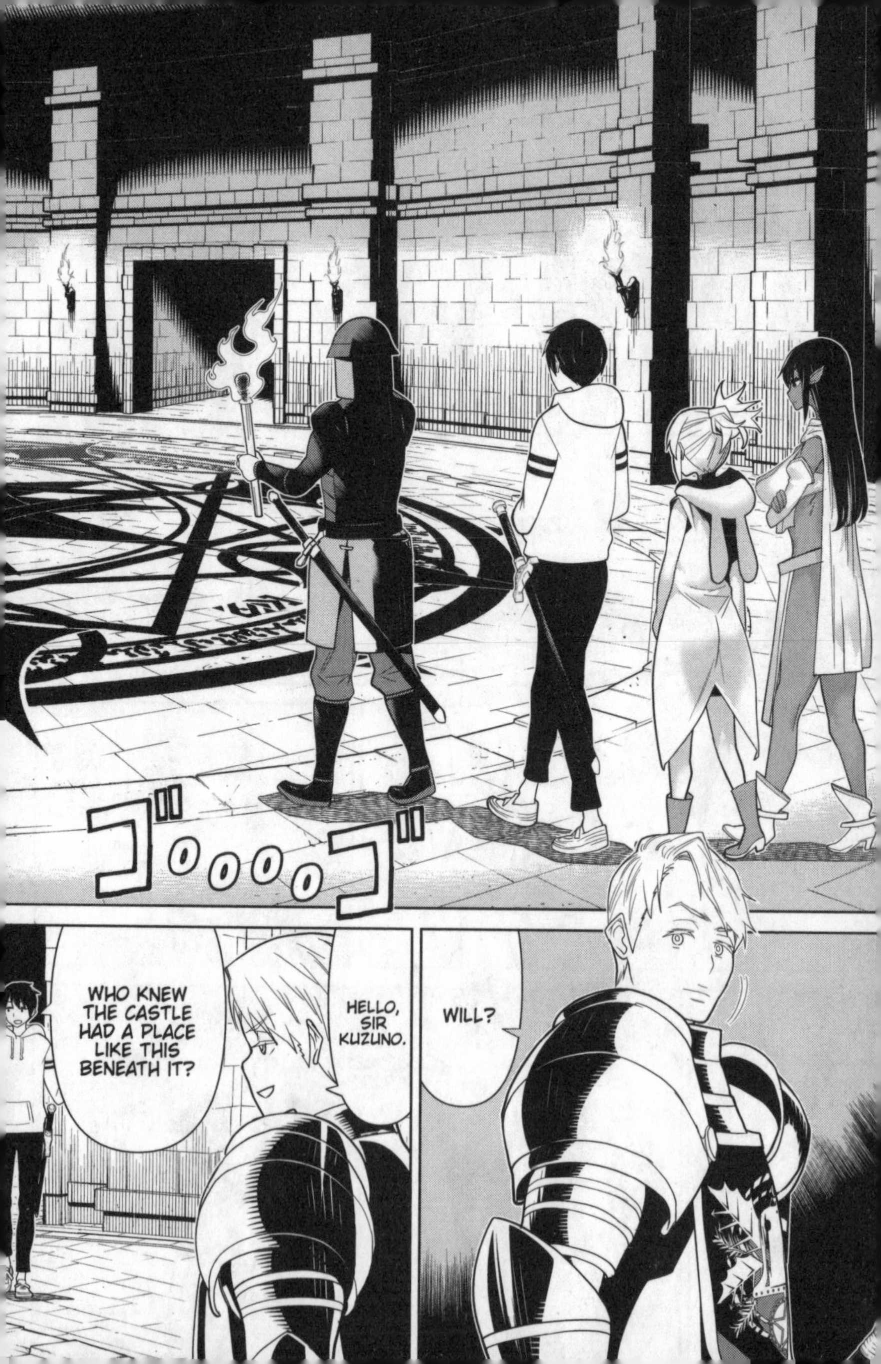
ゴooooゴ
WILL?
HELLO, SIR KUZUNO.
WHO KNEW THE CASTLE HAD A PLACE LIKE THIS BENEATH IT?

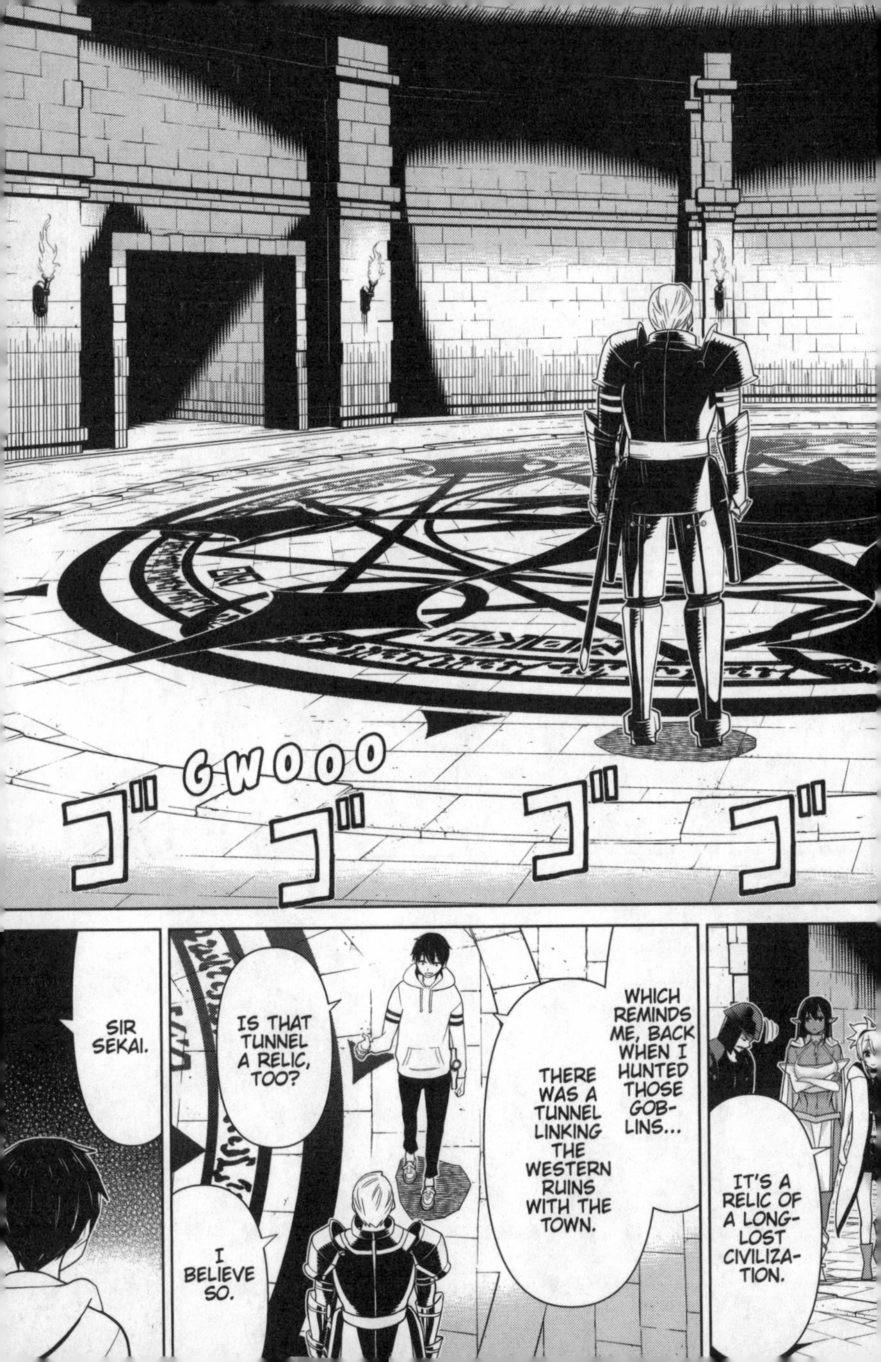
GWOOO
ゴゴゴゴ
IT'S A RELIC OF A LONG-LOST CIVILIZATION.
WHICH REMINDS ME, BACK WHEN I HUNTED THOSE GOB-LINS...
THERE WAS A TUNNEL LINKING THE WESTERN RUINS WITH THE TOWN.
IS THAT TUNNEL A RELIC, TOO?
I BELIEVE SO.
SIR SEKAI.

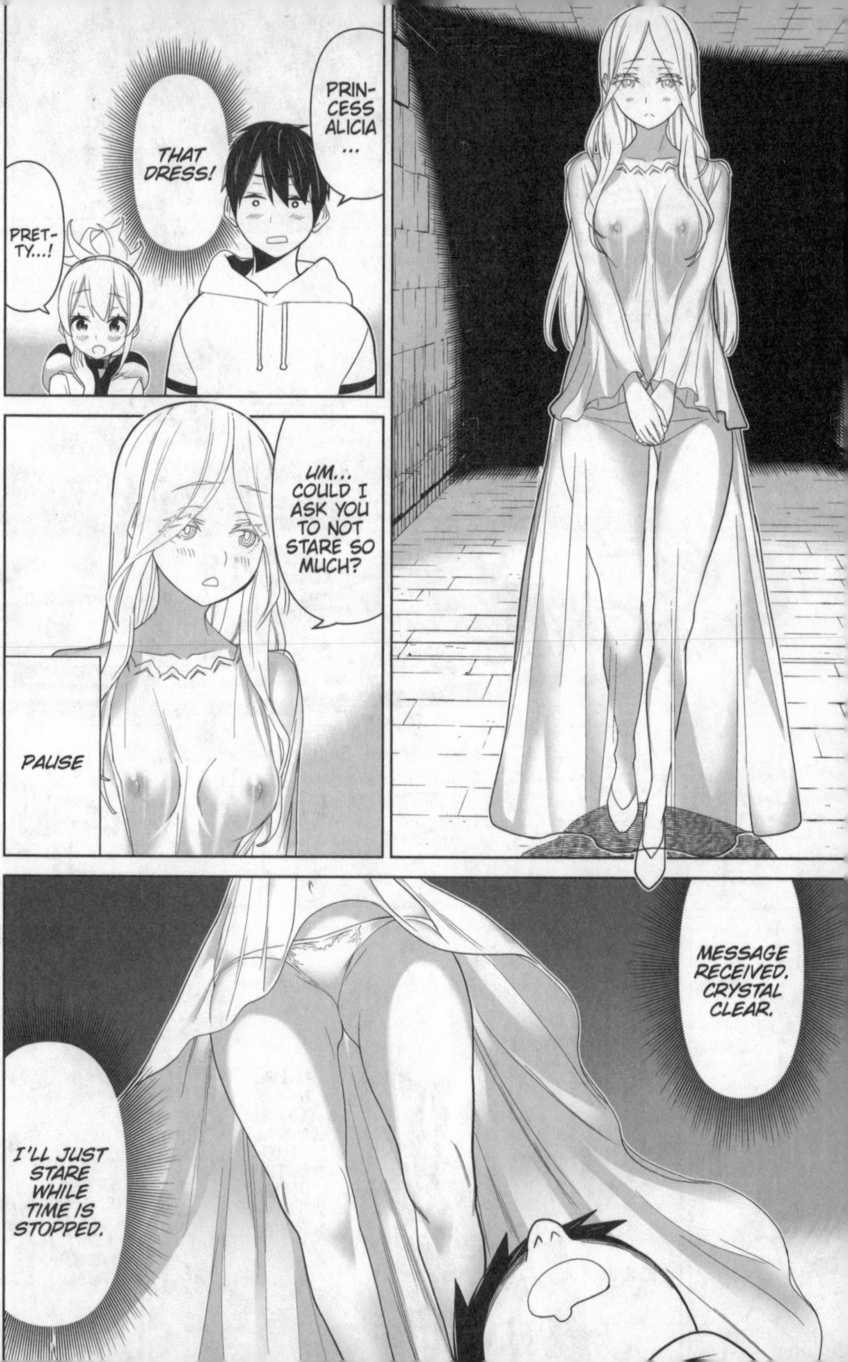
PRINCESS ALICIA...
THAT DRESS!
PRETTY...!
UM... COULD I ASK YOU TO NOT STARE SO MUCH?
PAUSE
MESSAGE RECEIVED. CRYSTAL CLEAR.
I'LL JUST STARE WHILE TIME IS STOPPED.

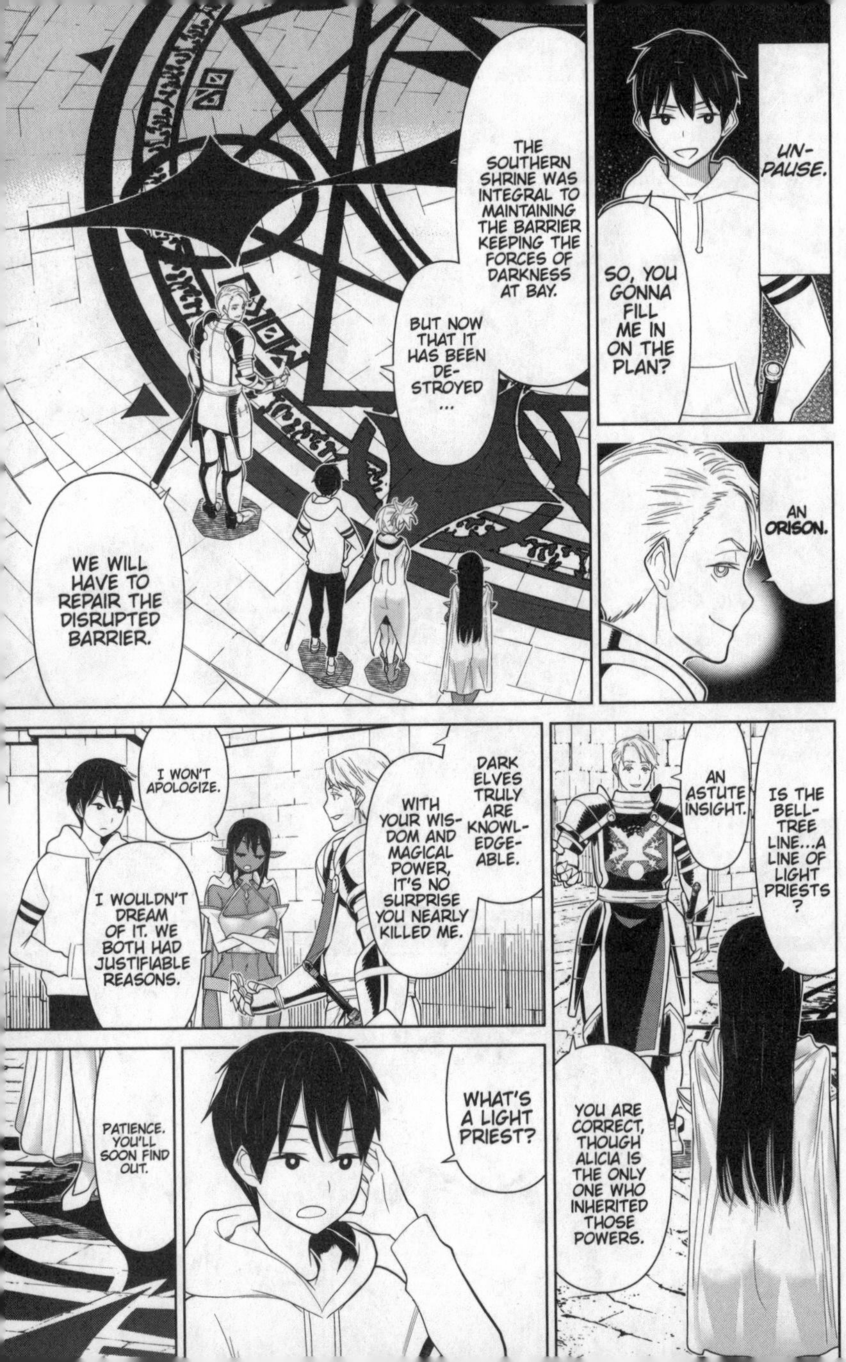
UN-PAUSE.
SO, YOU GONNA FILL ME IN ON THE PLAN?
AN ORISON.
THE SOUTHERN SHRINE WAS INTEGRAL TO MAINTAINING THE BARRIER KEEPING THE FORCES OF DARKNESS AT BAY.
BUT NOW THAT IT HAS BEEN DE-STROYED ...
WE WILL HAVE TO REPAIR THE DISRUPTED BARRIER.
IS THE BELL-TREE LINE...A LINE OF LIGHT PRIESTS?
AN ASTUTE INSIGHT.
DARK ELVES TRULY ARE KNOWL-EDGE-ABLE.
WITH YOUR WIS-DOM AND MAGICAL POWER, IT'S NO SURPRISE YOU NEARLY KILLED ME.
I WON'T APOLOGIZE.
I WOULDN'T DREAM OF IT. WE BOTH HAD JUSTIFIABLE REASONS.
YOU ARE CORRECT, THOUGH ALICIA IS THE ONLY ONE WHO INHERITED THOSE POWERS.
WHAT'S A LIGHT PRIEST?
PATIENCE. YOU'LL SOON FIND OUT.

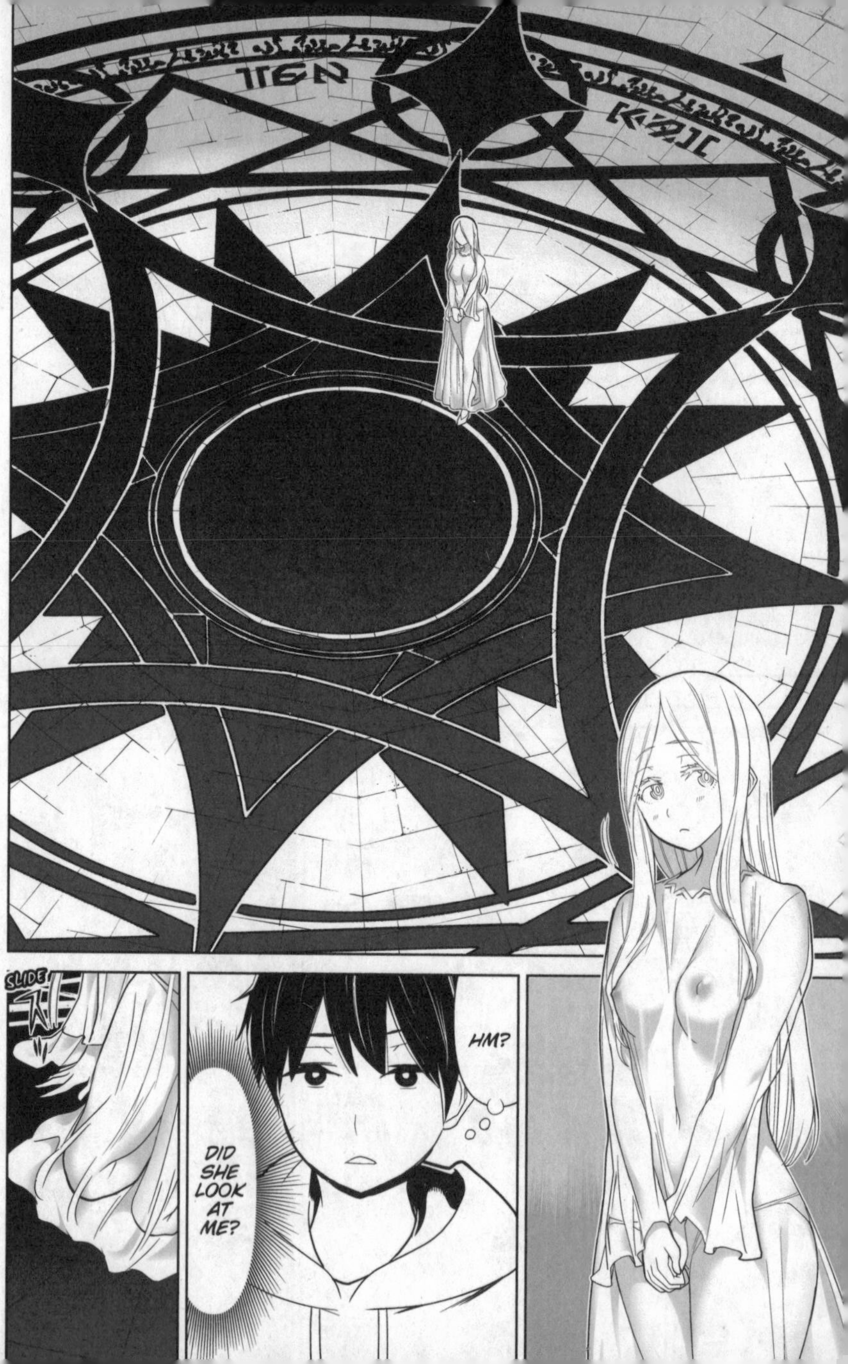
HM?
DID SHE LOOK AT ME?
SLIDE

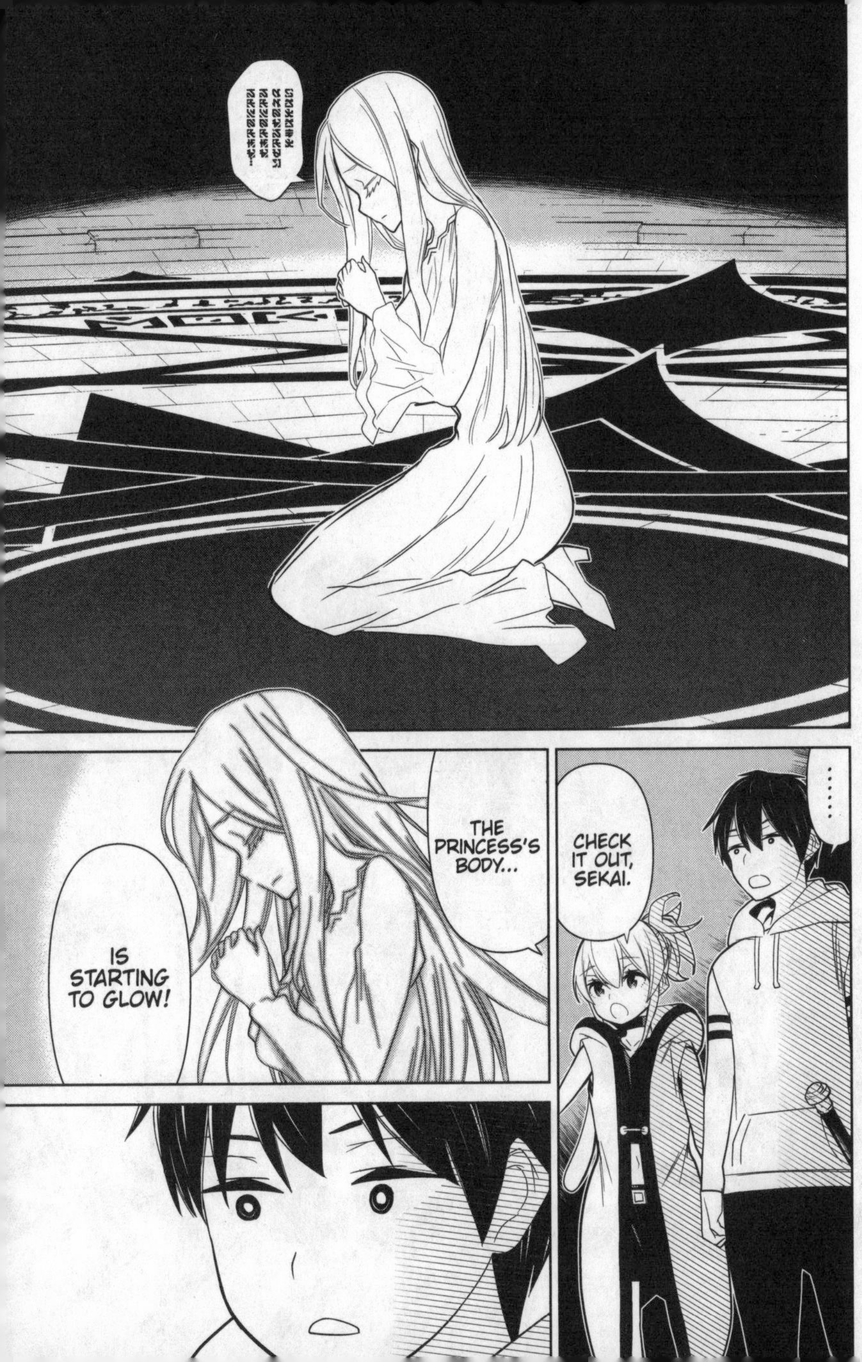
......
CHECK IT OUT, SEKAI.
THE PRINCESS'S BODY...
IS STARTING TO GLOW!

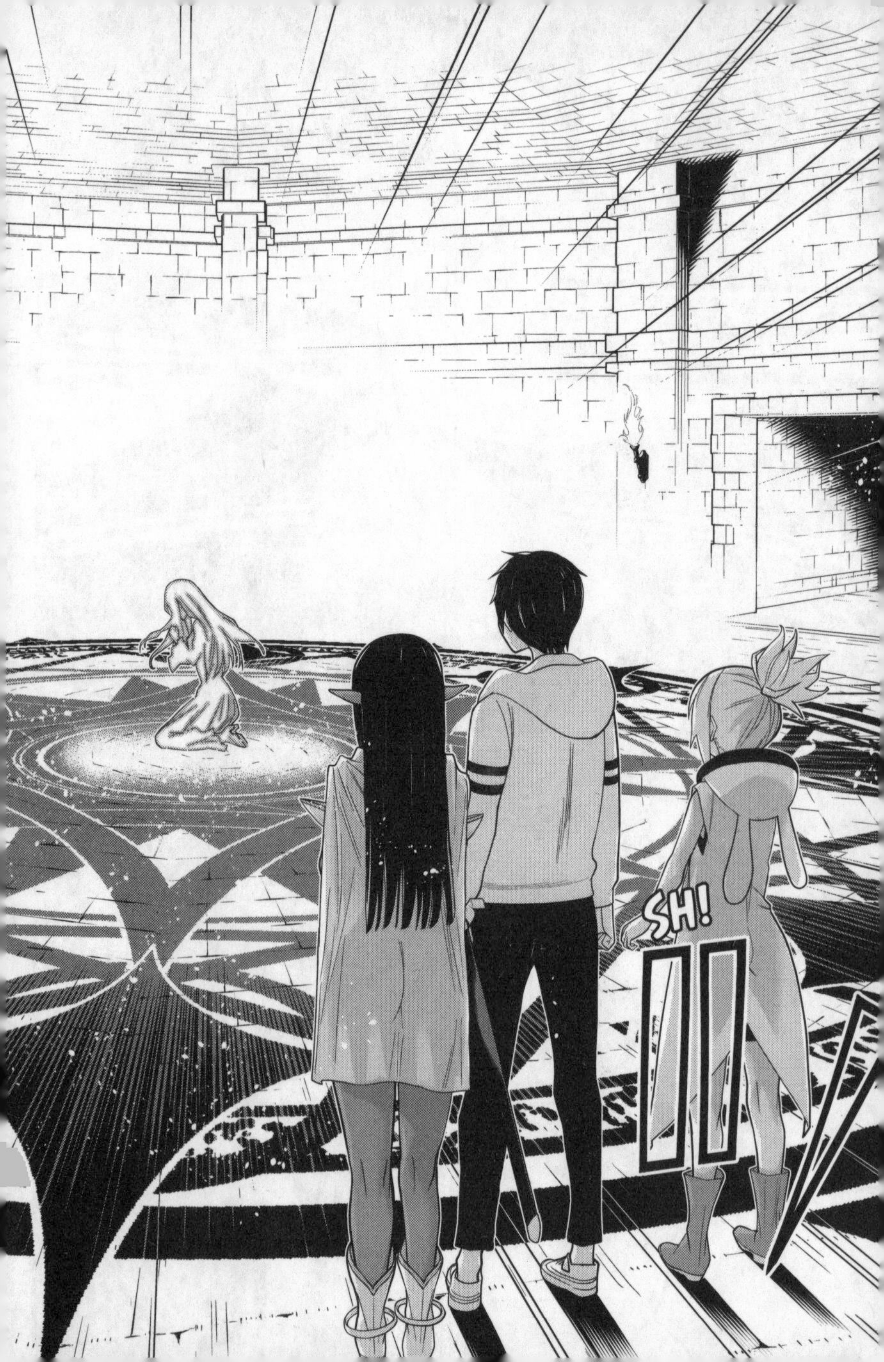
SH!

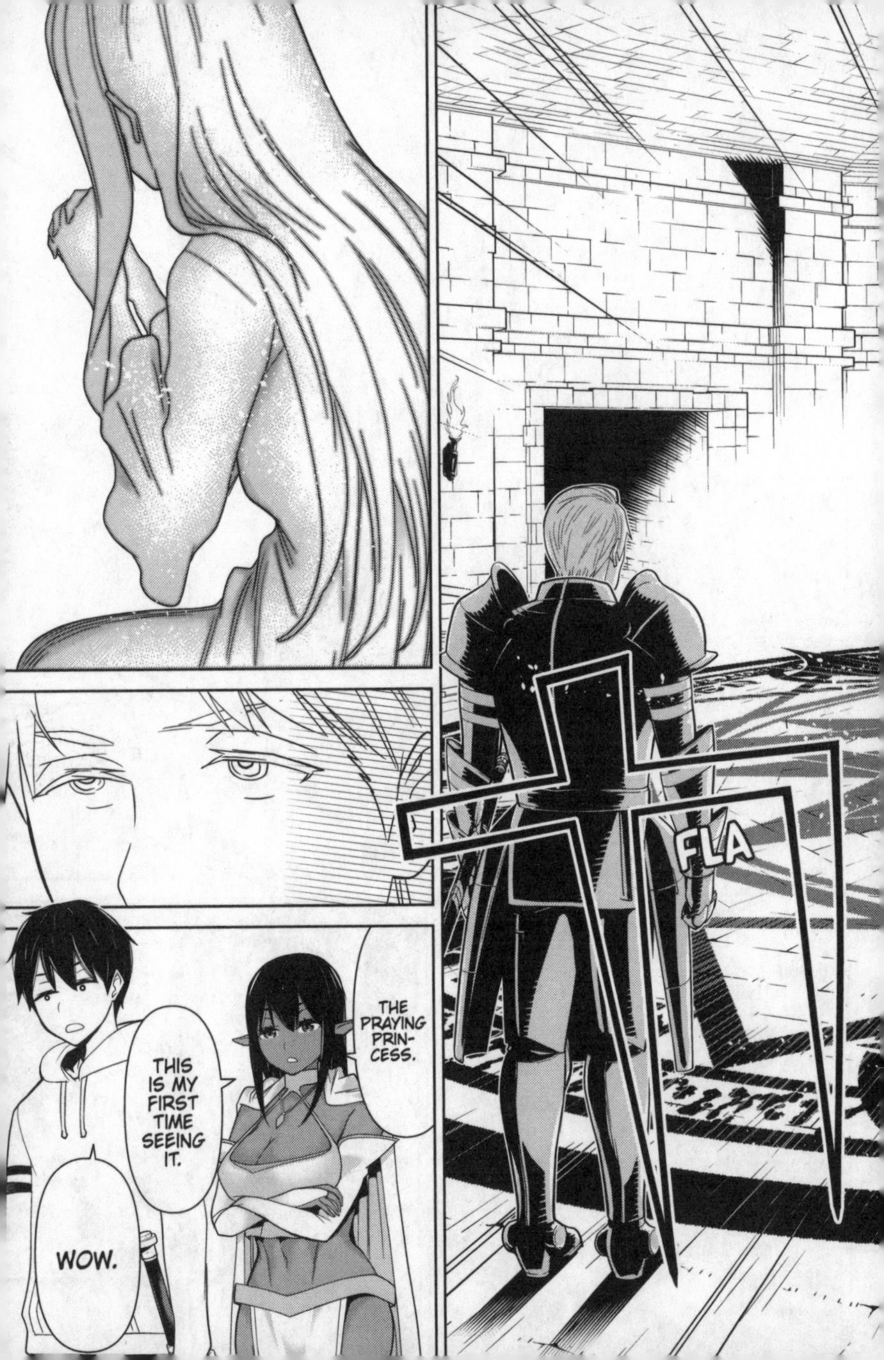
FLA
THE PRAYING PRIN-CESS.
THIS IS MY FIRST TIME SEEING IT.
WOW.

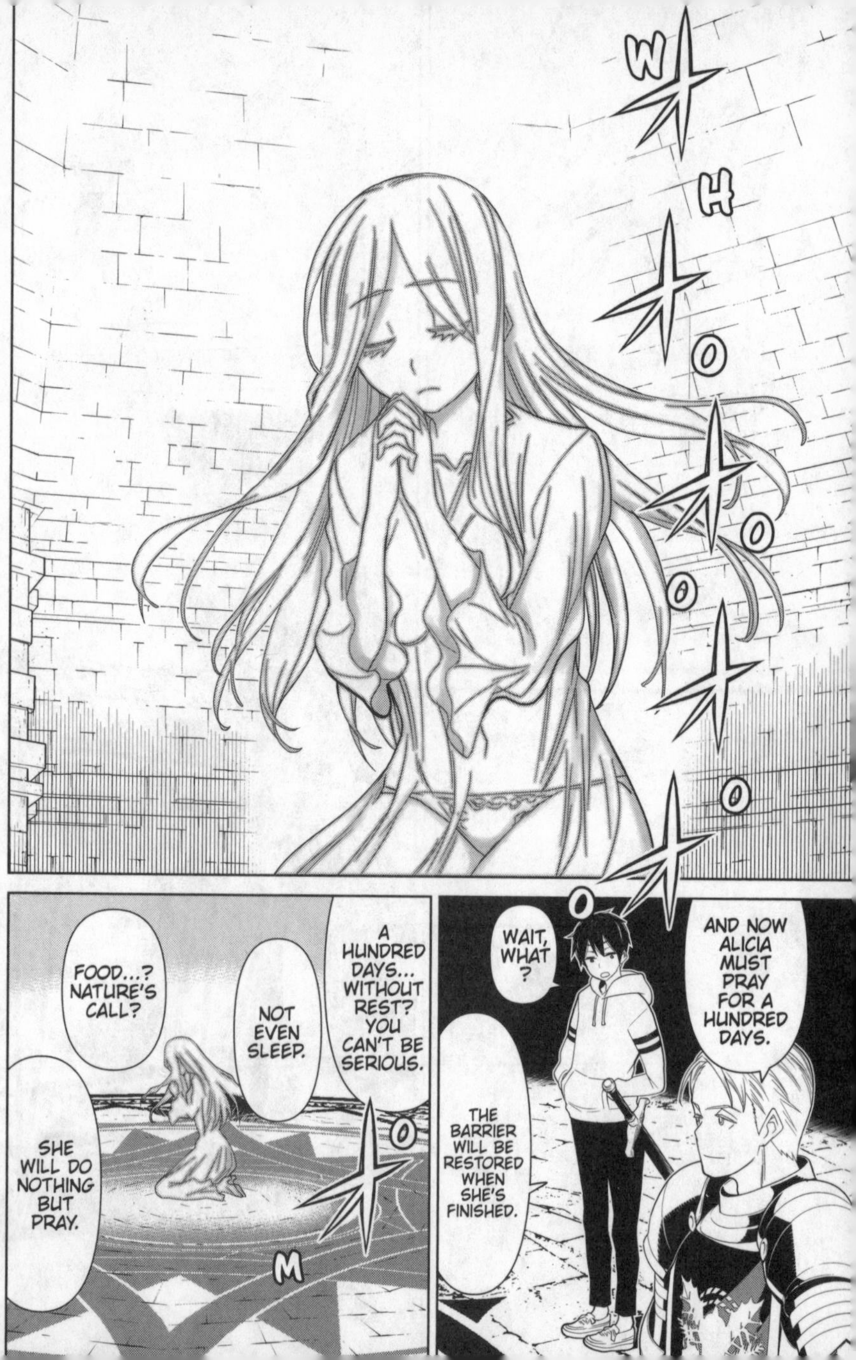
WHOOOOOOM
AND NOW ALICIA MUST PRAY FOR A HUNDRED DAYS.
WAIT, WHAT?
THE BARRIER WILL BE RESTORED WHEN SHE'S FINISHED.
A HUNDRED DAYS... WITHOUT REST? YOU CAN'T BE SERIOUS.
NOT EVEN SLEEP.
FOOD...? NATURE'S CALL?
SHE WILL DO NOTHING BUT PRAY.

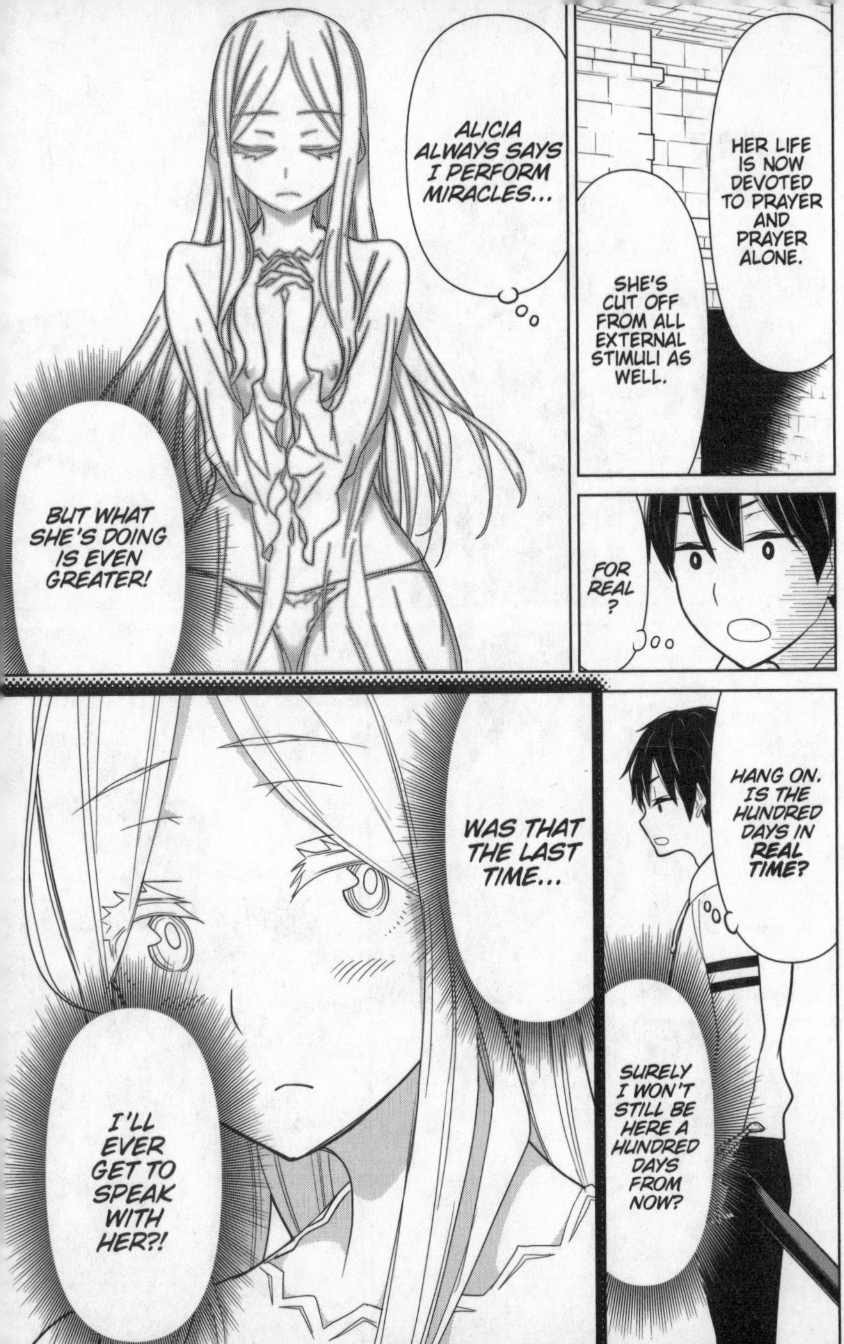
HER LIFE IS NOW DEVOTED TO PRAYER AND PRAYER ALONE.
SHE'S CUT OFF FROM ALL EXTERNAL STIMULI AS WELL.
FOR REAL?
ALICIA ALWAYS SAYS I PERFORM MIRACLES...
BUT WHAT SHE'S DOING IS EVEN GREATER!
HANG ON. IS THE HUNDRED DAYS IN REAL TIME?
SURELY I WON'T STILL BE HERE A HUNDRED DAYS FROM NOW?
WAS THAT THE LAST TIME...
I'LL EVER GET TO SPEAK WITH HER?!

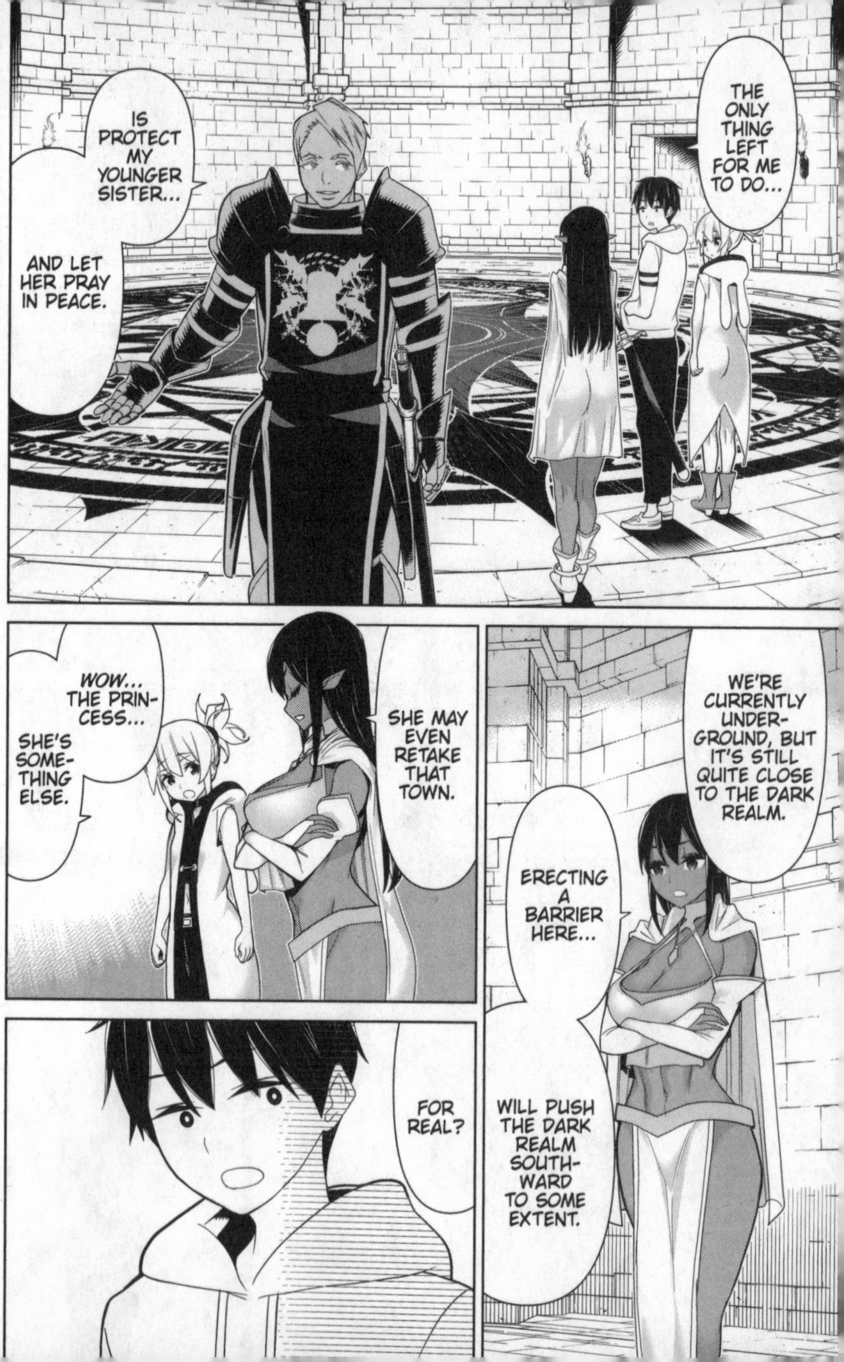
THE ONLY THING LEFT FOR ME TO DO...
IS PROTECT MY YOUNGER SISTER...
AND LET HER PRAY IN PEACE.
WE'RE CURRENTLY UNDERGROUND, BUT IT'S STILL QUITE CLOSE TO THE DARK REALM.
ERECTING A BARRIER HERE...
WILL PUSH THE DARK REALM SOUTHWARD TO SOME EXTENT.
SHE MAY EVEN RETAKE THAT TOWN.
WOW... THE PRINCESS... SHE'S SOMETHING ELSE.
FOR REAL?

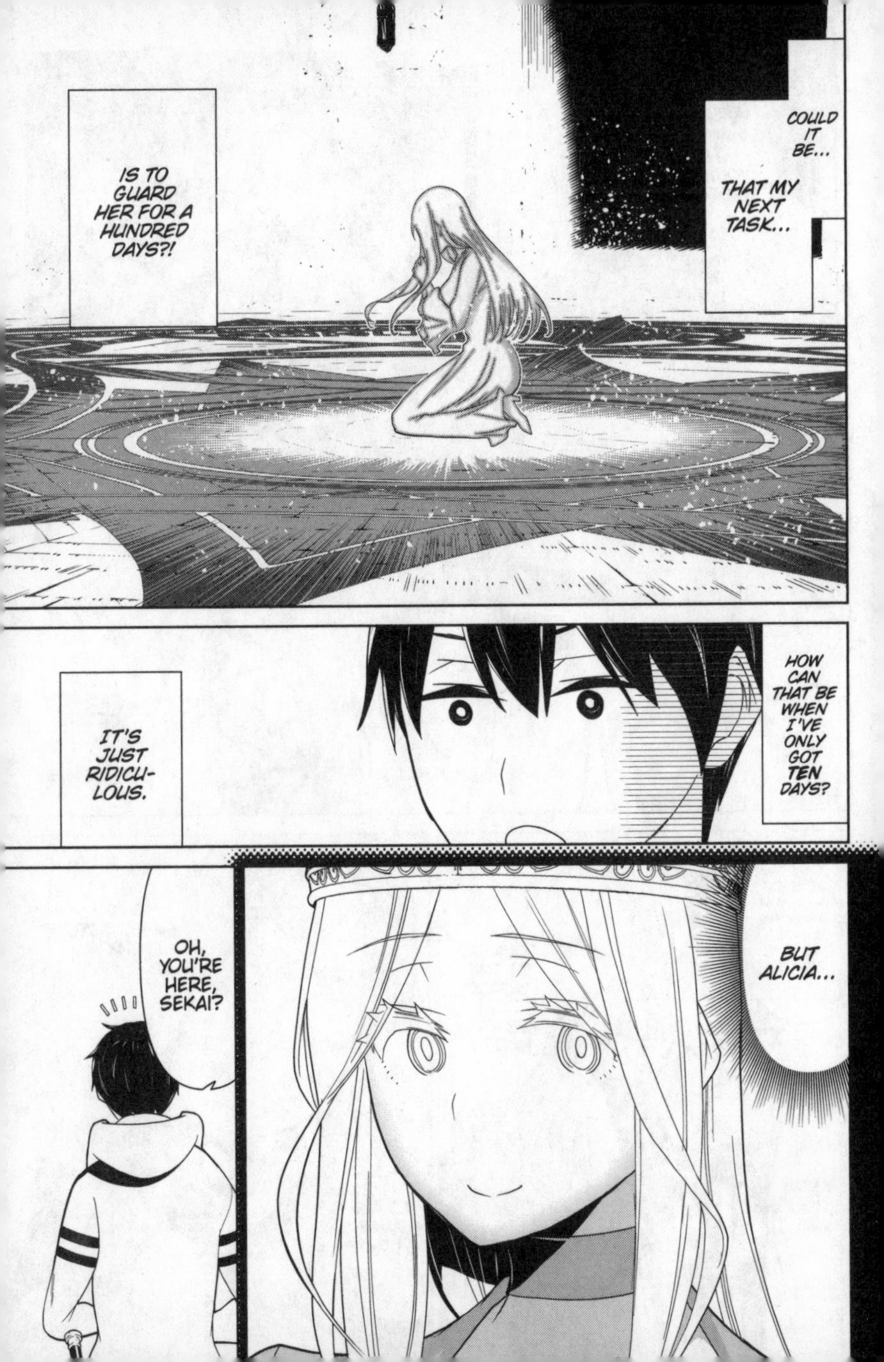
COULD IT BE...
THAT MY NEXT TASK...
IS TO GUARD HER FOR A HUNDRED DAYS?!
HOW CAN THAT BE WHEN I'VE ONLY GOT TEN DAYS?
IT'S JUST RIDICULOUS.
BUT ALICIA...
OH, YOU'RE HERE, SEKAI?

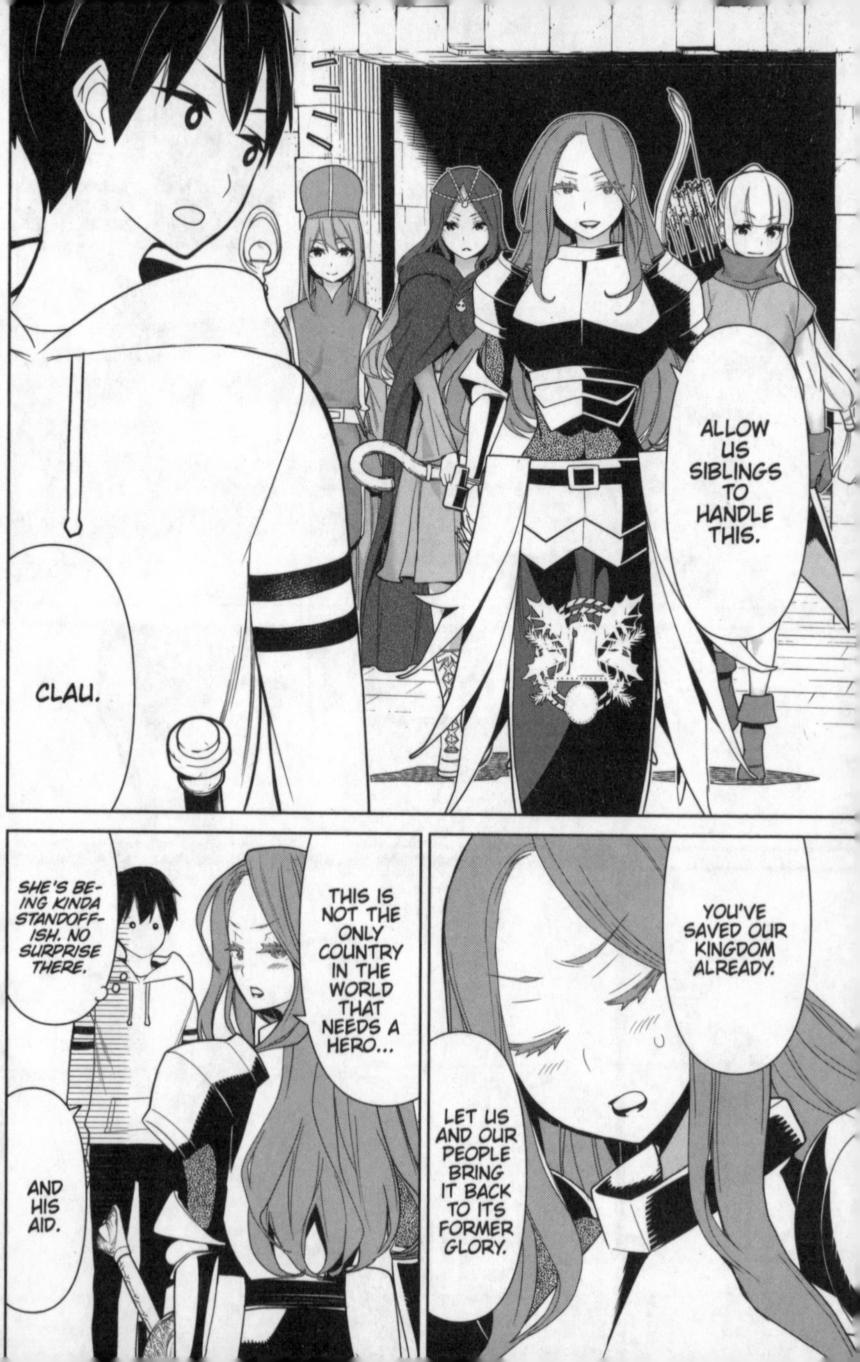
ALLOW US SIBLINGS TO HANDLE THIS.
CLAU.
YOU'VE SAVED OUR KINGDOM ALREADY.
LET US AND OUR PEOPLE BRING IT BACK TO ITS FORMER GLORY.
THIS IS NOT THE ONLY COUNTRY IN THE WORLD THAT NEEDS A HERO...
SHE'S BE-ING KINDA STANDOFF-ISH. NO SURPRISE THERE.
AND HIS AID.

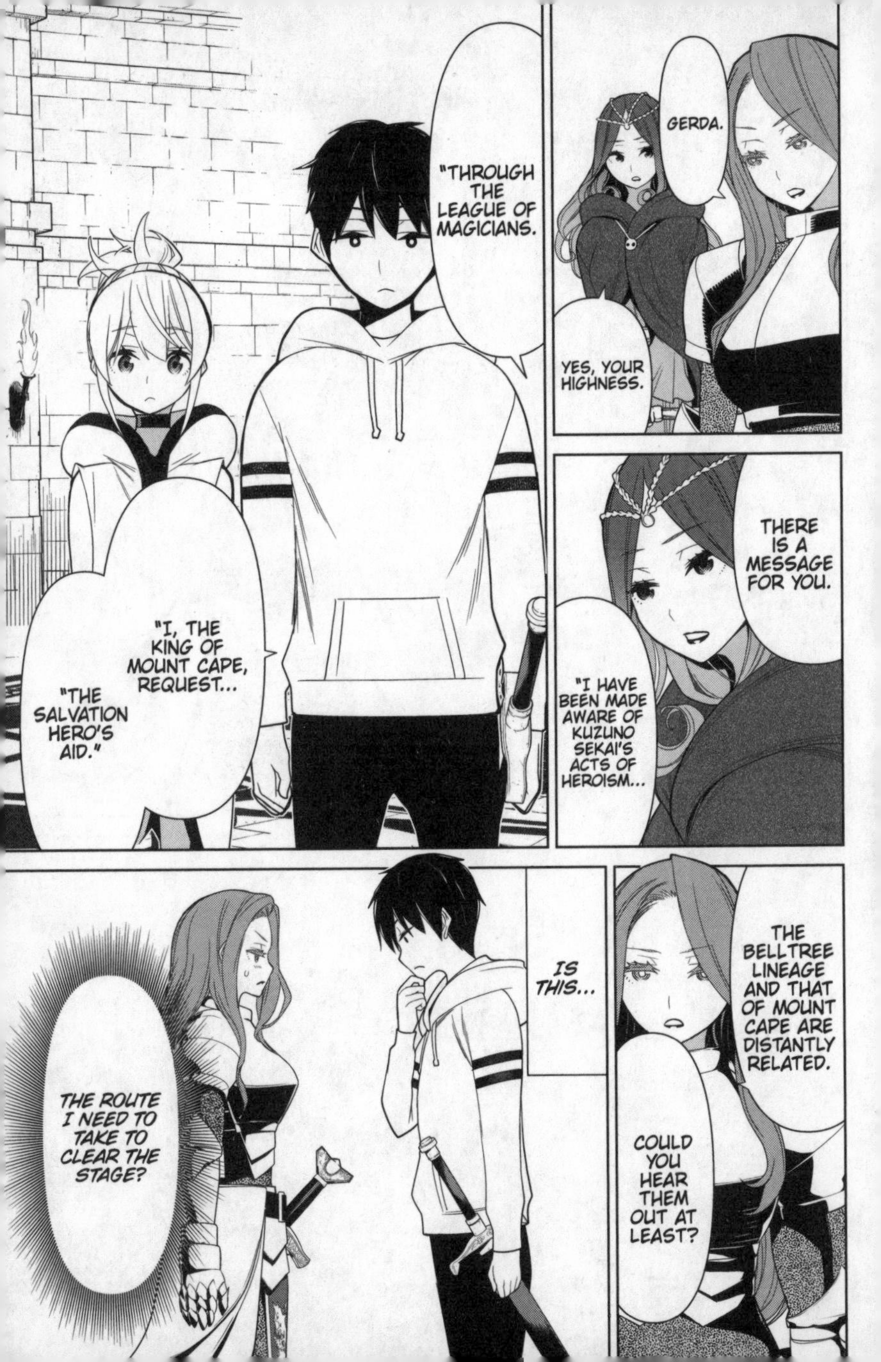
GERDA.
YES, YOUR HIGHNESS.
THERE IS A MESSAGE FOR YOU.
"I HAVE BEEN MADE AWARE OF KUZUNO SEKAI'S ACTS OF HEROISM...
"THROUGH THE LEAGUE OF MAGICIANS.
"I, THE KING OF MOUNT CAPE, REQUEST...
"THE SALVATION HERO'S AID."
THE BELLTREE LINEAGE AND THAT OF MOUNT CAPE ARE DISTANTLY RELATED.
COULD YOU HEAR THEM OUT AT LEAST?
IS THIS...
THE ROUTE I NEED TO TAKE TO CLEAR THE STAGE?

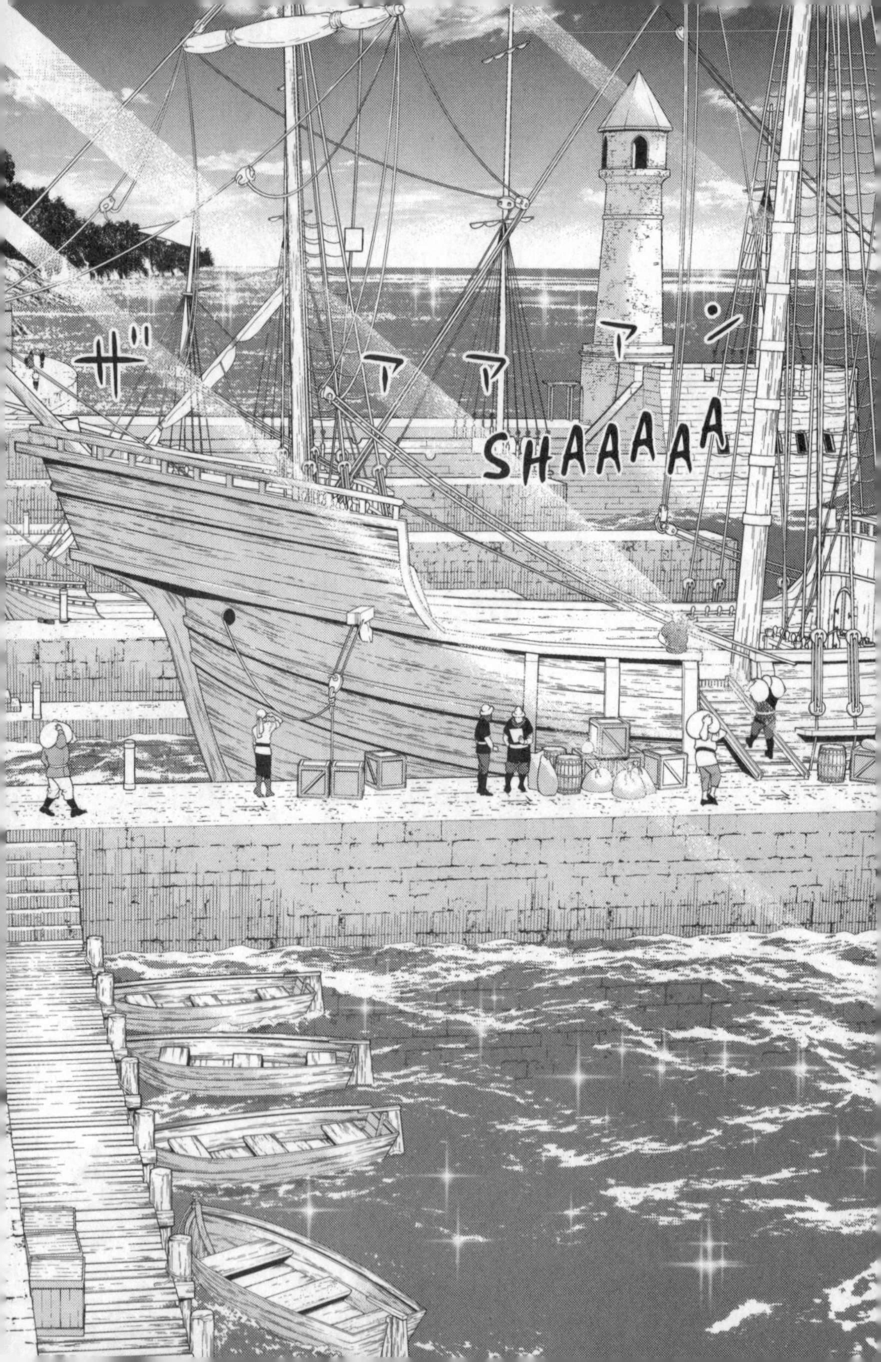
ザザァァ〜ン
SHAAAAA

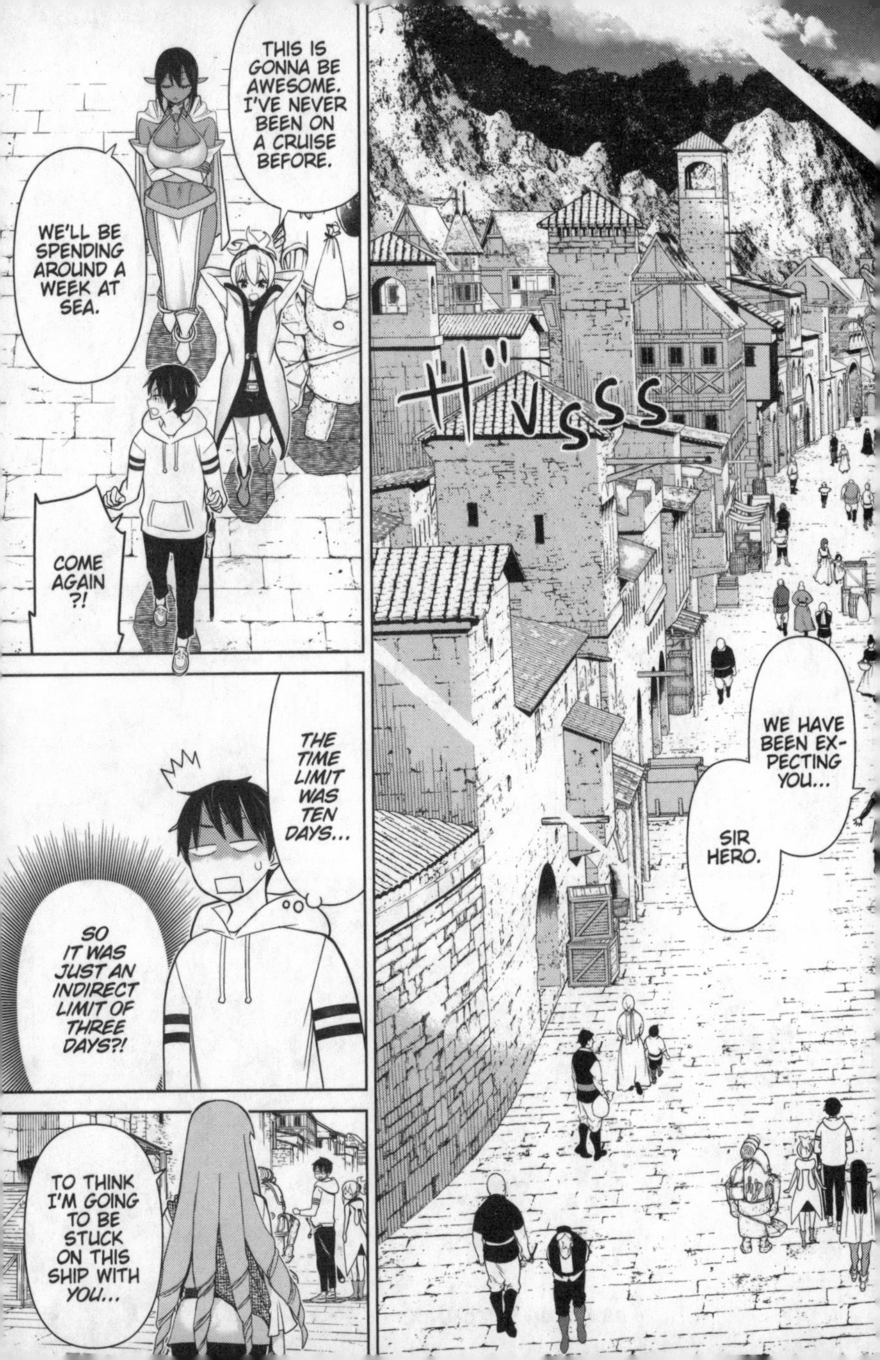
WE HAVE BEEN EX-PECTING YOU...
SIR HERO.
THIS IS GONNA BE AWESOME. I'VE NEVER BEEN ON A CRUISE BEFORE.
WE'LL BE SPENDING AROUND A WEEK AT SEA.
COME AGAIN?!
THE TIME LIMIT WAS TEN DAYS...
SO IT WAS JUST AN INDIRECT LIMIT OF THREE DAYS?!
TO THINK I'M GOING TO BE STUCK ON THIS SHIP WITH YOU...

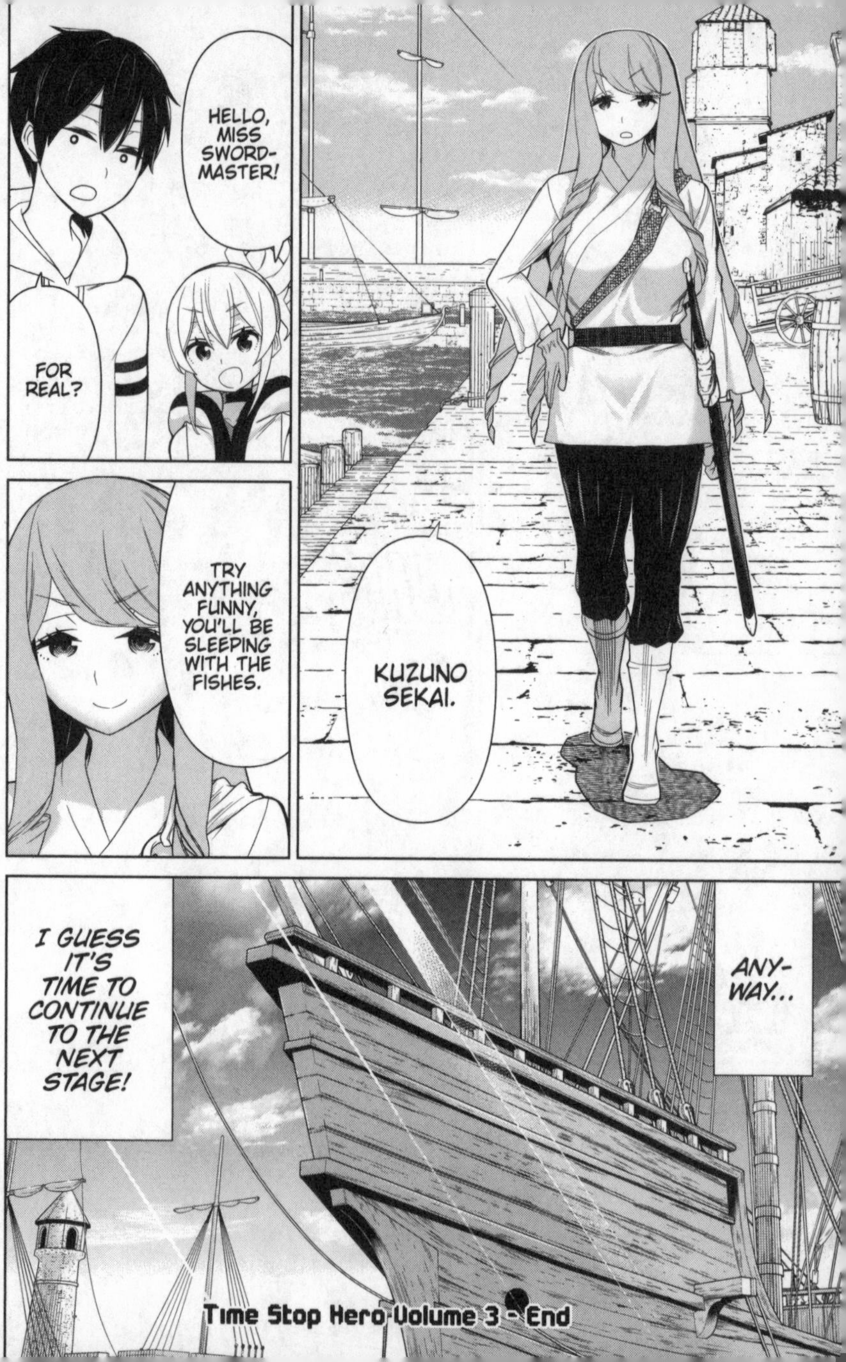
KUZUNO SEKAI.
HELLO, MISS SWORD-MASTER!
FOR REAL?
TRY ANYTHING FUNNY, YOU'LL BE SLEEPING WITH THE FISHES.
ANY-WAY...
I GUESS IT'S TIME TO CONTINUE TO THE NEXT STAGE!
Time Stop Hero Volume 3 - End

2 3 4 5 6 7 8

START
▶ PAUSE

▶START
PAUSE

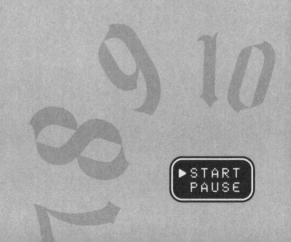

SEVEN SEAS ENTERTAINMENT PRESENTS

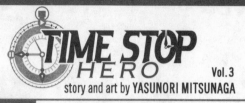

TIME STOP HERO

Vol. 3

story and art by YASUNORI MITSUNAGA

TRANSLATION
Mario Varo

ADAPTATION
Solo Mia

LETTERING
Erika Terriquez

COVER DESIGN
Hanase Qi

LOGO DESIGN
George Panella

PROOFREADER
Janet Houck

COPY EDITOR
Dawn Davis

EDITOR
Nick Mamatas

PREPRESS TECHNICIAN
Melanie Ujimori

PRINT MANAGER
Rhiannon Rasmussen-Silverstein

PRODUCTION MANAGER
Lissa Pattillo

MANAGING EDITOR
Julie Davis

ASSOCIATE PUBLISHER
Adam Arnold

PUBLISHER
Jason DeAngelis

Jikan Teishi Yusha vol. 3

First published in Japan in 2020 by Kodansha Ltd., Tokyo.
Publication rights for this English edition arranged through Kodansha Ltd., Tokyo.

Seven Seas press and purchase enquiries can be sent to Marketing Manager Lianne Sentar at press@gomanga.com. Information regarding the distribution and purchase of digital editions is available from Digital Manager CK Russell at digital@gomanga.com.

ISBN: 978-1-64827-640-8
Printed in Canada
First Printing: January 2022
10 9 8 7 6 5 4 3 2 1

READING DIRECTIONS

This book reads from ***right to left***, Japanese style. If this is your first time reading manga, you start reading from the top right panel on each page and take it from there. If you get lost, just follow the numbered diagram here. It may seem backwards at first, but you'll get the hang of it! Have fun!!

1
2
3
4
5
6
7
8
9

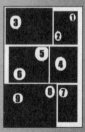

Follow us online: www.SevenSeasEntertainment.com